Aberrations in Black

Critical American Studies Series

George Lipsitz, University of California–San Diego, series editor

Aberrations in Black

Toward a Queer of Color Critique

Roderick A. Ferguson

Critical American Studies

University of Minnesota Press

Minneapolis :: London

An earlier version of chapter 3 was published as "The Nightmares of the Heteronormative," *Cultural Values* 4, no. 4 (October 2000).

Published by the University of Minnesota Press
111 Third Avenue South, Suite 290
Minneapolis, MN 55401-2520
http://www.upress.umn.edu

Library of Congress Cataloging-in-Publication Data

Ferguson, Roderick A.
    Aberrations in black : toward a queer of color critique / Roderick A. Ferguson.
        p.   cm. — (Critical American Studies series)
    Includes bibliographical references and index.
    ISBN 0-8166-4128-5 (HC : alk. paper) — ISBN 0-8166-4129-3 (PB : alk. paper)
        1. American fiction—African American authors—History and criticism.
    2. Homosexuality and literature—United States—History—20th century.
    3. American fiction—20th century—History and criticism.   4. Baldwin, James, 1924– Go tell it on the mountain.   5. Gays' writings, American—History and criticism.   6. Wright, Richard, 1908–1960. Native son.
    7. African American gays—Intellectual life.   8. Ellison, Ralph. Invisible man.   9. African Americans in literature.   10. Morrison, Toni. Sula.
    11. Gays in literature.   12. Canon (Literature)   I. Title.   II. Series.
    PS374.N4 F47 2003
    813'.509896073'008664—dc21

                                                                2003012779

Printed in the United States of America on acid-free paper

The University of Minnesota is an equal-opportunity educator and employer.

12 11 10 09 08 07 06 05 04   10 9 8 7 6 5 4 3 2 1

Contents

Preface

LC-USF33-001172-M4 is a picture, one that is a part of a Library of Congress exhibition, *The African-American Odyssey: A Quest for Full Citizenship.* The photo, taken in 1938, depicts a segregated railroad facility in Manchester, Georgia. Four African American men wait outside of what is probably the railroad employment office. Two sit on the steps outside a door that reads "Colored Waiting Room," while the other two—clad in overalls—stand to their right. The men donned in overalls are smoking cigarettes in front of a restroom with the words "Colored Men" written across the door.

I am drawn to this picture for several reasons—some that are purely scholastic, others that are outright personal. In many ways, the picture represents the traditional history of American race relations, cast in black and white, depicting racial exclusion in social accommodations and occupation. Like the picture, the traditional historiography of race in America presents black men as the central characters in a history of exclusion. That historiography casts the exclusion of African Americans from the rights and privileges of citizenship as part of the burgeoning industrialization taking place within the United States. The disciplinary machines of the modern academy historically have recycled that historiography. Indeed, we may presume without error that this picture appeals to a certain sociological rendering of African American racial formations. In this picture are the images that have become the emblem of the sociology of race relations, images suggesting the intersections of poverty, race, and economic discrimination. For canonical sociologists, that exclusion would eventually be resolved by the very political economy that initiated it, and African Americans would gradually be assimilated into the American political and economic spheres.

This sociological imagining of the picture coheres with the official memory of the American nation-state, as the photograph is housed in one of the government's main bureaucratic archives. The introduction to the exhibition reads,

> The major presentation in the Jefferson Building, *The African-American Odyssey: A Quest for Full Citizenship,* explores black America's quest for equality from the early national period through the twentieth century. The Library's materials . . . tell the story of the African-American experience through nine chronological periods that document the courage and

determination of blacks, faced with adverse circumstances, who overcame immense odds to fully participate in all aspects of American society.[1]

The archive solemnizes the image according to the same motivations that lead sociologists to approach racial discrimination—to mark the injustices of racial exclusion *and* to promote the state's ability to assimilate that which it formerly rejected. Like the introduction to the exhibit, canonical sociology has historically organized the meaning of African American history in terms of the nomenclature of liberal capital—"equality, full citizenship, full participation," the rewards subdued after "immense odds" have been "overcome." But what is the normative infrastructure of that language and its practices?

The picture itself suggests answers to this question. Behind the men clad in overalls—in the background—is a white woman. One can imagine that the words "Colored Men" not only identify the gender and racial specificities of the bathroom, but they announce an invisible line that separates her from the four African American men. The picture dramatizes what has become an established insight—that is, the ways in which a discourse of sexuality was inscribed into racial exclusion. As several authors have noted, racial segregation ostensibly worked to ensure the sexual purity of white women and the sexual mobility of white men. Assigning racial segregation the task of protecting gender and sexual norms, of course, made miscegenation one of segregation's signal anxieties. The danger of using this image to think about the intersections of race and sexuality is that miscegenation has often been interpreted separately from other transgressive sexual formations obtained in the context of racial exclusion. How might we see this picture in relation to other racial subjects? In other words, how do we speak of the picture as part of a dialogical and polymorphous network of perversions that contradicted notions of decency and American citizenship?

I am pulled to this picture for reasons that straddle distinctions between the epistemological and the personal. I know this railroad station. It is a ten-minute walk from the house I grew up in. I know as well that there are subjects missing who should be accounted for—the transgendered man who wore Levi's and a baseball cap and chewed tobacco; the men with long permed hair who tickled piano keys; the sissies and bulldaggers who taught the neighborhood children to say their speeches on Easter Sunday morning. Is there a way in which their emergence can be located within the social formations that the picture represents? And might their presence cause us to reconsider political economy and racial formation as they are normally pursued?

I offer this bit of personal detail not for purposes of autobiography, but to demonstrate the ways in which epistemology is encountered personally.

I come to this picture aware of the epistemological and official renderings of racial exclusion and the need to hold those renderings under inspection. I am principally interested in what the sociological and national depictions of that history leave out. My inspection is informed by a single assumption—that epistemology is an economy of information privileged and information excluded, and that subject formations arise out of this economy. I also know that canonical and national formations rarely disclose what they have rejected. Such disclosures require alternatives to those formations, alternatives expressed in those sites excluded from the so-called rigors and official imperatives of canons and archives. As the picture symbolizes the sociological and national depictions of racial exclusion, my personal encounter with it also symbolizes an epistemological engagement with what those depictions leave out.

This book tells a story of canonical sociology's regulation of people like the transgendered man, the sissy, and the bulldagger as part of its general regulation of African American culture. This book places that story within other stories—the narrative of capital's emergence and development, the histories of marxism and revolutionary nationalism, and the novels that depict the gendered and sexual idiosyncrasies of African American culture. In turn, this book tries to present another story—one in which the people that presumably evince the dysfunctions of capitalism are revised as sites that possibly critique state, capital, and social science. In this book, I wish to connect American cultural studies to questions from sociology, queer studies, postcolonial studies, African American studies, and ethnic studies. I do so for two reasons. I want to suggest that contrary to canonical claims, intellectual inquiry is always shaped out of heterogeneity, never neatly contained within the presumed homogeneous boundaries of a discipline. I would also like to point to the productive nature of that heterogeneity—that is, its ability to inspire new horizons for thought and action. I do not mean to establish some intellectual or political protocol with this book. I merely wish to offer a work whose insights and failures might incite other ways to be.

This book began in the restlessness of graduate school, and because of the support and intelligence of friends, colleagues, and teachers, I can now put this project to rest. I want to thank Ivan Evans, Harvey Goldman, Gershon Shafir, and Jonathan Holloway for their support as committee members. I thank my friends in sociology—Joann Ball, Doug Hartmann, Jeanne Powers, Jennifer Jordan, Jonathan Markovitz, and Beth Jennings—for knowing what I meant when I uttered our discipline's name. I thank Alex Halkias for being there when I first conceived of this project and for encouraging me with mentorship that was always gentle. I thank Susan Fitzpatrick for her interest in my work and her patience as an interlocutor. I thank Chanta Haywood for lovingly prodding me to keep writing. I thank Hassan Dhouti, John Berteaux, Jerry "Rafiki" Jenkins, Ann DuCille, Andrew Zimmerman, Janet Roberts, and Diane Bartlow for their generosity as readers. I thank Ruby's Reading Group (Ruby Tapia, Chandan Reddy, Victor Viesca, Maurice Stevens, Danny Widener, Gayatri Gopinath, Victor Bascara, and Kyungwon Grace Hong) for their rigor and their vision for contemporary scholarship in race, gender, sexuality, and political economy. My project is all the better because of the brilliance of their insights and the steadfastness of their rigor. It's been a few years since we were graduate students, but in many ways I still write for them. I thank Avery Gordon for spending time with me and helping me to think of ways to turn a dissertation into a book. I thank Judith Halberstam for clarification and for encouraging me to think of queer studies as a site of intervention. I thank Stephanie Smallwood for constant encouragement and conversation and for insisting that I keep African American studies on my mind. I thank Kulvinder Arora, Kara Keeling, Jodi Melamed, and Cynthia Tolentino for their enthusiasm and insight as listeners and readers. I thank Chandan Reddy for brilliance and friendship unparalleled, for making this project and my life all the sweeter. Finally, I thank George Lipsitz and Lisa Lowe for being the best mentors I could ever have: George—for abiding mentorship and for showing me that the creation of an alternative university is accomplished through work rather than personality; Lisa—for quietly and unconsciously insisting that our work live up to the difficulty and complexity of the formations that we address. I thank them for teaching me—as they did countless others—to see the complex and the difficult as my project's task, rather than its obstruction, and to regard the state of emergency as the moment of emergence. To them, I am forever grateful.

Since arriving at Minnesota, I have been fortunate to work in an environment that is both stimulating and democratic. My colleagues Jennifer Pierce, David Noble, and Jean O'Brien, especially, have made the Department of American Studies a welcoming place, going out of their way to make sure that a newcomer felt like an agent. In addition to the Department of American Studies, I have been deeply moved, informed, and inspired by colleagues outside of that department: Ananya Chatterjea, Anna Clark, Maria Damon, Qadri Ismail, Leola Johnson, Hiromi Mizuno, Gwendolyn Pough, Paula Rabinowitz (and the students in her seminar "Girls Read Marx"), and Michelle Wright. My friend Richard Morrison has been an attentive and unobtrusive editor. This text is all the better because of his talents and expertise, and because of the craftsmanship of the University of Minnesota Press staff. These are the people who labored with me, and to them I owe my all.

Introduction

Queer of Color Critique, Historical Materialism, and Canonical Sociology

In Marlon Riggs's *Tongues Untied*, a black drag-queen prostitute sashays along a waterfront. She has decked herself in a faux leather bomber and a white tiger-striped dress that stops just below her knees. Her face is heavy with foundation as she ponders into the distance. She holds a cigarette between fingers studded with cheap press-on nails, dragging on it with lips painted red. A poem by Essex Hemphill and a ballad by Nina Simone drum in the background. It is difficult to discern whether she is melancholic about her life or simply satisfied. This uncertainty, this hint of pleasure and alrightness, flies in the face of those who say that her life is nothing more than a tangle of pathologies and misfortunes. In the pleasure of her existence lies a critique of commonplace interpretations of her life. Doubtless, she knows that her living is not easy. But that's a long way from reducing the components of her identity to the conditions of her labor. Conceding to the meanness of life, probably for her, is a far cry from assuming that her gender and sexual difference are the reason for her poverty and that who she is attests to the absence of agency.

This scene captures the defining elements of this book. In the film, the drag-queen prostitute is a fixture of urban capitalism. Figures like her, ones that allegedly represent the socially disorganizing effects of capital, play a powerful part in past and contemporary interpretations of political economy. In those narratives, she stands for a larger black culture as it has engaged various economic and social formations. That engagement has borne a range of alienations, each estrangement securing another: her racial difference is inseparable from her sexual incongruity, her gender eccentricity, and her class marginality. Moreover, the country of her birth will call out to "the American people" and never mean her or others like her. She is multiply determined, regulated, and excluded by differences of race, class, sexuality, and gender. As drag-queen prostitute, she embodies the intersections of formations thought to be discrete and transparent, a confusion of that which distinguishes the heterosexual (i.e., "prostitute") from the homosexual (i.e., "drag queen"). She is disciplined by those within and outside African American communities,

1

reviled by leftist-radicals, conservatives, heterosexuals, and mainstream queers alike, erased by those who wish to present or make African American culture the embodiment of all that she is not—respectability, domesticity, heterosexuality, normativity, nationality, universality, and progress. But her estrangements are not hers to own. They are, in fact, the general estrangements of African American culture. In its distance from the ideals upheld by epistemology, nationalisms, and capital, that culture activates forms of critique.

The scene, thus, represents the social heterogeneity that characterizes African American culture. To make sense of that culture as the site of gender and sexual formations that have historically deviated from national ideals, we must situate that culture within the genealogy of liberal capitalist economic and social formations. That genealogy can, in turn, help us perceive how the racialized gender and sexual diversity pertaining to African American cultural formations is part of the secular trends of capitalist modes of production. These are trends that manifest themselves globally, linking terrains separated by time and space.

Queer of Color and the Critique of Liberal Capitalism

The preceding paragraphs suggest that African American culture indexes a social heterogeneity that oversteps the boundaries of gender propriety and sexual normativity. That social heterogeneity also indexes formations that are seemingly outside the spatial and temporal bounds of African American culture. These arguments oblige us to ask what mode of analysis would be appropriate for interpreting the drag-queen prostitute as an image that allegorizes and symbolizes that social heterogeneity, a heterogeneity that associates African American culture with gender and sexual variation and critically locates that culture within the genealogy of the West. To assemble such a mode of interpretation, we may begin with the nascent and emergent formation known as queer of color analysis.[1]

In "Home, Houses, Nonidentity: 'Paris Is Burning,'" Chandan Reddy discusses the expulsion of queers of color from literal homes and from the privileges bestowed by the nation as "home." Reddy's essay begins with the silences that both marxism and liberal pluralism share, silences about the intersections of gender, sexual, and racial exclusions. Reddy states,

> Unaccounted for within both Marxist and liberal pluralist discussions of the home and the nation, queers of color as people of color . . . take up the critical task of both remembering and rejecting the model of the "home" offered in the United States in two ways: first, by attending to the ways in which it was defined over and against people of color, and second, by expanding the locations and moments of that critique of the

home to interrogate processes of group formation and self-formation from the experience of being expelled from their own dwellings and families for not conforming to the dictation of and demand for uniform gendered and sexual types.[2]

By identifying the nation as the domain determined by racial difference and gender and sexual conformity, Reddy suggests that the decisive intervention of queer of color analysis is that racist practice articulates itself generally as gender and sexual regulation, and that gender and sexual differences variegate racial formations. This articulation, moreover, accounts for the social formations that compose liberal capitalism.

In doing so, queer of color critique approaches culture as one site that compels identifications with and antagonisms to the normative ideals promoted by state and capital. For Reddy, national culture constitutes itself against subjects of color. Alternatively, culture produces houses peopled by queers of color, subjects who have been expelled from home. These subjects in turn "collectively remember home as a site of contradictory demands and conditions."[3] As it fosters both identifications and antagonisms, culture becomes a site of material struggle. As the site of identification, culture becomes the terrain in which formations seemingly antagonistic to liberalism, like marxism and revolutionary nationalism, converge with liberal ideology, precisely through their identification with gender and sexual norms and ideals. Queer of color analysis must examine how culture as a site of identification produces such odd bedfellows and how it—as the location of antagonisms—fosters unimagined alliances.

As an epistemological intervention, queer of color analysis denotes an interest in materiality, but refuses ideologies of transparency and reflection, ideologies that have helped to constitute marxism, revolutionary nationalism, and liberal pluralism. Marxism and revolutionary nationalism, respectively, have often figured nation and property as the transparent outcome of class and racial exclusions. Relatedly, liberal pluralism has traditionally constructed the home as the obvious site of accommodation and confirmation. Queer of color analysis, on the other hand, eschews the transparency of all these formulations and opts instead for an understanding of nation and capital as the outcome of manifold intersections that contradict the idea of the liberal nation-state and capital as sites of resolution, perfection, progress, and confirmation. Indeed, liberal capitalist ideology works to suppress the diverse components of state and capitalist formations. To the extent that marxism and revolutionary nationalism disavow race, gender, and sexuality's mutually formative role in political and economic relations is the extent to which liberal ideology captivates revolutionary nationalism and marxism. To restate, queer of color analysis presumes that liberal ideology occludes the intersecting saliency of race, gender, sexuality, and class in forming social practices. Approaching ideologies of transparency as formations that have worked to conceal those intersections means that queer of color analysis has to debunk the idea that race, class, gender, and sexuality are discrete formations, apparently insulated from one another. As queer of color critique challenges ideologies of discreteness, it attempts to disturb the idea that racial and national formations are obviously disconnected. As an intervention into queer of color analysis, this text attempts to locate African American racial formations alongside other racial formations and within epistemological procedures believed to be unrelated or tangential to African American culture.

To Disidentify with Historical Materialism

By relating queer of color subjects and practices to marxism and liberal pluralism, Reddy suggests that queer of color analysis must critically engage the genealogy of materialist critique. In his book, *Disidentifications: Queers of Color and the Performance of Politics*, José Esteban Muñoz argues, "Disidentification is the hermeneutical performance of decoding mass, high, or any other cultural field from the perspective of a minority subject who is disempowered in such a representational hierarchy."[4] As Munoz suggests, queer of color critique decodes cultural fields not from a position outside those fields, but from within them, as those fields account for the queer of color subject's historicity. If the intersections of race, gender, sexuality, and class constitute social formations within liberal capitalism, then queer of color analysis obtains its genealogy within a variety of locations. We may say that women of color feminism names a crucial component of that genealogy as women of color theorists have historically theorized intersections as the basis of social formations. Queer of color analysis extends women of color feminism by investigating how intersecting racial, gender, and sexual practices antagonize and/or conspire with the normative investments of nation-states and capital.

As queer of color analysis claims an interest in social formations, it locates itself within the mode of critique known as historical materialism.[5] Since historical materialism has traditionally privileged class over other social relations, queer of color critique cannot take it up without revision, must not employ it without disidentification. If to disidentify means to "[recycle] and [rethink] encoded meaning" and "to use the code [of the majority] as raw material for representing a disempowered politics of positionality that has been rendered unthinkable by the dominant culture,"[6] then disidentification resembles Louis Althusser's rereading of historical materialism. Queer of color analysis disidentifies with historical materialism to *rethink* its categories and how they might conceal the materiality of race, gender, and sexuality. In this instance, to disidentify in no way means to discard.

Addressing the silences within Marx's writings that enable rather than disturb bourgeois ideology, silences produced by Marx's failure to theorize received abstractions like "division of labor, money, value, etc.," Althusser writes in *Reading Capital,*

> This silence is only "heard" at one precise point, just where it goes unperceived: when Marx speaks of the initial abstractions on which the work of transformation is performed. What are these initial abstractions? By what right does Marx accept in these initial abstractions the categories from which Smith and Ricardo started, thus suggesting that he thinks in continuity with their object, and that therefore there is no break in object between them and him? These two questions are really only one single question, precisely the question Marx does not answer, simply because he does not pose it. Here is the site of his silence, and this site, being empty, threatens to be occupied by the "natural" discourse of ideology, in particular, of empiricism. . . . An ideology may gather naturally in the hollow left by this silence, the ideology of a relation of real correspondence between the real and its intuition and representation, and the presence of an "abstraction" which operates on this real in order to disengage from it these "abstract general relations," i.e., an empiricist ideology of abstraction.[7]

As empiricism grants authority to representation, empiricism functions hegemonically, making representations seem natural and objective. To assume that categories conform to reality is to think with, instead of against, hegemony. As he uncritically appropriated the conceptions of political economy formulated by bourgeois economists, Marx abetted liberal ideology. He identified with that ideology instead of disidentifying with it. Disidentifying with historical materialism means determining the silences and ideologies that reside within critical terrains, silences and ideologies that equate representations with reality. Queer of color analysis, therefore, extends Althusser's observations by accounting for the ways in which Marx's critique of capitalist property relations is haunted by silences that make racial, gender, and sexual ideologies and discourses commensurate with reality and suitable for universal ideals.

An ideology has gathered in the silences pertaining to the intersections of race, gender, sexuality, and class. We may locate that silence within one "tendency" of marxism. Writing about that tendency as part of marxism's critique of Western civilization, Raymond Williams states, "'Civilization' had produced not only wealth, order, and refinement, but as part of the same process poverty, disorder, degradation. It was attacked for its 'artificiality'—its glaring contrasts with a 'natural' or 'human' order."[8] As it kept silent about sexuality and gender, historical materialism, along with liberal ideology, took normative heterosexuality as the emblem of order, nature, and universality, making that which deviated from heteropatriarchal ideals the sign of disorder. In doing so, marxism thought in continuity with bourgeois definitions of "Civilization." Moreover, the distinction between civilization as progress versus civilization as disorder obtained meaning along the axes of race, gender, sexuality, and class. Hence, the distinction between normative heterosexuality (as the evidence of progress and development) and non-normative gender and sexual practices and identities (as the woeful signs of social lag and dysfunction) has emerged historically from the field of racialized discourse. Put plainly, racialization has helped to articulate heteropatriarchy as universal.

Marx universalized heteropatriarchy as he theorized property ownership. In *The German Ideology,* he bases the origins of property ownership within the tribe, stating,

> The first form of ownership is tribal . . . ownership. . . . The division of labor is at the stage still very elementary and is confined to a further extension of the *natural* division of labour existing in the family. The social structure is, therefore, limited to an extension of the family; patriarchal family chieftains, below them the members of the tribe, finally slaves.[9]

For Marx, tribal ownership presumed a *natural* division of labor symbolized by the heterosexual and patriarchal family. This definition of the "tribe" as a signifier of natural divisions cohered with the use of that category in the nineteenth century. "Tribe" described a "loose *family* or collection headed not by a 'king' but by a 'chief' and denoted a *common essence associated with the premodern.*"[10] "Tribe" was a racialized category emerging out of the history of colonial expansion from the seventeenth to the nineteenth centuries. Tribes marked racial difference, securing and transmitting that difference from one person to the next through heteropatriarchal exchange and reproduction. As a racial category, "tribe" illustrates the ways in which racial discourses recruited gender and sexual difference to establish racial identity and essence.

In addition, Marx characterized communal essence and identity as a founding prerequisite for property relations. As he states,

> The spontaneously evolved tribal community, or, if you will, the herd—the common ties of blood, language, custom, etc.—is the first precondition of

the appropriation of the objective conditions of life, and of the activity which gives material expression to, or objectifies it (activity as herdsmen, hunters, agriculturalists, etc.).[11]

The property relations presumed within tribal communities suggested a racialized essence garnered through heterosexual and patriarchal familial arrangements. Another way of wording this would be to say that Marx imagined social relations and agency—or as he says, "appropriation" and "activity"— through heteropatriarchy and racial difference simultaneously. Explicating this assumption about social relations and agency, Marx argues in *The German Ideology,* man, who "daily [remakes his] life . . . enters into historical development" by "[making] other men" and "[propagating] their kind."[12] Even earlier, in the *Economic and Philosophic Manuscripts,* Marx stated, "This direct, natural, and necessary relation of person to person is *the relation of man to woman.* In this natural species relationship, man's relation to nature is immediately his relation to man, just as his relation to man is his relation to nature—his own *natural* destination."[13] For Marx, heteropatriarchy was the racialized essence of Man and the standard of sociality and agency.

If a racially secured and dependent heteropatriarchy underlies Marx's origin narrative of social relations and historical agency, then capitalist property relations represent the ultimate obstacle to heteropatriarchal practice and being. In disrupting heteropatriarchy, capital disrupted man's fundamental essence. Locating this disruption within the emergence of the commodity form, Marx argues that

[p]roduction does not simply produce man as a *commodity,* the *human commodity,* man in the role of *commodity*; it produces him in keeping with this role as a *mentally* and physically *dehumanized* being.—Immorality, deformity, and dulling of the workers and the capitalists.—Its product is the *self-conscious* and *self-acting* commodity . . . the human commodity. Great advance of Ricardo, Mill, etc., on Smith and Say, to declare the existence of the human being—the greater or lesser human productivity of the commodity—to be *indifferent* and even *harmful.*[14]

The commodity disrupts the moral parameters of subjectivity and agency. As Marx states, the commodification produces man as a "mentally and physically dehumanized being," deforming agency and distorting subjectivity.[15]

For Marx, the symbol of that dehumanization could be found in none other than the prostitute. He writes,

Prostitution is only a *specific* expression of the *general* prostitution of the laborer, and since it is a relationship in which falls not the prostitute alone, but also the one who prostitutes—and the latter's abomination is still greater—the capitalist, etc., also comes under this head. . . . In the approach to woman as the spoil and handmaid of communal lust is expressed the infinite degradation in which man exists for himself.[16]

The prostitute proves capital's defilement of man. She symbolizes man's dehumanization or more specifically, man's feminization under capitalist relations of production. While man's essence in heteropatriarchy suggests undeterred connections with other humans, with one's self, and with nature, the prostitute represents the ways that capital disrupts those connections. Capital now violently mediates man's relationship to himself, to others, and to nature. As a figure of self-interest, the prostitute represents man's descent into vulgar egoism. Suggesting this egoism spawned by capitalist alienation, Marx argues, "[Alienated labor] estranges man's own body from him, as it does external nature and his spiritual essence, his human being."[17] We can see that violent mediation very clearly as the worker who—like all prostitutes—must sell his own labor to survive. Castrated from the means of production, the worker has only that labor that resides in his body to sell. As the prostitute is regarded as the property of "communal lust," the worker is "branded . . . as the property of capital."[18] As Marx imagines capitalist expansion through the disruption of heteropatriarchy, capital implies the mobility of vice, the spread of immorality, and the eruption of social transgressions.

It was precisely this sort of eruption that bourgeois ideologues in nineteenth-century Britain feared the most. During this period, middle-class observers conflated the anarchic possibilities of economic production with a presumably burgeoning sexual deviancy among working-class communities, in general, and working-class women, in particular.[19] The prostitute symbolized poor and working-class communities' potential threat to gender stability and sexual normativity. As mills throughout London employed young British girls, enabling them to buy clothes and other items that were previously inaccessible, middle-class citizens often saw working-class girls' tastes in commodities as signs of awakening sexual appetites. Desires for ribbon, lace, and silks, those citizens reasoned, could entice young girls into a life of prostitution.[20] As Thomas Laquer notes, "[W]orking-class women were thought to bear the dangers of uncontrolled desire that seemed to flow freely from one domain to another, from legitimate consumption to illegitimate sex."[21] Giving credence to the idea that industrialization was engendering prostitution, the French socialist and feminist Flora Tristan alleged that there were in "'London from 80,000–100,000 women—the flower of the population—living off prostitution'; on the streets and in 'temples raised by English materialism to their gods . . . male guests come to exchange their gold for debauchery.'"[22] Reports of out-of-wedlock births, prenuptial pregnancy, early marriage, masturbation, sexually active youth, and so forth arose during this period and were for the British middle class evidence of a peaking sexual chaos. In doing so, they conflated the reality of changing gender and sexual relations with the representation of the prostitute and the working class as pathologically sexual. As middle-class witnesses to industrialization understood their own families to be sufficiently anchored against the moral disruptions of capital, they regarded the working class as "rootless and un-controlled—a sort of social correlative to unrestrained id."[23] Corroborating presumptions about industrial capital's encouragement of libertinism, Frederick Engels argued, "[N]ext to the enjoyment of intoxicating liquors, one of the principal faults of the English working-men is sexual license."[24] Marx's use of the prostitute as the apocalyptic symbol of capital's emergence points to his affinity with bourgeois discourses of the day. Both bourgeois ideologues and their radical opponents took the prostitute as the sign for the gendered and sexual chaos that commodification was bound to unleash.

More to the point, pundits understood this gender and sexual chaos to be an explicitly racial phenomenon. Indeed, in nineteenth-century Britain, the prostitute was a racial metaphor for the gender and sexual confusions unleashed by capital, disruptions that destabilized heteropatriarchal conformity and authority.[25] In fact, nineteenth-century iconography used the image of Sarah Bartmann, popularly known as the Hottentot Venus, who was exhibited in freak shows throughout London, to link the figure of the prostitute to the alleged sexual savagery of black women and to install nonwhite sexuality as the axis upon which various notions of womanhood turned.[26] As industrial capital developed and provided working-class white women with limited income and mobility, the prostitute became the racialized figure that could enunciate anxieties about such changes. Conflating the prostitute with the British working class inspired racial mythologies about the supposedly abnormal reproductive capacities and outcomes of that class. One tale suggested that the bodies of British working-class women could produce races heretofore unforeseen. One magistrate warned that if "empty casks were placed along the streets of Whitechapel," it would help spawn species of tub men who would wreak havoc on communities in Britain, creating the conditions by which "savages [would live] in the midst of civilization."[27]

The universalization of heteropatriarchy produces the prostitute as the other of heteropatriarchal ideals, an other that is simultaneously the effect of racial, gender, sexual, and class discourses, an other that names the social upheavals of capital as racialized disruptions. Unmarried and sexually mobile, the prostitute was eccentric to the gendered and sexual ideals of normative (i.e., patriarchal) heterosexuality. That eccentricity denoted the pathologies, disorders, and degradations of an emerging civilization. Rather than embodying heteropatriarchal ideals, the prostitute was a figure of nonheteronormativity, excluded from the presumed security of heteropatriarchal boundaries.

As such, she and others like her were the targets of both liberal *and* revolutionary regulations. Those regulations derived their motives from the fact that both bourgeois and revolutionary practices were conceived through heteropatriarchy. We may imagine Marx asking, "How could she—the prostitute—be entrusted with the revolutionary transformation of society?" Likewise, we could imagine the bourgeoisie declaring, "Never could whores rationally administer a liberal society." Historical materialism and bourgeois ideology shared the tendency to read modern civilization as the racialized scene of heteronormative disruption. Marx fell into that ideology as he conflated the dominant representation of the prostitute with the social upheavals wrought by capital. Put differently, he equated the hegemonic discourse about the prostitute, a discourse that cast her as the symbol of immorality, vice, and corruption, with the reality of a burgeoning capitalist economy. Taking the prostitute to be the obvious and transparent sign of capital, at what point could Marx approach the prostitute and her alleged pathologies as discursive questions, rather than as the real and objective outcomes of capitalist social relations? At what point might he then consider the prostitute and others like her to be potential sites from which to critique capital?

Naturalizing heteropatriarchy by posing capital as the social threat to heteropatriarchal relations meant that both liberal reform and proletarian revolution sought to recover heteropatriarchal integrity from the ravages of industrialization. Basing the fundamental conditions of history upon heterosexual reproduction and designating capital as the disruption of heterosexual normativity did more than designate the subject of modern society as heteronormative. It made the heteronormative subject the goal of liberal and radical practices. Under such a definition of history, political economy became an arena where heteronormative legitimation was the prize. Universalizing heteropatriarchy and constructing a racialized other that required heteropatriarchal regulation was not the peculiar distinction of, or affinity between, Marx and his bourgeois contemporaries. On the contrary, the racialized investment in heteropatriarchy bequeathed itself to liberal and revolutionary projects, to bourgeois and revolutionary nationalisms alike. Queer of color analysis must disidentify with historical materialism so as not to extend this legacy.

The Multiplications of Surplus: U.S. Racial Formations, Nonheteronormativity, and the Overdetermination of Political Economy

Queer of color analysis can build on the idea that capital produces emergent social formations that exceed the racialized boundaries of gender and sexual ideals, can help explain the emergence of subjects like the drag-queen prostitute. At the same time, queer of color critique can and must challenge the idea that those social formations represent the pathologies of modern society. In other words, queer of color work can retain historical materialism's interest in social formations without obliging the silences of historical materialism.

Capital is a formation constituted by discourses of race, gender, and sexuality, discourses that implicate nonheteronormative formations like the prostitute. In addition, capitalist political economies have been scenes for the universalization and, hence, the normalization of sexuality. But those economies have also been the arenas for the disruption of normativity. If we are to be sensitive to the role that those normalizations and disruptions have played within liberal capitalism, we can only take up historical materialism by integrating the critique of normative regimes with the analysis of political economy. In doing so, we must clarify the ways in which our knowledge of liberal capitalism implies this contradiction—that is, the normalization of heteropatriarchy on the one hand, and the emergence of eroticized and gendered racial formations that dispute heteropatriarchy's universality on the other. Understanding the drag-queen prostitute means that we must locate her within a national culture that disavows the configuration of her own racial, gender, class, and sexual particularity and a mode of production that fosters her own formation.

While Marx, like his liberal antagonists, was seduced by the universalization of heteropatriarchy, he can also help us locate procedures of universalization within state formations. As he writes in "On the Jewish Question,"

> [The state] is conscious of being a political state and it manifests its universality only in opposition to these elements [private property, education, occupation, and so forth]. Hegel, therefore, defines the relation of the political state quite correctly when he says: "In order for the state to come in to existence as the self-knowing ethical actuality of spirit, it is essential that it should be distinct from the forms of authority and of faith. But this distinction emerges only in so far as divisions occur within the ecclesiastical sphere itself. It is only in this way that the state, above the particular churches, has attained to the universality of thought—its formal principle—and is bringing this universality into existence."[28]

For Marx, the state establishes its universality in opposition to the particularities of education, property, religion, and occupation. For our own purposes, we may add that this universality exists in opposition to racial, gender, class, and sexual particularities as well. As heteropatriarchy was universalized, it helped to constitute the state and the citizen's universality. Lisa Lowe's arguments about the abstract citizen's relationship to particularity and difference prove instructive here. She writes,

> [The] abstraction of the citizen is always in distinction to the particularity of man's material condition. In this context, for Marx, "political emancipation" of the citizen is the process of relegating to the domain of the private all "nonpolitical" particulars of religion, social rank, education, occupation, and so on in exchange for representation on the political terrain of the state where "man is the imaginary member of an imaginary sovereignty, divested of his real, individual life, and infused with an unreal universality."[29]

The universality of the citizen exists in opposition to the intersecting particularities that account for material existence, particularities of race, gender, class, and sexuality. As a category of universality, normative heteropatriarchy or heteronormativity exists in opposition to the particularities that constitute nonheteronormative racial formations. In this formulation, the citizen is a racialized emblem of heteronormativity whose universality exists at the expense of particularities of race, gender, and sexuality.

Ironically, capital helps produce formations that contradict the universality of citizenship. As the state justifies property through this presumed universality, through claims about access, equivalence, rights, and humanity, capital contradicts that universality by enabling social formations marked by intersecting particularities of race, gender, class, and sexuality. Those formations are the evidence of multiplications. By this I mean the multiplication of racialized discourses of gender and sexuality and the multiplication of labor under capital. Addressing the multiplication of discourses and their relationship to modernity, Foucault argues, "The nineteenth century and our own have been rather the age of multiplication: a dispersion of sexualities, a strengthening of their disparate forms, a multiple implantation of 'perversions.' Our epoch has initiated sexual heterogeneities."[30] For Marx, the multiplication of class divisions and economic exploitation characterizes modernity. As he states, "Growth of capital implies growth of its constituent, in other words, the part invested in labour-power."[31] Despite conventional wisdom, we may think of these two types of multiplication in tandem. For instance, in "On the Jewish Question," Marx states, "Man, in his most *intimate* reality, in civil society, is a profane being. Here, where he appears both to himself and to others as a real individual he is an *illusory* phenomenon."[32] Man, the subject of civil society, is not an unmediated figure. As an illusory phenomenon, Man is constituted within discourse. Like the British prostitute and the race of tub men, Man testifies to capital as a simultaneously discursive and material site. The growth of capital implies the proliferation of discourses.

The gendered and eroticized history of U.S. racialization compels us to address both these versions of multiplication. Indeed, my use of nonheteronormativity attempts to name the intersection between the racialized multiplication of gender and sexual perversions and the dispersion of capitalist property relations. Anxieties about this multiplication characterized American industrialization. The migrations of Asians, Europeans, Mexicans, and African Americans generated anxieties about how emerging racial formations were violating gender and sexual norms. As racialized ethnic minorities became the producers of capitalist surplus value, the American political economy was transformed into an apparatus that implanted and multiplied intersecting racial, gender, and sexual perversions. Nonwhite populations were racialized such that gender and sexual transgressions were not incidental to the production of nonwhite labor, but constitutive of it. For instance, industrial expansion in the southwest from 1910 to 1930, as George Sanchez notes, "created an escalating demand for low-wage labor" and inspired more than one million Mexicans to immigrate to the United States.[33] The entrance of Mexican immigrant labor into the U.S. workforce occasioned the rise of Americanization programs designed to inculcate American ideals into the Mexican household. Those programs were premised on the racialized construction of the Mexican immigrant as primitive in terms of sexuality, and premodern in terms of conjugal rites and domestic habits.[34] In the nineteenth century as well, San Francisco's Chinatown was the site of polymorphous sexual formations that were marked as deviant because they were nonreproductive and nonconjugal. Formed in relation to exclusion laws that prohibited the immigration of Asian women to the United States and out of U.S. capital's designation of Asian immigrants as surplus and redundant labor, Chinatown became known for its bachelor societies, opium dens, and prostitutes. Each one of these formations rearticulated normative familial arrangements and thereby violated a racialized ideal of heteropatriarchal nuclearity.[35] Likewise, as African American urban communities of the North were created out of the demands of northern capital in the early twentieth century, they gave birth to vice districts that in turn transformed gender and sexual ideals and practices in northern cities. As Kevin Mumford notes, spurred by a wartime economy and "in protest of outrageous repression" in the South, the Great Migration—through the production of speakeasies, black and tans, intermarriage, and fallen women—caused a change in "gender roles, standards of sexuality," and conjugal ideals.[36]

As capital solicited Mexican, Asian, Asian American, and African American labor, it provided the material conditions that would ultimately disrupt the gender and sexual ideals upon which citizenship depended. The racialization of Mexican, Asian, Asian American, and African American labor as contrary to gender and sexual normativity positioned such labor outside the image of the American citizen. The state's regulation of nonwhite gender and sexual practices through Americanization programs, vice commissions, residential segregation, and immigration exclusion attempted to press non-whites into gender and sexual conformity despite the gender and sexual diversity of those racialized groups. That diversity was, in large part, the outcome of capital's demand for labor. As a technology of race, U.S. citizenship has historically ascribed heteronormativity (universality) to certain subjects and nonheteronormativity (particularity) to others. The state worked to regulate the gender and sexual nonnormativity of these racialized groups in a variety of ways. In doing so, it produced discourses that pathologized nonheteronormative U.S. racial formations. In the case of Mexican immigrants, Americanization programs attempted to reconstitute the presumably preindustrial Mexican home, believed to be indifferent to domestic arrangements and responsibilities. Doing so meant that the Mexican mother had to be transformed into a proper custodian who would be fit for domestic labor in white homes, as well as her own. As George Sanchez notes, "By encouraging Mexican immigrant women to wash, sew, cook, budget, and mother happily and efficiently, Americans would be assured that Mexican women would be ready to enter the labor market, while simultaneously presiding over a home that nurtured American values of economy."[37] In the case of Asian Americans, immigration exclusion laws worked to ensure that the gender and sexual improprieties of Asian Americans would not transgress U.S. boundaries as residential segregation worked to guarantee that such impropriety among Asian and Asian American residents would not contaminate white middle-class neighborhoods. In like fashion, vice commissions in New York and Chicago, along with antimiscegenation laws, attempted to insulate middle-class whites from the real and presumed gender and sexual nonnormative practices of African Americans and Asian Americans.

Despite his naturalization of gender, sexuality, and race, Marx is useful for thinking about how capital fundamentally disrupts social hierarchies. Those disruptions account for the polymorphous perversions that arise out of the production of labor. Marx defines surplus labor as that labor that capitalist accumulation "constantly produces, and produces indeed in direct relation with its own energy and extent." Surplus populations are populations that are "relatively redundant working populations . . . that is superfluous to capital's average requirements for its own valorization."[38] Surplus populations exist as future laborers for capital, "always ready for exploitation by capital in the interests of capital's own changing valorization requirements."[39] Both superfluous and indispensable, surplus populations fulfill *and* exceed the demands of capital.

In the United States, racial groups who have a history of being excluded from the rights and privileges of citizenship (African Americans, Asian Americans, Native Americans, and Latinos, particularly) have made up the surplus populations upon which U.S. capital has depended. The production of such populations has accounted for much of the racial heterogeneity within the United States. As mentioned before, the heterogeneity represented by U.S. surplus populations was achieved to a large degree because of capital's need to accumulate labor.

As capital produced surplus populations, it provided the contexts out of which nonheteronormative racial formations emerged.[40] As U.S. capital had to constantly look outside local and national boundaries for labor, it often violated ideals of racial homogeneity held by local communities and the United States at large. As it violated those ideals, capital also inspired worries that such violations would lead to the disruption of gender and sexual proprieties. If racialization has been the "site of a contradiction between the promise of political emancipation and the conditions of economic exploitation,"[41] then much of that contradiction has pivoted on the racialization of working populations as deviant in terms of gender and sexuality. As formations that transgress capitalist political economies, surplus populations become the locations for possible critiques of state and capital.

Marx addresses many of the ways in which capital fosters social heterogeneity and therefore nonequivalent formations. For instance, he states,

> As soon as capitalist production takes possession of agriculture, and in proportion to the extent to which it does so, the demand for a rural working population falls absolutely, while the accumulation of the capital employed in agriculture advances, without this repulsion being compensated for by a greater attraction of workers, as is the case in non-agricultural industries. Part of the agricultural population is therefore constantly on the point of passing over into an urban or manufacturing proletariat, and on the lookout for opportunities to complete this transformation. . . . There is thus a constant flow from this source of the relative surplus population.[42]

Moreover, as capital produced certain working populations as redundant, it inspired rural populations to migrate in search of employment, a move that ensured greater and greater heterogeneity in urban areas. The constant flow of surplus populations from the rural to the urban captures the diverse histories of nonwhite migrations within and to the United States. For instance, this movement from the rural to the urban denotes the history of African American migration.

As well as exceeding local and regional boundaries, surplus populations disrupt social hierarchies of race, gender, age, and sexuality. As it produces surplus, capital compels the transgression of previously established hierarchies and provides the context for the emergence of new social arrangements, identities, and practices. As Marx states,

> We have further seen that the capitalist buys with the same capital a greater mass of labour-power, as he progressively replaces skilled workers by less skilled, mature labour-power by immature, male by female, that of adults by that of young persons or children. (788)

To adapt this insight to the circumstances of U.S. working populations we might add "immigrant" and "nonwhite" to that of "less skilled," "female," and "child." Hence, the creation of surplus is the violation of the boundaries of age, home, race, and nation.

Surplus populations point to a fundamental feature of capital: It does not rely on normative prescriptions to assemble labor, even while it may use those prescriptions to establish the value of that labor. Capital is based on a logic of reproduction that fundamentally overrides and often violates heteropatriarchy's logic. Subsequently, capital often goes against the state's universalization and normalization of heteropatriarchy. Discussing the ways in which capital bypasses heterosexual means of reproduction, Marx argues,

> The expansion by fits and starts of the scale of production is the precondition for its equally sudden contraction; the latter again evokes the former, but the former is impossible without disposable human material, without an increase in the number of workers, which must occur *independently of the absolute growth of the population.* (785–86)

Continuing with this argument, he states

> Capitalist production can by no means content itself with the quantity of disposable labour-power which the natural increase of population yields. It requires for its unrestricted activity an industrial reserve army which is *independent of these natural limits.* (788, italics mine)

Capital is based on a fundamentally amoral logic. Capital, without pressures from the state or citizenry, will assemble labor without regard for normative prescriptions of race and gender. Capital, on the other hand, will oblige normative prescriptions, especially in those moments in which it wants to placate the interests of the state.

While capital can only reproduce itself by ultimately transgressing the boundaries of neighborhood, home, and region, the state positions itself as the protector of those boundaries. As the modern nation-state has historically been organized around an illusory universality particularized in terms of race, gender, sexuality, and class, state formations have worked to protect and guarantee this universality. But in its production of surplus populations unevenly marked by a racialized nonconformity with gender and sexual norms, capital constantly disrupts that universality. As the state and heteronormativity work to guarantee and protect that universality, they do so against the productive needs and social conditions set by capital, conditions that produce nonheteronormative racial formations. If heteronormativity is racialized, as I have been arguing, then it is not only gender and sexual integrity that are at stake for heteronormative formations, like the state, but racial integrity and purity as well. As capital disrupts social hierarchies in the production of surplus labor, it disrupts gender ideals and sexual norms that are indices of racial difference. Disrupting those ideals often leads to new racialized gender and sexual formations. To restate, capital requires the transgression of space and the creation of possibilities for intersection and convergence. Capital, therefore, calls for subjects who must transgress the material and ideological boundaries of community, family, and nation. Such transgressions are brought into relief through the capitalist production of labor. As surplus labor becomes the impetus for anxieties about the sanctity of "community," "family," and "nation," it reveals the ways in which these categories are normalized in terms of race, gender, sexuality, and class. Indeed, the production of labor, ultimately, throws the normative boundaries of race, gender, class, and sexuality into confusion.

Nonheteronormative racial formations represent the historic accumulation of contradictions[43] around race, gender, sexuality, and class. The variety of such racial formations (Asian, Asian American, Mexican, Chicano, Native American, African American, and so forth) articulates different racialized, gendered, and eroticized contradictions to the citizen-ideal of the state and the liberatory promise of capital. In doing so, they identify the ways in which race, gender, and sexuality intersect within capitalist political economies and shape the conditions of capital's existence. To address these formations as an accumulation means that we must ask the question of what possibilities they offer for agency. We must see the gendered and eroticized elements of racial formations as offering ruptural—i.e., critical—possibilities. Approaching them as sites of critique means that we must challenge the construction of these formations as monstrous and threatening to others who have no possibility of critical agency and instead engage nonheteronormative racial formations as the site of ruptures, critiques, and alternatives. Racial formations, as they are constituted nonnormatively by gender and sexual differences, overdetermine[44] national identity, contradicting its manifold promises of citizenship and property. This overdetermination could compel intersecting antiracist, feminist, class, and queer struggles to emerge.

Epistemology, Political Economy, and Regulation

Historical materialism is not the only inquiry into social formations characterized by investments in normative epistemes. Canonical American sociology betrays those investments as well. Canonical sociology denotes a discursive formation that emerges out of Enlightenment claims to rationality and scientific objectivity. These claims entail an investment in heterosexual patriarchy as the appropriate standard for social relations and the signature of hegemonic whiteness. As canonical sociology has racialized heteropatriarchy through whiteness, the discipline has excluded and disciplined those formations that deviate from the racial ideal of heteropatriarchy.

We can see the exclusionary and disciplinary techniques at work in the discipline's engagement with African American culture. American sociology has historically understood civilization as the production of wealth and order and as the spread of disorder and dehumanization. American sociology, like historical materialism, has proffered heteronormativity as the scene of order and rationality and nonheteronormativity as the scene of abandonment and dysfunction. In doing so, the discipline has contributed to the discursivity of capital. I turn now to canonical sociology because it has contributed to that discursivity as it has produced racial knowledge about African American culture. Indeed, sociology has been a hegemonic site of reflection about African American culture and has read that culture consistently through a heteronormative lens. American sociology has deployed liberal ideology as the main paradigm through which to read American racialization. Historical materialism has provided the means by which canonical sociology could translate processes of state and capital into a narrative of African American racial formation and disruptions to gender and sexual ideals.[45] In fact, universalizing heteropatriarchy and understanding that universalization as whiteness and through American citizenship defined the core of sociological reflection about African American culture. As it has done so, formations like the drag-queen prostitute have been a constant preoccupation that canonical sociology has constructed as pathologies emblematic of African American culture. Looking at canonical sociology's relationship to African American nonheteronormative formations can help us see how U.S. capital has also been regarded as a site of pathologies and perversions that have designated racialized nonwhite communities as the often ominous outcome of capital's productive needs. As I stated earlier, queer of color analysis attempts to explain how gender and sexuality variegate racial formations and how that variety indexes material processes. We must engage racial knowledge about African American culture as it was produced by sociology if we are to understand the gender and sexual variation within African American culture as the outcome of material and discursive processes.

In *Modernity and Self-Identity*, Anthony Giddens argues that reflection is one of the institutional traits of modernity and that "[sociology], and the social sciences more widely conceived, are inherent elements of the institutional reflexivity of modernity."[46] In the United States, the social changes that characterized American modernity brought different peoples and cultures within close proximity to one another. Because of these changes, sociology sought to "understand the ways in which societies (or cultures or peoples) differed from one another,"[47] initiating a foundational concern with difference into sociology's reflexive project. We can see American sociology's interest in difference in the discipline's fascination with the social conditions of African American existence. For early American sociologists of racial relations, the question of African American culture became the location within which sociologists could speculate about the relationships between modernization and cultural difference. Even though these sociologists of race often presumed that they were studying racial phenomena that were external to them, the sociology of race was, in fact, a site for the production of racial knowledge that "consisted *ex hypothesi* in the making of difference."[48] The sociological writings about race "[were] part of the *reflexivity* of modernity: they [served] routinely to organise and alter the aspects of social life they [reported] on or [analysed]."[49]

American sociology began as a way to reflect on "the vast dislocations from extremely rapid urbanization and industrialization. [It] was shaped from the start by a *moral response to immediate national social problems—racial and cultural concerns prominent among them.*"[50] The social problems that occasioned sociological interest were ones posed by migrations to urban areas. In sociological discourses, African American migration loomed largely in narratives of urban and industrial dislocations and in the moral responses to national and social problems enunciated on the axes of race and culture. Whereas in 1910, 637,000 African Americans lived in cities in the North and the West, by 1930 that number had grown to 2,228,000.[51] Sociologists worried that African American migrants from rural beginnings were culturally unfit and morally unversed for the demands of city life. Canonical sociology imagined African American culture as the site of polymorphous gender and sexual perversions and associated those perversions with moral failings typically. During this period, sociologists broke with prior formulations of African American racial difference by eschewing explanations of biological inferiority but revised those formulations by offering the cultural inferiority of African Americans as an explanation for urban poverty and social upheaval. Often sociologists explained African American poverty and upheaval through what was considered African American gender, sexual, and familial eccentricity. Sociological arguments about African American cultural inferiority were racialized discourses of gender and sexuality. As Kobena Mercer argues, "[A]ssumptions about black sexuality lie at the heart of the ideological view that black households constitute deviant, disorganized and even pathological familial forms that fail to socialize their members into societal norms."[52]

At the base of sociological arguments about African American cultural inferiority lay questions about how well African Americans approximated heteronormative ideals and practices embodied in whiteness and ennobled in American citizenship. For instance, African Americans' fitness for citizenship was measured in terms of how much their sexual, familial, and gender relations deviated from a bourgeois nuclear family model historically embodied by whites.[53] The sexualized construction of African Americans was both a way of grounding African American racial difference within the so-called vagaries of the sexual and a way of locating African Americans within liberal capitalism. Liberal ideology has typically understood the family as that institution that provides stability and civility against the instability and ruthlessness of civil society.[54] That ideology has historically constructed the African American family as an insufficient tether against the chaos of civil society. The advancement of capitalism, therefore, has occasioned the state's efforts to displace the social burdens of that advancement onto relations within the private sphere, making the African American family the bearer of those burdens. Liberal ideology has recommended conforming to the heterosexual nuclear family model as the appropriate way to bear such burdens.[55] Canonical sociology has consistently abutted that ideology by demanding the heteronormalization of African Americans as the primary resolution to economic devastation. By "[naturalizing] heterosexuality as the only possible, sensible, and desirable organizing principle by which society and social relations can function,"[56] canonical sociology aligned itself with the regulatory imperatives of the state against African Americans.

African American culture has historically been deemed contrary to the norms of heterosexuality and patriarchy. As its embodiment in whiteness attests, heteronormativity is not simply articulated through intergender relations, but also through the racialized body. Sociology helped to establish African American corporeal difference as the sign of a nonheteronormativity presumed to be fundamental to African American culture.[57] Marking African Americans as such was a way of disenfranchising them politically and economically. In sum, the material and discursive production of African American nonheteronormativity provided the interface between the gendered and eroticized properties of African American racial formation and the material practices of state and civil society.

I theorize African American nonheteronormative difference as a way of thinking discourse and contradiction in tandem. Foucault argues against the presumption that the modern age was simply about the repression of sexuality, arguing instead that scientific discourses have produced a multiplicity of sexual perversions. Foucault is also arguing against narratives that locate the age of repression within the development of capitalism and bourgeois order.[58] We may extend and revise Foucault's argument by addressing the ways in which sociological discourse produced multiple sexual and gender perversions coded as nonwhite racial difference and as the study of African American culture. By engaging capital as a site of contradictions that compels racial formations that are eccentric to gender and sexual normativity, I have also attempted to revise the presumption that capital is the site of gender and sexual uniformity.

But canonical sociology has produced that heterogeneity to discipline it. In *The Dialogic Imagination,* Mikhail Bakhtin defines canonization as a process that attempts to suppress the heterogeneity of meaning. For Bakhtin, the heterogeneity refers to the multiplicity that characterizes a given social context. Sociology, when incarnated canonically, attempts to discursively suppress an actual material heterogeneity. The material heterogeneity that I've been discussing is one that critically exposes the gender and sexual diversity within racial formations. That multiplicity points to the illusions of universal claims as they are taken up by canonical sociology and the American state. As canonical sociology suppresses heterogeneity in the name of universality, it becomes an epistemological counterpart to the state's enforcement of universality as the state suppresses nonheteronormative racial difference. Pathologizing the material heterogeneity embodied in African American nonheteronormative formations disciplines its critical possibilities. As a site that arches toward universality, canonical sociology can only obscure the ways that nonheteronormative racial formations point to the contradictions between the promise of equality and the practice of exclusions based on a racialized gender and sexual eccentricity, an eccentricity produced through discourse and articulated in practice. As the universal has been the justification for political and economic regulations of those formations deemed antithetical to it, canonical sociology has intersected with forms of nationalism and capital over the gendered and sexual regulation of nonwhite populations.

As canonical formations suppress the multiplicity of a social context, they also regulate the diversity that constitutes a discipline. As canonical formations are constituted through claims to universality, they oblige themselves to the regulatory and exclusionary imperatives of those claims. They must present their own histories as ones emptied of formations that contradict universality. In the context of canonical sociology, black sociologists occupy such a position. During periods of segregation and industrialization, African American sociologists were incapable of claiming the illusory universality fostered by canonical sociology. Black sociologists such as St. Claire Drake, Horace Cayton, and E. Franklin Frazier operated within a historical moment that constructed the black body as the antithesis of the rationality and universality of Western epistemology and American citizenship. Whereas the bodies of canonical (i.e., "white") sociologists were unmarked by particularities of gender, sexuality, class, and race, the bodies of black sociologists were the signs of racial differences that placed the rationality of African American sociologists into question. The nonheteronormative racial difference associated with black bodies prevented them from claiming canonical status. For instance, during the 1930s the Carnegie Corporation asked a "neutral" and "objective" Swedish sociologist—Gunnar Myrdal—to head the major study of race relations within the United States rather than E. Franklin Frazier, despite Frazier's status as the authority on race within the states.[59] Canonical sociology excluded black sociologists as subjects who could not claim the universal properties of the rational subject of epistemology and the citizen-subject of the United States.

Without a doubt, black sociologists from the thirties to the seventies contributed to the body of sociological knowledge. We need only think of how influential Charles Johnson's work was to Gunnar Myrdal's *American Dilemma* or to how E. Franklin Frazier's theories about the black family laid the groundwork for Daniel Patrick Moynihan's *The Negro Family*. As a regulatory and exclusionary formation, canonical sociology has subjugated the history of African American sociology, making authors like Myrdal, Moynihan, Park, and Burgess the spectacular representatives of American sociology's interest in social relations during periods of industrialization. In turn, canonical sociology has made black sociologists such as Du Bois, Horace Cayton, St. Clair Drake, E. Franklin Frazier, Charles Johnson, Kelly Miller, and Monroe Work part of the unread genealogy of American sociology. Canonical sociology expresses an ideological imperative, one that calls for the subjugation of the historical roles of African American sociologists. Hence as I address canonical sociology throughout this text, I am not referring to black sociologists. While these authors may be canonical to African American studies, they are part of the unseen and subterranean layers of American sociology. While seemingly a progressive and democratic move, including African American sociologists within the definition of canonical sociology actually denies the regulatory and exclusionary practices of canonical formations and suggests the perfection of the discipline. This sort of move is really liberal ideology applied to epistemology. Rather than reifying the suppression of African American sociologists by not addressing them at all, I attempt to demonstrate the ways in which canonical sociology has usurped their intellectual work and banished them from the taken-for-granted and lived history of American sociology.

As it has imputed African American culture with hegemonic meanings, canonical sociology is part of the genealogy of African American nonheteronormativity. It has constructed African American racial difference as the exemplar of social pathologies that suggest gender and sexual disorders. Moreover, it has affixed that meaning to African American culture and to African American bodies. Canonical sociology has consistently said that these hegemonic formulations are appropriate to understanding the upheavals formed by industrialization.

Culture, Heterogeneity, and Rupture

In their introduction to *The Politics of Culture in the Shadow of Capital*, Lisa Lowe and David Lloyd make the following argument:

> We suggest "culture" obtains a political force when a cultural formation comes into contradiction with economic or political logics that try to refunction it for exploitation or domination. Rather than adopting the understanding of culture as one sphere in a set of differentiated spheres and practices, we discuss "culture" as a terrain in which politics, culture, and the economic form an inseparable dynamic.[60]

I have been implying throughout this chapter that epistemology, along with politics and economics, composes the cultural terrain as well. Indeed, African American culture obtains a political force as American sociology has attempted to retool African American nonheteronormative difference for state and economic exploitation and domination. As the site of nonheteronormative difference, African American culture materially and discursively registers the gender and sexual heterogeneity of African American racial formations as critiques of the contradictions of state and capital and the regulations of canonical sociology.

This book critiques canonical sociology by concentrating on a cultural form that negotiates with the material and discursive components of African American culture. That cultural form is the African American novel. Indeed, the material and discursive multiplicity of African American culture registers upon African American novels. As I have been suggesting, the gender and sexual heterogeneity of that culture interrogates the singularity, normativity, and universality presupposed by national culture. As minority cultural forms, African American novels record that interrogation. Produced within a history of exclusion and nonwhite racialization, these forms are both within and outside canonical genealogies. Hence, we cannot assume that African American cultural forms interrogate national culture in ways that are transparent or intentional. Canonical formations pressure cultural forms, in general, but literature in particular. The contradictory formation of African American literature—as both within and outside of canonical genealogy—means that we can exploit its alienation from canonical presumptions of universality and normativity to provide a critique of the ways in which African Americans have been racialized as pathologically nonheteronormative. We may even use this cultural form to deepen our understanding of the gender and sexual multiplicity that constitutes African American culture. If we were to relate this sort of interrogation to queer of color analysis, we might say that queer of color critique employs cultural forms to bear witness to the critical gender and sexual heterogeneity that comprises minority cultures. Queer of color analysis does this to shed light on the ruptural components of culture, components that expose the restrictions of universality, the exploitations of capital, and the deceptions of national culture.

As an example of the ways in which canonical ideologies pressured African American literature, we need only look at the historical and ideological circumstances out of which black writing arose. In *Figures in Black: Words, Signs, and the "Racial" Self,* for instance, Henry Louis Gates identifies the ways that African American literature arose as a way to claim humanity for African Americans, and in doing so, took up Enlightenment practices of recognition and legitimation. He argues,

> [The] black tradition's own concern with winning the war against racism had led it not only to accept this arbitrary relationship but to embrace it, judging its own literature by a curious standard that derived from the social applications of the metaphors of the great chain of being, the idea of progress and the perfectibility of man, as well as the metaphor of capacity derived initially from eighteenth-century comparative studies of the anatomy of simian and human brains and then translated into a metaphor for intelligence and the artistic potential of a "race."[61]

Inasmuch as African American writing thematized progress and perfectibility, it located itself within the signature preoccupations of modernity.

Aesthetic culture has pronounced progress and perfectibility within the intertwining languages of nationalism and normativity. The nineteenth-century French intellectual and Enlightenment exponent Germaine de Staël defined the relationship between canonical literature, nationalism, and morality when she wrote, "Literature can derive its enduring beauty only from the most perfect morality. . . . If Literature can serve morality, it must also have a powerful influence upon renown, for there can be no enduring honor in a country where there is no public morality."[62] As literature upholds public morality, it gives honor to the nation. According to Madame de Staël, literature's aesthetic function is inseparable from its normative and political function. David Theo Goldberg situates the Enlightenment's reformulation of classical aesthetics within eighteenth-century practices of racialization. He states, "[N]atural qualities of beauty and perfection were supposed to be established on a priori grounds of racial membership."[63] Progress and perfection became the racialized tropes of the Enlightenment and were immediately associated with aesthetic culture. Celebrating the dictates of morality would assure literature its universality and grant distinction to the nation-state, a distinction and universality that, in the context of the eighteenth and nineteenth centuries, were racialized *and* normalized.

In *Democracy in America*, Alexis de Tocqueville echoed Madame de Staël's sentiments. Discussing the relationship between the life of the mind and the rational individual who is the epistemological counterpart of the liberal citizen-subject, Tocqueville states that "[poetry], eloquence, memory, the graces of the mind, the fires of the imagination and profundity of thought, all things scattered broadcast by heaven, were a profit to democracy, and . . . served its cause by throwing into relief the natural greatness of man."[64] Tocqueville, like Madame de Staël, assumes intellectual and aesthetic work will promote the normalizing knowledges of the liberal state. Those knowledges distinguish between the rational citizen, who embodies and claims the rights and privileges of citizenship, versus the irrational other, who can never possess those rights and privileges.[65] If morality is that which legitimates certain social practices, then liberal ideology delegated aesthetic culture to justify normative social relations and the liberal nation-state. Moreover, aesthetic culture could demonstrate moral fitness for citizenship, demonstrating that the citizen-subject is idealized through race and conceived in normativity.

Accordingly, liberal ideology has often presented literature as a mechanism by which marginalized groups can bid for the normative positions of state and civil society. Abolitionists used the poetry of Phyllis Wheatley and the letters of Ignatius Sancho to show "that the untutored African may possess abilities equal to an European."[66] Aesthetic practices would grant access to national culture and Western civilization and would bestow the properties of the rational (i.e., "white") citizen-subject onto the irrational other. As canonical interpretations format literature to enable morality, they presume literature's obligation to normalize and universalize heteropatriarchal relations. As we saw with canonical sociology and historical materialism, universalizing and normalizing heteropatriarchal relations would also necessitate disciplining nonheteronormative formations. Indeed, regulating nonheteronormative elements exposes a nationalist imperative at work within aesthetics. As it responds to canonical pressures, literature engages the racialized genealogy of citizen and state formations.

As queer of color critique addresses minority cultural forms as both within and outside canonical genealogies, pointing to the ruptural possibilities of those forms means that culture is not simply exhausted by its complicity with regulation. Inasmuch as minority cultural forms are eccentric to the normative and racialized properties of canonical formations, they suggest possibilities outside the normative parameters and racialized boundaries of those canonical structures. For instance, following Homi Bhabha, we may say that African American novels, as minority cultural forms that suggest the racialized gender and sexual nonnormativity of African American culture, only mimic the properties of canonical literature. As discourses of mimicry, they estrange themselves from the normalizing knowledges upon which canonical literature is founded, namely its reliance upon and privileging of the normative heterosexual subject idealized by the West. Apprehending African American literature as a critical cultural site means that we must read it not simply as consistent with the universalist ideals of nationalism. We must read African American literature as a cultural form, that is, to show how it disrupts those ideals by referring to a gender and sexual multiplicity constitutive of African American culture.

As African American cultural forms distance themselves from the normative claims of canonical formations, they simultaneously estrange themselves from liberal articulations of aesthetics and canonical enunciations of sociology. Historically even African American novels, as cultural forms, often converged with American sociology in a contest over African American representation, naming sociology as a contradictory and *ambivalent*[67] enterprise located between the humanities and the natural sciences and positioned as both the critic and the supplicant of the American state.[68] As such, sociology's claims to objectivity were often dogged by suggestions of discursivity, especially where racial matters were concerned. And its declarations of progressive solidarity with racially egalitarian projects were questioned on the basis of sociology's discursive practices, which often enabled, rather than disabled, racial regulation. Hence, in saying that African American culture is a site of contradiction, I do not mean to suggest that sociology is not contradictory. I simply mean to suggest that African American culture's own particular contradiction of being racialized as nonheteronormative produces nonheteronormativity as a site of rupture. Canonical sociology could not produce nonheteronormativity as a site of rupture because whether as supplicant or as critic, sociology universalized and racialized heteropatriarchy and pathologized nonheteronormativity as nonwhite difference. In this book, I have juxtaposed sociological texts alongside African American novels to demonstrate how African American culture as a site of reflection compelled struggles and confrontations over the meaning of the gendered and sexual diversity associated with African American culture. In other words, I situate African American novelists alongside canonical sociologists to illuminate how African American culture as an epistemological object produced dialogical relations that both exceeded the formal parameters of its interlocutors and confused the distinctions between factual and fictive enterprises.

In chapter 1 I address the formation of nonheteronormative subjects and practices in industrial Chicago during the 1930s. I analyze Richard Wright's *Native Son*; Robert Park, Ernest Burgess, and Roderick McKenzie's *The City*; and an unpublished ethnography about a transgender ball on Chicago's South Side. Each of these texts refers to the discursive explosion around a heterogeneously constituted African American culture. Moreover, they point to the ways in which U.S. industrialization disrupted hegemonic gender and sexual ideals and how that disruption was spoken as racial difference.

Chapter 2 analyzes an unpublished chapter from Ralph Ellison's *Invisible Man*. In this chapter, a black queer university professor named Woodridge calls for a critique of the ways in which canonical literary and sociological formations serve as discursive locations that produce racial and sexual knowledge about African Americans. Chapter 2 interrogates the ways that nonheteronormative subject formations critique developmental narratives of migration, narratives that figure nonwhite migration as witness to the liberal state's perfection and to capital's benevolence. Such narratives presume a subject whose ethical development is organized normatively. As nonheteronormative subjects of color are estranged from the normativity of ethical development, African American nonheteronormative subjects rebut social science, literature, state, and capital's presumptions about progress, perfectibility, and recognition. Disputing those presumptions offers insights about the migratory narratives of other racial formations. This chapter then evokes canonical sociology's role in creating a discourse around African American nonheteronormativity to reconsider Foucault's theory of how sexual knowledge is produced and upon what subjects that knowledge is based.

As chapter 2 critiques developmental narratives from the vantage point of nonheteronormative social and subject formations, chapter 3 analyzes rationality as a subject and social formation that linked the racialization of African Americans to racialization within colonial regimes. As the book approaches racialization as the production of gender and sexual heterogeneity, chapter 3 interrogates diaspora as a gendered and eroticized process as well. The chapter engages African American nonheteronormative formations to refuse the discrete presumptions of national identity and to link up with the anticolonial struggles of diasporic blacks. To do so, I juxtapose Gunnar Myrdal's *American Dilemma: The Negro and American Democracy* with James Baldwin's *Go Tell It on the Mountain* to highlight the gender and sexual regulations of American citizenship and to locate those regulations within Western nation-state formations, in general. In the chapter, I read *Go Tell It on the Mountain* as an analysis of the ways in which Western rationality is a technique of racialization that requires erotic subjugation. I go on to locate critiques of rationality's disciplinary imperatives within the genealogy of decolonization. I conclude by insisting that diasporic critiques integrate analyses of gender and sexual normativity.

Taking the gender and sexual exclusions of decolonizing and civil rights struggles as its point of departure, chapter 4 explores the emergence of black lesbian feminist critiques in the 1970s, analyzing how woman of color theorizations of intersections index the rise of transnational capital as an economic formation that commodifies nonwhite female labor for surplus extraction. By locating the emergence of black lesbian feminism within the exclusions of anticolonial, revolutionary, and cultural nationalist social movements, I argue that black lesbian feminist formations attempted to disrupt the normative genealogy of oppositional movements. To contextualize this emergence, the chapter creates a dialogue between Toni Morrison's *Sula* and Daniel Patrick Moynihan's 1965 text, *The Negro Family: A Case for National Action*, popularly known as *The Moynihan Report*. The chapter analyzes how *The Moynihan Report*, through its theory of black matriarchy, presented the grammar of state and citizen formation as the one most appropriate for decolonizing subjects, a grammar that insisted on the disciplining of gender and sexual nonnormativity. As an example of how revolutionary nationalism intersects with the normative protocols of canonical sociology, the chapter attempts to show how investments in heteronormativity provided occasions for unlikely alliances between radical movements and liberal social science. For instance, the chapter looks at the way in which revolutionary nationalism invested in Moynihan's theory of matriarchy, arguing that the theory displaced anxieties about the destabilization of heteropatriarchy onto black women's hunger for castration and occluded the gendered exploitations of capital. Black lesbian feminists attempted to theorize these displacements and occlusions and address contemporary capital as a set of relations characterized by an unprecedented gender and racial diversity. Hence, theorizing intersections was a way of naming the manifold outcomes of that diversity and determining what new strategies and opportunities for coalition could arise from it. In this context, black lesbian feminists engaged Toni Morrison's *Sula* as a means to fashion a subject who could critique the aforementioned displacements and create alternatives to them.

The conclusion to this book explores the ways that contemporary state formations lubricate the mobility of capital by enlisting middle-class minorities to regulate the gender and sexual eccentricities of nonwhite populations. The present moment requires a critique of canonical social science, and state and revolutionary nationalisms as they all participate in the gendered and sexual regulation of nonwhite peoples. In the conclusion, I acknowledge the complicity between state formations under globalization and minority middle classes as the cooptation of prior social movements. I argue that contemporary globalization is one in which normativity still organizes state and citizen formations, but apprehends subjects previously excluded from the normative privileges of sovereignty and rights. This chapter also theorizes postnationalist American studies as one epistemic formation that might presume the relations specific to woman of color and queer of color subjects as a way of imagining forms of sociality and agency that exceed the normative binds of citizenship.

We need a study of racial formations that will not oblige heteropatriarchy, an analysis of sexuality not severed from race and material relations, an interrogation of African American culture that keeps company with other racial formations, and an American studies not beguiled by the United States. This book represents an attempt to theorize queer of color critique as an answer to these needs. As an inquiry into the nonnormative components of racial formations and as a challenge to the manifold restrictions of normative epistemes, queer of color analysis can be another step in the move beyond identity politics and toward what Angela Davis calls "unlikely and unprecedented coalitions."[69]

1

The Knee-pants of Servility: American Modernity, the Chicago School, and *Native Son*

> As the night wears on some of them begin to wear makeup, even going so far as to put on artificial eyelashes. Quite a number have painted fingernails. . . . Are such places as the one described a detriment to society? It is a question that requires careful analysis and consideration. It does provide an outlet for these unstable people who are forced to repress their feelings in the normal group. But still we wonder if this process of conditioning and obvious approval doesn't encourage those on the borderline to slip into this role of uncertainty.
>
> —Conrad Bentzen, "Notes on the Homosexual in Chicago"

In 1938, South Side streets were full of wonders that, for many, testified to the swing of city life and the march of industry. And on one night the celebrants at a South Side party for black homosexuals observed a stranger in their midst. Some drag queen, whose nerves had been tried, thought to herself, "Oh, there goes another white boy tourist come to slum with faggots." But little did she know that his gall went a step further. For the white boy descended upon the South Side not to satisfy sexual curiosity, but to pursue intellectual interests. His name was Conrad Bentzen, and he wished to know of the homosexual and his habitat. And the knowledge that came out of this and other endeavors provided the foundation not only for an academic discipline, but for black radicalism as well.

The student's assumptions about the South Side—that it illustrated the racialized nature of gender and sexual nonnormativity—provide a glimpse of canonical sociology's own presumptions about African American culture. In particular, the Chicago School of Sociology understood American modernity through the category of social disorganization and lifted African American culture up as evidence of modernity's course and society's disorganization. During the period of industrialization within the United States, texts by Chicago School sociologists intersected with the black nationalist writings of Richard Wright through their mutual interests in African American culture as the recipient of modern social formations, but also through their shared assumptions about gender and sexual heterogeneity.

The Disruptions of Modernity: Racialized Migration and New Deal Social Policy

Racial difference formed the basis of American sociology's conception of industrial and commercial capitalism. In the context of the international migrations of people, U.S. scholars and lay persons in the early twentieth century believed that capitalist political economy promoted racial heterogeneity. Those same persons believed that such intercourse disrupted traditional gender and sexual identities and social formations and subsequently gave birth to formations that transgressed heteropatriarchal ideals and institutions. As a matter of fact, these nonheteronormative changes in urban areas provided the context and the motivation for the emergence of Chicago School sociology. As sociologists reformulated the meaning of political economy to account for the new racial formations taking place in the United States, they naturalized heteropatriarchal relations and pathologized nonheteronormative racial formations in the process.

In 1942, Robert Park observed that modernizing processes in the United States were bringing the discontents of progress to America's shores. For Park, global commerce and trade were inspiring new and unforeseen racial formations.[1] Cities, media technologies, migration, and international commerce were making racial interaction the signal feature of modernity in general and American modernity in particular.[2] As Park argued, "Every civilization, in extending the area of human intercourse, has invariably brought new concentrations of population and a new intermingling of races."[3]

In a social moment characterized by the intermingling of races, intimacy became the framework for understanding the changes in urban environments. Drawing on this framework, Park imagined that assimilation and modern economic formations encouraged modes of intimacy.[4] Modern capital brought different groups of people into intimate contact with one another in the modern city. That contact became the yardstick for measuring "the rapidity and completeness of assimilation."[5] For instance, as U.S. capital promoted immigration for the purposes of surplus extraction, heterosexual reproduction became the organizing logic for racial assimilation. Park believed, as did others, that such merging took place through sexual contact. In the essay, "Human Migration and the Marginal Man," he wrote:

> In the long run, however, peoples and races who live together, sharing the same economy, inevitably interbreed, and in this way, if no other, the relations which were merely co-operative and economic become social and cultural. When migration leads to conquest, either economic or political, assimilation is inevitable.[6]

Park thus imagined the American political economy as promoting a greater concentration of culturally and racially diverse groups. This concentration then led to sexual exchange and reproduction. Heterosexual reproduction thus functioned as the starting point for social and cultural relations.

Park was not the only one who imagined migration and assimilation through heterosexual reproduction. Theodore Roosevelt endorsed the naturalization of European immigrants on the basis that native whites could intermarry with European immigrants. According to Roosevelt, this "mixture of blood" through intermarriage could produce a "new ethnic type in this melting pot of nations."[7] The creation of this new ethnic type depended on heterosexual reproduction. When the federal government conflated citizenship with whiteness in the post–World War One era, it was asserting that European immigrants could attain the ideals of both whiteness and heteropatriarchy, that they could be candidates for racialized heteronormativity. In doing so, Roosevelt—like Park—was attempting to argue that Southern and Eastern European immigrants were corporeally similar to native whites and therefore eligible partners for heterosexual reproduction and marriage. While ethnically different, European immigrants enjoyed racial similarity to native whites. Rather than threatening racial virility, such immigrants enhanced it. The category of ethnicity extended white racial difference to European immigrants, concealing its role as a technology of race by insisting on European corporeal similarity to native whites.

By insisting on corporeal similarity as a criterion for heterosexual marriage, ethnicity worked also as a technology of sexuality. The logic of ethnicity designated marriage as the site for naturalizing white racial difference and—in Roosevelt's eyes—augmenting racial integrity and virility during the eras of immigration and migration. In such an ideological and political climate, racial purity was idealized in the white family. Heterosexual reproduction by European immigrants and native whites would lead to more advanced social and cultural formations in the United States.

But arguing for the corporeal and thus racial similarity of Eastern and

Southern European immigrants was no small matter. Such arguments were roundly and vehemently contested. In an era in which race was associated with national difference, miscegenation would symbolize the violation of racialized heteronormativity and its guarantee of American (i.e., "white") racial purity. Indeed, miscegenation, for many, typified the nonheteronormative. A German American woman, during the depression, lamented her marriage to a Greek American, "a half-nigger."[8] In addition, the *Saturday Evening Post* extolled Madison Grant's 1916 text *The Passing of the Great Race,* which upheld "the purity of the 'Nordic,' the race of the white man par excellence against 'Alpine,' 'Mediterranean' and Semitic invaders."[9] Moreover, native whites flooded their congresspersons with letters advocating immigration restriction and the "preservation of a 'distinct American type.'"[10] For many, unrestricted immigration would eventually lead to "race suicide." Acknowledging that immigration restriction was largely motivated by a concern for the purity of American racial stock, the director of the National Industrial Conference Board argued that the restriction of immigration was "essentially a racial question."[11] During this period, native whites asserted that Eastern and Southern Europeans were pathogenically nonheteronormative, countering the assertion of the federal government, reformers, and sociologists that Eastern and Southern Europeans could comfortably inhabit the idealized terrain of the racially heteronormative. To regulate the polymorphous perversions produced by an economy based on racial differentiation, the state imposed a formidable arsenal of exclusionary devices. At the same time that the state granted white citizenship to European immigrants, it denied citizenship and property status to Asian immigrants through the Alien Land Laws of 1913, 1920, and 1923.[12]

Consequently, American onlookers regarded the racial features of industrialization and urbanization as the signs of liberal capitalism's perverse and disorganizing underside. These onlookers regarded that underside as perverse because of the ways in which racial contact promoted sexual and gender transgressions. For Park, Ernest Burgess, and Roderick D. McKenzie, the distribution of labor and subsequent residential proximity so fundamental to urbanization disrupted the "intimate relationships of the primary group" and "the moral order which rested upon them." In the city, they argued, the primary group had to compete with other institutions and social forces. Movies, parties, automobiles, and other features of urban life exposed the city's residents to other truths that provided both context and access to alternative subject and social formations. Prostitution, homosexuality, miscegenation, "liquor traffic,"[13] and juvenile delinquency evidenced such alternatives and were very often addressed as the negative and perverse outcomes of industrialization and urbanization. Thematized as the side effects of immigration and migration, miscegenation, juvenile delinquency, prostitution, and homosexuality constituted a constellation of nonheteronormative formations.

While Park and other Chicago sociologists believed that social interaction moved toward social equilibrium and that immigration and migration would eventually lead to assimilation, contradictions within their theory of societal development disrupted their faith in the inevitability of social harmony and assimilation. For example, the very secondary contacts that promoted civilization by generating mobility and individuation could also promote what Chicago sociologists called "social disorganization." In *The City*, Park charged that individualization was the subjective counterpart of social disorganization. As he stated,

> With the growth of great cities, with the vast division of labor which has come in with machine industry, and with movement and change that have come about with the multiplication of the means of transportation and communication, the old forms of social control represented by the family, the neighborhood, and the local community have been undermined and their influence greatly diminished. . . .
>
> This process by which the authority and influence of an earlier culture and system of social control is undermined and eventually destroyed is described by [William I.] Thomas—looking at it from the side of the individual—as a process of *individualization*. But looking at it from the point of view of society and the community it is *social disorganization*.[14]

As social disorganization's counterpart, individualization was a demoralizing feature of modern society, "[breaking] up the habits upon which the existing social organization rests, [destroying] that organization itself."[15] While Park argued that intimate contact completed assimilation, he also believed that the intimacy afforded by the growth of cities, division of labor, transportation, and communication could undo social stability. For Park, social unrest was guaranteed if such secondary agencies as "juvenile courts, juvenile protective associations, parent-teachers' associations, Boy Scouts, Young Men's Christian Association settlements, boys' clubs of various sorts, and . . . playgrounds and playground associations"[16] did not restore the foundations that primary institutions once provided.

As assimilation was imagined through heterosexual procreation and marriage, so was social disorganization. As a concept, social disorganization worked to reinforce heteropatriarchal ideals. Anxious about the stability of those ideals, Chicago School sociologists derived their theory of social disorganization from W. I. Thomas and Florian Znaniecki's *The Polish Peasant in Europe and America*, originally published in 1918. Indeed, Thomas and

Znaniecki addressed social disorganization through the disruption of the romantic love ideal. For the authors, love arose as a conjugal ideal in the moment that familial respect ceased to be the overarching motivation for heterosexual marriage. Rather than being promoted by external cultural forces, in this new context, heteropatriarchal marriage depended on individual motivation and consent. Cultural norms no longer governed heteropatriarchal marriage solely. Instead they had to negotiate with individual desire.

Basing heteropatriarchal marriage on the vagaries of individual desire was costly, to say the least. Those costs had far-reaching effects. As the authors state,

> Perhaps . . . [the dissolution of the monogamous marriage] . . . would not constitute a social danger if among the immigrants of peasant origin disorganization of marriage were not as closely connected as it is with demoralization in other fields, and if it did not affect the children as it does. . . . The only possible way to counteract this degeneration of marriage is to give the Polish-American society new ideals of family life or help it develop such ideals. And this can be done only by its actual incorporation into American society.[17]

Indeed, the sociologists believed that immigration and industrialization produced a crisis in the authority of heteronormative cultural norms and the stability of the heteropatriarchal family, a crisis that—these scholars believed—would lead to pauperism, sexual depravity, and juvenile delinquency.

Reinforcing the idea that those boundaries were endangered by urban economy, Park argued, "[marriage] takes place later in the city, and sometimes it doesn't take place at all."[18] As political economy weakened the authoritative range of primary institutions, heteronormativity became the hegemonic mode for regulating not only sexual practice, but sexual desire as well. As capital was imagined through the framework of intimacy and racial transgression, a new ethical relation of the self arose to reassert the racial and sexual boundaries of household and neighborhood. In a moment that disrupted those boundaries, that ethic worked to keep desire within the racialized confines of the heteropatriarchal household and the segregated neighborhood. In addition, that racially heteronormative ethic worked to constitute the subject as eligible for citizenship. That work, if done successfully, would culminate in an American citizen who conformed to the racialized boundaries of heteropatriarchal marriage.

As sociologists were concerned with the transgressions inspired by capital, social reformers during the 1930s and 1940s responded to those transgressions by designing social policy that would restore responsible intimacy to economically, ethnically, and racially marginalized communities. For New

Dealers, restoring responsible intimacy meant eradicating the nonhetero-normative formations that obstructed gender and sexual ideals held dear by middle-class whites.[19] Restoring responsible intimacy also meant establishing heteropatriarchal households within minority communities. Allocating bene-fits on the basis of women's status as wives and mothers, New Deal social policy tied women's economic security to men's wages, Aid to Dependent Children (ADC), and widow's benefits. Men's economic security, in turn, was tied to fair wages, unions, and social insurance. Social policy worked to ar-range men and women within heteropatriarchal family structures.[20]

As female-headed families characterized a fourth of African American households during the depression, blacks were regarded as outside the moral ideals of New Deal social reformers and were often excluded from New Deal policies on this basis. As the federal government deferred to states in mat-ters of coverage, "local determination of need and fitness permitted varia-tions in grant levels and exclusion on moral grounds of families otherwise eligible."[21] State-level prohibitions and regulations against unwed mother-hood made illegitimacy the nonheteronormative formation justifying the denial of protection. Even those states that did not exclude unwed mothers commanded social workers to subject them to relentless observation and regulation to determine if black mothers were making attempts to conform to heteropatriarchal ideals.

During the period of the New Deal, particularly after wage-earning and unwed mothers predominated the rolls of Aid to Dependent Children (ADC), policy analysts and social reformers conceptualized African American cul-ture through a moral, and not simply an economic, lens. In doing so, New Deal reformers identified culture rather than biology as the locus of African American racial difference. New Deal reformers pointed to sociology as the epistemological lens through which they could read African American famil-ial diversity. As one reformer argued, "[S]ociologically, at least, we have in the illegitimate family a survival of an outgrown and therefore destructive form of family organization—the mother and child, biologic unit—in a culture which is striving to bring in the third member into responsible intimacy."[22] Those reformers believed that African Americans would be full-fledged hetero-patriarchal subjects if not for the gendered and sexual transgressions of Af-rican American culture. If culture was the basis of African American racial difference, according to the reformers, then policy must at least target culture to remedy economic inequality. While New Deal reformers believed that the exclusion of African Americans from programs like ADC was racist, they supported that exclusion inasmuch as they deemed African Americans in-eligible for assimilation because of nonheteronormative cultural, gender, and familial differences. Reformers thus designed policies that ostensibly ensured the welfare of children by "encouraging Black mothers' social reform." As it excluded black families from protection because of their "cultural difference," New Deal social policy designated African American culture as the site for producing national identification. This identification hinged on that culture's proximity to heteropatriarchal standards.

As they became indices of national belonging and estrangement, African American familial, gender, and sexual relations became morally and culturally significant for policy considerations as well. About liberal capitalism, Marx writes, "It claims . . . to have created pure morality and an agreeable degree of culture."[23] As Marx suggests, one of the staple features of liberal capitalism is the way in which it enlists culture as the moral agent of capital. As such, liberal capitalism gives culture the task of regulating citizens and noncitizens for the good of capitalist relations of production. Culture was given such a task under the ideology of the New Deal. Insisting that minority assimilation would resolve both inequality and indigence, the New Deal designated heteropatriarchal culture as the horizon of morality and agreeable culture and the ticket to minority assimilation. New Deal reformers insisted that social policy must provide "gender and cultural services" to African American communities during the 1930s and 1940s if reform was going to be effective. New Deal reformers and social policies made racialized gender and racialized sexuality the pivot upon which national identity turned. As national identity was articulated through gender and sexual conformity, African American racial difference placed African American culture outside national identity inasmuch as that difference was taken to symbolize gender and sexual nonconformity.

By investing culture with moral agency, New Deal ideology obscured the contradictions between the state's enforcement of heteropatriarchal ideals and capital's encouragement of African American nonheteronormative formations. Even as the state decried African American female-headed households and sexual nonconformity among blacks, the Social Security Act Amendment of 1939 excluded personal servants, domestics, and casual and agricultural workers from coverage, hence denying African American men the very economic protections that were said to restore heteropatriarchal family structures. At the same time that New Deal reformers sought to keep white women from wage-earning work so as to guarantee the stability of the heteropatriarchal household, they deemed black women appropriate wage earners. They saw "no reason why the employable Negro mother should not continue her usually sketchy seasonal labor or indefinite domestic service rather than receive a public assistance grant."[24] Such race-based disparities contradicted the state's efforts at heteropatriarchal regulation. Those contradictions were extended as state and capital conspired to lure black women's labor away from the private sphere and as they worked to preclude black men from forming and sustaining heteropatriarchal households. Hence, African American racial and communal formations became sites of contradiction and negation that opened up alternative subject and social formations around race, class, gender, and sexuality.

When the Transgendered Mulatta Throws a Party: African American Sexual Heterogeneity

American modernity in early twentieth-century industrialization provided contexts for the emergence of polymorphous nonheteronormative formations. In the 1930s, these formations were racialized in terms of urban black racial and cultural difference. And as nonwhite communities were racialized as nonheteronormative, heteropatriarchal regulation enforced the racialized boundaries of neighborhood and community. For example, in June 1913 Congress passed the Mann Act. Also known as the "White Slave Traffic Act," the Mann Act attempted to "regulate prostitution by prohibiting the transportation of women across state lines."[25] The law was designed to protect white men's access to white women against the presumed desires of black men. Black critics, in turn, charged that the law made white women the only worthy beneficiaries of state protection, while black women were the legitimate prey of white men.[26] As white women and black men who crossed racial boundaries were stigmatized as prostitutes and rapists, the Mann Act worked to curb their mobility for fear that it would violate the heteropatriarchal authority of the white household. The victims of the Mann Act were charged with committing "unlawful sexual intercourse," "debauchery," and "crimes against nature." Taunted as "nigger-lovers," white women involved with black men were reracialized as black. As whiteness was the horizon of racial and sexual purity, black racial difference became one of the origins and outcomes of polymorphous perversions.[27]

After immigration exclusion, anxieties about the polymorphous perversions of industrial capital were relocated onto African American communities. Those fears were to a large degree motivated by the way in which African American migration threatened sexual and racial segregation within northern cities. Black male workers who heard the call of capital had unprecedented access to white women because of the growth of commercialized sex. Black women migrants, after World War I, had come to predominate as sex workers. Because of labor marginalization during the 1920s, black women often opted for sex work as a means of employment. In the 1920s, as well, prostitution in Chicago had moved from suburban areas to the African American neighborhoods of the South Side.[28]

As Thomas and Znaniecki suggested, the industrializing city led to an assortment of polymorphous perversions that could (and would) challenge regulatory agencies. As marriage became the indicator of social organization in the industrial economy, the stability of the neighborhood was imagined in terms of the predominance of heteropatriarchal monogamous families. In this context, black racial difference and black neighborhoods became the signs of moral instability and alternative gender and sexual formations. Those individuals, families, and neighborhoods that contradicted the logic of the heteropatriarchal family were placed in the political category of "vice" and its sociological counterpart, "deviance." Both categories had sexual connotations and admitted those practices and identities that were deemed contrary to the ideals of the heteropatriarchal family unit, practices that could lead to social disorganization.

As sites of alternative gender and sexual relations, African American vice districts were socially heterogeneous zones in which blacks and whites, as well as heterosexuals and homosexuals, could congregate. The intersection of the black and the nonblack, the heterosexual and the homosexual, the young and the seasoned in black neighborhoods was of interest to Chicago School sociologist Ernest Burgess. In 1938, one of Burgess's students, Conrad Bentzen, conducted an ethnography of a black and tan cabaret. Black and tans during this period were parties known for open displays of sex, for their inversion of racial hierarchies, for "race mixing," and as sites from which same-sex relationships and identities could emerge. Taking the black and tan as a metaphor for African American urban communities, Bentzen argued that the South Side of Chicago was ripe for "homosexual congregation." As he stated, "the social taboos of a conventional society have been raised and the repressed individual can find full expression for the smoldering desires burning within." Bentzen writes,

> Every night we will find the place crowded with both races, the black and
> the white, both types of lovers, the homo and the hetro [sic]. . . . Before
> long the orchestra strikes up a tune and the master of ceremonies appears
> on the stage. This person is a huge mulatto with wide shoulders and narrow
> hips. It wears a white satin evening gown that reveal [sic] the unmistakable
> breasts of a woman. The lips are heavily painted and are so full that they
> make a red block against the ghostly white countenance. It is a lascivious
> creature that strikes the normal as extremely repulsive. With a deep husky
> voice it begins to sing a wild song and as the tempo increases the stage rap-
> idly fills with a remarkable collection of sexual indeterminants.[29]

For Bentzen, the transgendered mulatta embodies the charismatic and contagious nature of sexual vices that, in the 1930s, were imagined through the lens of race.[30] For Bentzen, she is the siren of the straight and the queer, the black and the white, the mature and the juvenile. While sociology established an epistemological proximity to blackness and homosexuality, vice districts helped to render them as materially proximate.

Generally, the sexualized perversions of industrialization in the 1920s and 1930s were scripted onto the racialized meanings of U.S. urban landscapes. Sociologists argued that the moral and temperamental specificity of minority groups drove residential segregation, such that "[every] neighborhood, under the influences which tend to distribute and segregate city populations, may assume the character of a 'moral region,'" or moral zone.[31] In such a formulation, African American neighborhoods, popularized as the terrain of prostitutes, homosexuals, rent parties, black and tans, interracial liaisons, speakeasies, and juvenile delinquency, epitomized moral degeneracy and the perverse results of industrialization. As symbols of intersecting racial, gender, and sexual transgressions, African American communal and corporeal difference became the symbol of the nonheteronormative perversions of industrializing and urbanizing economies.

Anxieties about the sexual transgression of racial boundaries inspired city governments, such as Chicago's, to enact laws against vice. Ostensibly, these laws would rid Chicago of vice, but in fact, they located vice to African American neighborhoods in the South Side. White real estate agents in the early 1900s rented apartments in the same neighborhoods to black middle-class persons and their counterparts in the "sporting life," people who partied to "rag time music far into the night."[32] Chicago police during this period worked to restrict vice to African American neighborhoods, concentrating nonheteronormative subjects in black neighborhoods, safe from the hallowed domain of white residents. The police would often raid "black and tan resorts" like the one described by Bentzen because of their interracial clientele. Hence, vice worked in tandem with residential segregation and thereby established a formal relationship between racial exclusion and sexual regulation.

The Chicago School's construction of African American neighborhoods as outside heteropatriarchal normalization underwrote municipal government's regulation of the South Side, making African American neighborhoods the point at which both a will to knowledge and a will to exclude intersected. If the city necessitated that its residents internalize a heteronormative ideal, as Thomas and Znaniecki stated, African American neighborhoods represented the impossibility and often the rejection of those ideals.

The transgendered mulatta and the other party goers embodied what for many were the worst of migration's transgressive potentials. As figures that exist outside the gender and sexual dictates of heteropatriarchy, they represent a refusal of heteropatriarchal regulation. Describing the party goers, Bentzen argues,

> Some of them seem to be more feminine than others but before long you began to realize that they are changing their roles from time to time. They all act far more feminine than a normal girl, carrying filmy handkerchiefs which they draw out of their sleeves and flutter around. . . . It would seem the effeminate men would like a masculine mate but that is not the case. Inasmuch as their libido is divided they find difficulty in finding a summation of great enough intensity that it can be satisfied by either sex. Only by attaching themselves to a person who has the qualities of both sex [sic] can they find the realization of their sex desires. They are so effeminate that it is quite impossible to know which is playing what role. They talk and joke about girdles and braziers [sic] which seems to be the source of most of their humor.[33]

As Bentzen implies, the party goers are all the more scandalous because they perform the fluidity of gender identity. While acknowledging the regulatory nature of a social order arranged around heterosexuality, Bentzen arranges his observations within the normative logic of heterosexuality. He ends by stating, "[The black and tan] does provide an outlet for these *unstable* people who are forced to repress their feelings in the normal group. But still we wonder if this process of conditioning and obvious approval doesn't encourage those on the borderline to slip into this role of uncertainty?"[34]

The threat to racial and sexual boundaries inspired the meanings of women's gender identities to change as well. For Park, Burgess, and McKenzie, the commercialization of vice and the disruption of sexual mores were "coincident with the entrance of women into a greater freedom, into industry, the professions, and party politics."[35] For these sociologists and lay onlookers, the meaning of womanhood was destabilized as the category "Woman" was translated and renegotiated with the advancement of industrial intercourse. Womanhood, in general, was reshaped as middle class and working women entered the public sphere for work and leisure, coming into contact with new styles of dress and commercialized entertainment and leisure. The meaning of womanhood was dialectically related to the changing meaning of black womanhood. With African American women dominating the ranks of prostitution in cities like New York and Chicago, and because of the already existent discourse of black women's sexual appetites, urban black womanhood became synonymous with prostitution.[36] While opening them to modes of regulation *and* freedom, the entrance of black women in particular and women in general into the public sphere took them outside the regulatory strictures of the heteropatriarchal household. They often elaborated identities and social relations alternative and very frequently antagonistic to that household. In the language of the sociology of that era, the prostitute, the black and tan, the mulatta, and the other nonheteronormative subjects who contradicted heteronormative ideals confirmed and exemplified the social disorganization of U.S. industrialization and urbanization.

Such subjects could only come to canonical sociology as formations that critically exceeded that discipline's epistemological reach. As they idealized heterosexuality and patriarchy, Chicago School sociologists could only respond to nonheteronormative racial formations by insisting on heteropatriarchal regulation and decrying capitalist change for bringing about nonheteronormative modes of intercourse. In this sense, sociology ratified the regulatory mechanisms of the U.S. state and municipal government. As the hysteria over vice districts attests, African American nonheteronormativity became capital's most obvious defilement, as well as the law and social science's most urgent problem.

Regulating the Nonheteronormative: Wright, Sociology, and Cultural Nationalism

Cedric Robinson notes in *Black Marxism: The Making of the Black Radical Tradition* that Richard Wright was part of a stellar group of black intellectuals like W. E. B. Du Bois, C. L. R. James, Oliver Cox, and George Padmore, who used marxism to articulate a black radical tradition that could oppose "Western racism and bourgeois society."[37] Wright's life and work, in particular, present an interesting intersection between sociology and marxism. As a student of sociology, Wright was interested in the ways in which urbanization and industrialization impacted the lives of African Americans and shaped African American communities formed out of migration. Sociology's interest in how capital brought diverse groups of people into contact with one another as laborers informed Wright's interest in marxism as a revolutionary force that could unite those groups. As he remarked, he was captivated "by the similarity of the experiences of workers in other lands, by the possibility of uniting scattered but kindred peoples into a whole."[38]

Classical marxism, I have argued, interprets capitalist exploitation as a process that feminizes the alienated worker. And nothing illustrates this more than a vague memory that Wright had of growing up in the then sexually explosive city of Memphis, Tennessee. In this memory, he wanders the streets of the industrial city as a drunken or drugged hermaphrodite, or as his notes say, as a "kind of devil without a tail."[39] The dream betrays not only an anxiety about homosexuality, but *an anxiety* about the ways in which industrialization made nonheteronormative difference so pervasive that Wright could imagine himself as the horrible embodiment of that difference. The absence of a tail is the evidence of castration. More to the point, the memory of homosexuality provided the backdrop for Wright's theory of nationalism. Wright drew upon marxism and sociology to narrate the gendered and sexual transgressions inspired by industrial capital. Borrowing from sociology, Wright's work located African American nonheteronormative formations within the feminizing dysfunctions of capital. In doing so, Wright's work denied nonheteronormative figures oppositional agency. We can see this in Wright's early writings, but also in his novel *Native Son.* In fact, through its main character, Bigger Thomas, Wright suggested that economic subordination intersected with racial subordination through the denial of patriarchal status to black men. We may only look to Bigger's name as a registrar of an anxiety about feminization and castration. While sociologists like Park may not have been interested in the oppositional tenor of marxism, Wright claimed marxism's radical nature as a way of imagining a program of black liberation. As Abdul JanMohamed argues, "Wright's overall fictive project consisted of an archaeological excavation of the racialized subject, of the various discursive strata that gradually sediment to construct that subject."[40] Differences of gender and sexuality were important components of those strata.

Discussing his interest in sociology, Wright made the following statement in the introduction to Horace Cayton and St. Clair Drake's *Black Metropolis*:

> The huge mountains of fact piled up by the Department of Sociology at the University of Chicago gave me my first concrete vision of the forces that molded the urban Negro's body and soul. . . . It was from the scientific findings of men like the late Robert E. Park, Robert Redfield, and Louis Wirth. With that I drew the meanings for my documentary book, *12,000,000 Black Voices*; for my novel *Native Son*; it was from their scientific facts that I absorbed some of the quota of inspiration necessary for me to write *Uncle Tom's Children* and *Black Boy*.[41]

Rightly so, Bernard Bell argues that Park's theories on social disorganization helped form the basis of Wright's beliefs about African American culture and his writings.[42] As the use of social disorganization to describe vice districts attests, this epistemology made African American communities and persons in Chicago synonymous with nonheteronormative transgressions.

Amid the gendered and sexual transgressions taking place in an industrializing United States, Richard Wright would be introduced to and would read the works of Chicago School sociologists. This nonheteronormative environment, replete with polymorphous perversions, inspired Wright to formulate his version of cultural nationalism. To do so, he employed sociological theories of social disorganization. As capital's burden was imagined in the frame of feminization and disorganizing gender and sexual transgressions, Wright's nationalism called for a specifically masculine revolutionary agency to oppose that feminization. While installing an antiracist practice, this version of nationalism proved aggressively heteropatriarchal. Emerging out of the context of gender and sexual fluidity and diversity, Wright's nationalism worked to keep that fluidity and diversity at bay through heteropatriarchal regulation.

"Blueprint for Negro Writing" expressed this theory most succinctly. The article was published in the autumn 1937 issue of *New Challenge,* a magazine begun by Wright and Dorothy West to "present the literature and conditions of life of American Negroes in relationship to the struggle against war and Fascism."[43] In contrast to the radical potentials of African American revolutionary nationalism, the article evoked the Harlem Renaissance as the horizon of intellectual and political effeminacy. Wright said,

> Generally speaking, Negro writing in the past has been confined to humble novels, poems, and plays, *prim* and *decorous* ambassadors who went *a-begging* to white America. They entered the Court of American Public Opinion dressed in the *knee-pants* of servility, *curtsying* to show that the Negro was not inferior, that he was a human, and that he had a life compatible to other people. For the most part these artistic ambassadors were received as though they were *French poodles* who do clever tricks.[44]

The essay calls for an African American intellectual production and political praxis that imagines African Americans as the ideal audience of African American writing and the real constituents of African American politics, a production and praxis that differs from Wright's view of the Harlem Renaissance in that it does not "plead with White America for justice." "Blueprint" summons African American writers to shirk bourgeois notions of progress that, according to Wright, rendered Harlem Renaissance writing into a "sort of conspicuous ornamentation, the hallmark of achievement." The basis of Wright's feminization is the white patron/black artist relationship that characterized much of the literary production during the Harlem Renaissance and, for many, represented racial accommodation during the contentious period of industrialization, racial segregation, and racial violence. For Wright, the modus operandi of Harlem Renaissance writers was not manly agency.

Marxism, according to Wright, could provide the antidote to that feminization. As Paula Rabinowitz has argued, 1930s proletarian theorists "described class divisions through gender differences: the effeminate bourgeoisie was bound to be replaced by the virile working class. Knowledge was still deeply gendered, and this formula left out women as agents of history."[45] Accordingly, Wright believed that marxism could present African American writers with a "meaningful picture of the world today." Continuing this line of argument, he wrote, "[Marxism] creates a picture which, when placed before the eyes, should unify his personality, organize his emotions, buttress him with a tense, obdurate will to change the world." In contrast to the feminine complacency of the Harlem Renaissance, African American nationalism would endow African Americans with transformative agency. That agency would change not only the world, but the African American actor as well: "Marxist vision, when consciously grasped, endows the writer with a sense of dignity which no other vision can give. Ultimately, it restores to the writer his lost heritage, that is, his role as a creator of the world in which he lives, and as a creator of himself."[46] Marxism could restore the masculine dignity absent from the feminized social relations and subjectivities of the Harlem Renaissance.

With this restorative aim in mind, Wright demanded that African American writers invest in the revolutionary potential nascent within African American folklore. That potential was embedded in black male folk heroes. As he writes, "In the absence of fixed and nourishing forms of culture, the Negro has a folklore which embodies the memories and hopes of his struggle for freedom. . . . How many John Henry's have lived and died on the lips of these black people? How many mythical heroes in embryo have been allowed to perish for lack of husbanding by alert intelligence?"[47] In a world ravaged by the feminizing forces of industrialization and urbanization, Wright believed that African American nationalism could effectively restore African American masculinity and found a virile radical tradition.

Again, Wright understood social disorganization as a feminizing process that disrupted African American gender and sexual integrity. One of the signal disorganizing moments came when Wright's father deserted the family, leaving his mother as the head. It was in the midst of the father's absence that Wright had his first intense bout with hunger. Indeed he would associate the father's absence with those pains of hunger, thinking of his father with a "biological bitterness." After the father's desertion, Ella Wright told her two boys that now they were different from other children because they had no father.[48] Wright's family was now stigmatized because of their inability to conform to a heteropatriarchal ideal, a stigmatization made all the more real because of the hunger associated with it, an ideal made all the more desirable because of its promise of food and a stable roof.

Wright's anxieties about female-headed households and homosexuality were motivated, to a large degree, by the way in which industrialization was encouraging nonheteronormative gender, sexual, and familial formations in urban spaces. Like the anxiety of Chicago School sociologists about urban social disorganization and demoralization, Wright was anxious about the sexual and gender transgressions taking place in U.S. cities, about the adjacency of nonnormative sexualities (hetero and homo) as material outcomes of social disorganization.

As the essay insisted on the virile and masculine images of the folk hero, it used revolutionary nationalism to supplant the nonheteronormative and feminized figures of the black female head and the hermaphrodite. But Wright did not claim the folk hero as the basis for his most monumental work, *Native Son*. Instead, *Native Son* begins with a more modern social type—the juvenile delinquent. Basing Bigger Thomas on several black males Wright knew, Wright writes that "[t]he Bigger Thomases were the only Negroes I know of who consistently violated the Jim Crow laws of the South and got away with it, at least for a sweet brief spell."[49] If the novel was imagined as a critique of feminization, the character Bigger Thomas suggests that Wright's revolutionary nationalism understood feminization not only through effeminacy and heterosexual impotence, but through a castrating disfranchisement that could potentially result in a bullish and unregulated masculinity. As JanMohamed notes, "Wright proceeds from the perspective of a protagonist so profoundly castrated that he experiences himself as an already 'feminized' black male who needs to (re)assert his 'manhood' through rape and murder."[50] As a feminized figure who does not conform to heteropatriarchy or nationalism's regulated ideal, Bigger represents nonheteronormative dysfunction. There is ample justification for locating the figure of the juvenile delinquent within the sexual components of the discourse of social disorganization. Indeed, St. Claire Drake and Horace Cayton locate their discussion of juvenile delinquency within their chapter "Lower Class: Sex and Family." For the authors of *Black Metropolis*, juvenile delinquency within Chicago's inner city emerged from families that lacked a male head; in other words, as part of the disorganizing relations unleashed by an urban culture insufficiently socialized to gender and sexual propriety.

While "castrating" black men as economic and political agents, the industrializing city encouraged what for many observers were witless sexual transgressions. As Drake and Cayton argue, "'Sexual delinquency' was probably more widespread than petty thievery and violence."[51] Those transgressions could only take place in supposedly privatized spaces protected from public exposure. In a deleted passage from *Native Son*, one such place was the darkened movie theater. While sitting in a movie theater, Bigger discusses the prospect of working for a wealthy white family named the Daltons with his friend Jack. At first Bigger shuns the idea of working, saying he would sooner "go to jail than take that damn relief job." But then he warms up to the idea of working in the same household with Mr. Dalton's daughter. Jack says to him, "Man, you ought to take that job. You don't know what you might run into. . . . Ah, man, them rich white women'll go to bed with anybody from a poodle on up. Shucks, they even have their chauffeur." As Bigger and Jack's conversation about the presumed sexual habits of white women suggests, the theater was not only a technology of race and class,[52] it was also a technology of sexuality that established white women as the reigning objects of heterosexual male desire. By doing so, the theater initiated desires in Bigger and Jack that could potentially violate the sexualized boundaries inscribed in racial segregation.

We may situate the alleged dangers of the theater within larger anxieties about mass culture in the 1930s. Indeed, Chicago residents feared that mass culture, signified by such modern fixtures as the franchise movie theater and the automobile, would dilute class and social boundaries.[53] The franchise movie theater succeeded the neighborhood movie theater, once the symbol of neighborhood particularity and ethnic culture. The takeover of neighborhood theaters by movie chains like Paramount, Loew's, Fox, Warner Brothers, and R.K.O. represented the dissolution of ethnic culture and stability by modernizing forces. Bigger and Jack's use of the movie theater to stage a racially transgressive sexual fantasy bears witnesses to the disruptions of those forces.

Moreover, as an institution that Park, McKenzie, and Burgess conceived as contributing to general demoralization and vice, the motion-picture show threatened heteropatriarchal regulation.[54] In a passage that was originally deleted but has subsequently been restored, Bigger and Jack masturbate together—or to use their words, "polish their nightsticks."[55] Later the two watch a newsreel about the wealthy Mr. Dalton and his loving daughter, Mary. It is significant that Bigger and Jack masturbate together even before watching the film. Indeed, they do not masturbate to the image of the idealized white woman presented later on screen. Rather, they masturbate simply as part of their fraternal bond: "[Bigger] glanced at Jack and saw that Jack was watching him out of the corner of his eyes. They both laughed."[56] Within the polymorphously perverse environment of 1930s Chicago, the scene straddles the line between homosexual expression and heterosexual perversion. As revolutionary nationalism valorized self-possession and heteropatriarchal integrity, Bigger and Jack's mutual masturbation seems to exemplify the demoralizing effects of urbanization and industrialization upon African American youth. In addition to suggesting homoeroticism, the scene implies a proximity with other effects of social disorganization within an industrializing context, one of those effects being homosexuality. The scene imagines juvenile delinquency as dangerously close to outright homosexuality, a closeness institutionalized through urban life. Though nonnormative heterosexual practices and homosexual practices were not commensurate in the 1930s, they were indeed adjacent.

As a matter of fact, sociological studies that preceded *Black Metropolis* conceptualized the juvenile delinquent in relation to other practices that were designated as the demoralizing effects of social disorganization. In the sociological literature, "youth" was imagined as a period of rebellion against internally and externally generated mechanisms of self-control. According to Park, McKenzie, and Burgess, the city, by presenting its inhabitants with a multitude of temptations, thereby destabilized the traditional authority of family, robbing American youth of a primary form of social control. As the hysteria over vice districts and nonheteronormative familial forms attests, sociologists and local officials presumed that the identities of African Americans were formed in conditions that encouraged the rejection of rational regulation and self-control. Addressing the links between sexual vice and "forms of personal and social disorganization," the sociologist Walter Reckless argued in his 1933 text, *Vice in Chicago*, "Our immediate concern here is that the neighborhood conditions which enable prostitution to thrive are undoubtedly the same ones which tend to produce the highest rates of juvenile delinquency in Chicago."[57] And as Park argued in *The City*, "The enormous amount of delinquency, juvenile and adult, that exists today in the Negro communities in northern cities is due in part, though not entirely, to the fact that migrants are not able to accommodate themselves at once to a new and relatively strange environment."[58]

Like the movie theater, the automobile helped American youth commit social transgressions. In *The City* Park names the automobile as an instrument of social disorganization and vice. In a rapidly changing society fixated on borders and the weakening of "primal" truths and ties, the car facilitated access to the world outside the home and neighborhood.[59] After Bigger accepts the job at the Daltons', Mary asks Bigger to drive her to a university lecture, but later instructs him to drive her to meet Jan. Wright arranges this encounter as a series of social transgressions and thus suffuses Bigger's encounter with communism with varying degrees of eroticism: Mary—with "her face some six inches from [Bigger]"—teasingly asks Bigger, "You're not a tattletale, are you? . . . I'm not going to the University. . . . I'm going to meet a friend of mine who's also a friend of yours."[60] When Jan, Mary's boyfriend and fellow communist, arrives, instead of immediately entering the car he insists on standing outside the car to shake Bigger's hand. Later, Jan insists on driving and Bigger finds himself sandwiched between Jan and Mary. Bigger had never "been so close to a white woman. He smelt the odor of her hair and felt the soft pressure of her thigh against his own" (68). In the context of these encounters, Bigger is supremely aware of his "black body" and its impotence. While Bigger feels disqualified from such transgression, Mary and Jan are propelled by transgressive desires. Driving through the black neighborhoods of the South Side, Mary says, "You know, Bigger, I've long wanted to go into those houses. . . . I just want to see. I want to know these people. Never in my life have I been inside of a Negro home" (69–70). Transgressing the boundaries of racial segregation, Mary and Jan ask Bigger to take them to Earnie's Kitchen Shack, the all-black diner on the South Side.

Again, the car functions as the object that enables sexual transgressions that violate the boundaries of proper behavior between blacks and whites. After they return to the car, Jan and Mary have sex in the backseat as Bigger chauffeurs them around Washington Park.

> He looked at the mirror. Mary was lying flat on her back in the rear seat and Jan was bent over her. He saw a faint sweep of white thigh. They plastered all right, he thought. He pulled the car softly round the curves, looking at the road before him one second and up at the mirror the next. He heard Jan whispering; then he heard them both sigh. Filled with a sense of them, his muscles grew gradually taut. He sighed and sat up straight, fighting off the stiffening feeling in his loins. . . . A long time passed.[61]

Bigger is made aware of his body while in the company of whites, but this time that awareness is unmistakably sexual.

Bigger's feminized status compels him to comply with Jan and Mary's desire for transgression. By asking him to overstep the social boundaries of race, Jan and Mary presume they are demonstrating the racially progressive nature of communist party politics and thereby subverting Bigger's socialization as a racialized minority and the racial hierarchy of 1930s America. But for Bigger their gestures only confirm their racial privilege as whites and his subordination as an impoverished African American. While Jan and Mary encounter these transgressions as evidence of their communist liberation, Bigger confronts them as proof of his compulsion and regulation. Like those whites who descended on African American neighborhoods for pleasure and entertainment, Jan and Mary retain and extend their racial privilege by venturing into the South Side.

Wright relates Bigger's regulation as worker to his regulation as son. His mother prods him to take the job with the Daltons:

> "You going to take the job, ain't you, Bigger?" his mother asked. . . . "If you get that job . . . I can fix up a nice place for you children. You could be

comfortable and not have to live like pigs." . . . As [Bigger] ate he felt that they were thinking of the job he was to get that evening and it made him angry; he felt that they had tricked him into a *cheap surrender.*[62]

As Jan and Mary use the context of the job as the microcosm for a race and class utopia, Mrs. Thomas holds the job up as the vehicle to his confirmation as a patriarch. For Mrs. Thomas the arena of labor commodification is that domain that will bring her and her family closer to womanhood, manhood, and domesticity. Provided Bigger takes the job, she can be a proper woman who provides *a nice place for the children where they will not have to live like pigs.* Bigger encounters that sphere as the realm of humiliation, timidity, and regulation.

Bigger's feminization as a worker and as a son illustrates the gendered features of racial domination. As JanMohamed argues, "Wright focuses on one crucial mode by which racialized sexuality operates: the 'feminization' or 'infantilization' of the black man within the phallocentric system."[63] Feminizing and infantilizing Bigger, Mrs. Thomas yells, "We wouldn't have to live in this garbage dump if you had any manhood in you."[64] As *The Economic and Philosophic Manuscripts* used the feminized figure of the prostitute to apprehend capitalist alienation, *Native Son* feminized Bigger to narrate industrial capital's burden upon black men.

As the story proceeds, Bigger accidentally kills Mary. She gets drunk after her night with Bigger and Jan. Bigger helps Mary to her room, but Mary's blind mother walks into the room, calling out for Mary. To keep Mary from responding and thus exposing a black man in her bedroom, Bigger places a pillow over Mary's face and eventually suffocates her. To conceal the murder, Bigger destroys Mary's body in the furnace of the Dalton basement. At this point in the narrative, Bigger ceases to associate transgression with regulation and instead associates it with an intoxicating freedom:

> The thought of what he had done, the awful horror of it, the daring associated with such actions, formed for him for the first time in his fear-ridden life a barrier of protection between him and a world he feared. He had murdered and had created a new life for himself. It was something that was all his own, and it was the first time in his life he had had anything that others could not take from him. . . . His crime was an anchor weighing safely in time; it added to him a certain confidence which his gun and knife did not. He was outside of his family now, over and beyond them. . . . Now, who on earth would think that he, a black timid Negro boy, would murder and burn a rich white girl and would sit and wait for his breakfast like this? Elation filled him.[65]

The point at which Bigger feels intoxicated by transgression is as he enacts agency outside the regulatory gazes of his white employers and his "matriarchal" family.

Bigger also rapes and murders his girlfriend, Bessie, after she discovers that he has killed Mary Dalton. The novel thus pathologizes Bigger's nonnormative difference as juvenile delinquent as it positions him as rapist and murderer. As JanMohamed writes, "The fundamental premise of *Native Son*, which Wright entirely fails to examine critically, is that the protagonist can become a 'man' through rape and murder and overcome the racialization of his subjectivity."[66] Bigger understands his murder of a rich white girl and his rape and murder of Bessie as a challenge to the domination imposed on him by a racially segregated society.

While Wright rearticulates Bigger's own nonheteronormativity to suggest possibilities for revolutionary agency, his nonheteronormative character is constantly figured as an impediment to a fully rationalized (i.e., masculine) agency. Hence, Wright can only narrate Bigger as an example of the *precondition* rather than the condition of nationalism. In "How Bigger Was Born," Wright argues,

> He was an American because he was a native son; but he was also a Negro nationalist in a vague sense because he was not allowed to live as an American. Such was his way of life and mine; neither Bigger nor I resided fully in either camp.
>
> Of this dual aspect of Bigger's social consciousness, I placed the nationalistic side first, not because I agreed with Bigger's wild and intense hatred of white people, but because his hate placed him, like a *wild animal* at bay, in a position where he was most symbolic and explainable. In other words, his nationalist complex was for me a concept through which I could grasp more of the total meaning of his life than I could in any other way. I tried to approach Bigger's *snarled* and *confused* nationalist feelings with conscious and informed ones of my own. Yet, Bigger was not nationalist enough to feel the need of religion or the folk culture of his own people.[67]

Bigger is the precursor of masculine agency, because he lacks the nationalist consciousness that would transform his witless actions into fully virile agency. Even as Wright narrates Bigger's entrance into agency, Bigger is never a representative of fully consummated nationalist agency. To the extent that Bigger's actions are "wild," "snarled," and "confused," they are symptomatic of the feminizing and infantilizing outcomes of industrialization. For Bigger to transcend his own delinquent status and become a "conscious and informed" nationalist rather than a boy who simply had "snarled and confused nationalist feelings," he would have to "know [the] origins . . . [and]

limitations [of nationalism]."[68] To be a fully embodied nationalist, Bigger would have to be self-possessed and conscious of the "interdependence of people in modern society." Moreover, Bigger would have to be versed in African American folklore, which contains "the most powerful images of hope and despair [that still remain] in the fluid state of daily speech."[69] As someone who did not "feel the need for folk culture," Bigger lacked the literacy to be a nationalist. As someone who engaged in sexual and criminal exploits that violated sexual propriety, he lacked the regulatory properties of nationalism. His exploits in the theater and his murder of Mary and Bessie only confirm his inability to transcend the social disorganization of industrial society. These traits place Bigger alongside the other figures of African American nonheteronormativity during the period of 1930s industrialization—unwed mothers, transgendered persons, criminals, delinquents, and homosexuals. Because of this association with African American nonheteronormative subject and social formations, we cannot lift Bigger up as the stable representative of African American revolutionary nationalism.[70] Instead, Wright positions himself as the exemplar of a "conscious" and "informed" nationalism. The result is an African American nationalism secured by the normalizations of sociology and classical marxism. In this instance, a class bias inflected the normative hues of revolutionary nationalism.

Black subjects in general and working-class black subjects in particular were racialized as pathologically nonheteronormative. This nonheteronormativity was the discursive counterpart to capital's maneuvers through industrialization and urbanization. Revolutionary nationalism responded to those maneuvers by claiming heteronormativity as the most appropriate and viable challenge to capital and its presumed nonheteronormative dysfunctions. In doing so, nationalists such as Wright ratified a distinctly sociological and contemporary message, contemporary in the sense that canonical sociology was providing a language for thinking modernity within the United States. As a discursive formation, sociology defined migration, mass culture, and urbanization as processes that not only signaled the benefits of progress, but portended its ominous potential as well. The threat of progress denoted the myriad ways in which modernization was producing racial heterogeneity that state, political, and epistemological forces could only imagine as upheavals to gender and sexual normativity. In such a climate, liberal and revolutionary politics defined their tasks as the reappropriation of normativity. As the reclamation of normativity outlined the parameters of political engagement, African American nonheteronormative differences could only then "strike the normal as repulsive." But as the next chapter will illustrate, the maligned and misrecognized figure of the nonheteronormative subject is that formation that can "read"[71] normativity in its varied iterations and strip it bare.

2

The Specter of Woodridge: Canonical Formations and the Anticanonical in *Invisible Man*

> "I wipe my ass with this literature, this condom to abort reality! This dirty shuck literature they drop to soil our hearts and minds. I mean it," he shouted as he turned suddenly to the bookshelf and I could hear a ripping sound as he turned, seized a book from the shelf and ripped out its pages, scattering them about before my shocked eyes.
>
> —Passage from an unpublished chapter in Ralph Ellison's *Invisible Man*

Readers of *Invisible Man* have no recollection of this passage or its diatribe. The character and the scene to which the passage refers were excised from the final version of the novel. But some characters refuse to lie in the grave of anonymity. This character's name was Woodridge, and he was a teacher at the college that the main character attended. He was both respected and reviled—a thinker who would take solace neither in the "objectivity" of sociology, nor in the "humanness" of literature. And because of the dubious esteem in which the teacher is held, the protagonist will seek him out in the middle of the night.

The unpublished chapter is part of the Ralph Ellison Papers at the Library of Congress. To date, there has been no mention of this chapter's existence. While it would be worthwhile to discover why it was left out of the published version of *Invisible Man*, my curiosities lie elsewhere. I am interested in the chapter as an intellectual document that critiques sociology and literature as sites of knowledge production about African Americans, a production that has everything to do with modern formulations of sexuality, racialization, and citizenship.

Woodridge's critique targets literature as well as canonical sociology. In doing so, his rant expresses an interest in the strategies of power that are immanent in canonical sociology's will to knowledge about African American culture and in canonical literature's extension of humanity to the dispossessed. It is important to note that this will to knowledge and the bestowal of humanity connote a sexual knowledge insinuated through racial discourses. As we will see, Woodridge's denunciation addresses the regulatory presumptions that underlie canonical literature and canonical sociology, especially as literature and sociology promote ideals of progress and development. Those ideals simultaneously organize the aesthetic subject of canonical literature, the epistemological subject of canonical sociology, and the citizen-subject of the United States. As Woodridge's tirade suggests a critique of the aesthetic subject, it refutes the ideals of the epistemological subject of sociology and the citizen-subject of the U.S. nation-state. During the period of industrialization especially, canonicity was a discourse of progress, as well as a technology of race and sexuality. The canonical narratives of progress implied by the aesthetic, epistemological, and citizen-subjects helped constitute African Americans not only as people who might fit within the normative bounds of citizenship, but as subjects who are ethically obliged to those bounds. This narrative lives at the center of *Invisible Man*. To paraphrase Farah Jasmine Griffin, African American migration narratives like *Invisible Man* explicate the complexities of modern power.[1] Woodridge's critique of canonical literature and sociology opens itself to an analysis of power, especially as power within the context of industrialization arose out of normative investments in progress and ethical development.

Regarded as one of the most canonical texts in American literature, *Invisible Man* won the National Book Award in 1953 and has been hailed as a tribute to American literature and diversity.[2] The award indicates a fundamental feature of canonical formations—that is, their attempt to unify aesthetic and intellectual culture by reconciling material differences and strata. In such instances, canonical formations have to elide material differences of race, class, gender, and sexuality in the name of aesthetic ideals such as diversity. This chapter investigates the limits of Ellison's own identification with canonical literature and how that identification aligns canonical literary formations with canonical sociology. With these limits in mind, I examine canons as aesthetic and epistemological projects that fail to achieve their aims because the material differences of race, gender, class, and sexuality never cease to contradict pronouncements of unity. In the name of unity, canonical formations proffer strategies for ethical development, which form the basis of national identification. As they claim to secure national affiliation, canonical formations pressure subjects to conform to the gender and sexual ideals of the nation. In addition, they posit this conformity as the standard of ethical development. For racialized minorities, this means trying to assume gender and sexual normativity against technologies of race that locate them outside heteropatriarchal ideals. In such a context nonheteronormative formations become that volatile admixture of differences that threatens the authority of canons—literary and sociological—as canonical formations attempt to resuscitate the normative ideals of liberal citizenship.

Chicago School Sociology and the "Lady among the Races"

We can begin to understand the context of Woodridge's harangue by addressing canonical sociology not as a solely intellectual formation, but as a discursive one that soldered the production of knowledge to the extension of power. While Wright employed sociological theory to presumably clarify the position of African Americans within the social and economic transformations of the 1930s, Ellison regarded sociological theory as fundamentally distorting. As sociology was laying its canonical foundations, it did so by locating African Americans outside of heteropatriarchal norms and relations. In his introduction to *Shadow and Act*, Ellison describes his first encounter with sociology as part of his literary and racial trajectory:

> In this quest, for such it soon became, I learned that nothing could go unchallenged; especially that feverish industry dedicated to telling Negroes who and what they are, and which can usually be counted upon to deprive both humanity and culture of their complexity. I had undergone, not too many months before taking the path which led to writing, the humiliation of being taught in a class in sociology at a Negro college (from Park and Burgess, the leading textbook in the field) that Negroes represented the "lady of the races." This contention the Negro instructor passed blandly along to us without even bothering to wash his hands, much less his teeth.[3]

As the passage attests, Ellison's interest in sociology was not informed by canonical mandates; it was not inspired by his desire to become the subject of sociology. Indeed, the essay implies an interest in sociology's construction of African Americans as objects of study. Realizing that he was implicated in sociology's production of racial knowledge, his interest in the discipline was informed by his racial status as an African American, a status worried over and determined—in part—by the epistemological prowess of American social science.[4]

The essay to which the epigraph to this chapter refers is "Temperament,

Tradition, and Nationality," which was published in the leading textbook in the field, *Introduction to the Science of Sociology*. The book was compiled by Robert Park and Ernest Burgess in 1921 and became the "bible for more than a generation of Chicago students."[5] "Temperament, Tradition, and Nationality" was actually a shorter version of an address entitled "The Conflict and Fusion of Cultures with Special Reference to the Negro," which was delivered at the 1918 meeting of the American Sociological Association. In that address, Park argued that the immigration of Asians and Europeans to the United States during the first two decades of the twentieth century occasioned the ASA address and his remarks about African Americans. Park believed that African Americans were convenient in that they allowed sociologists to speculate about the ability of "foreign groups" to assimilate into American society.[6] Park, like many white elites in and outside of the academy, wondered how to Americanize a culturally diverse population and thus to domesticate its cultural particularities, which could otherwise threaten national unity. For Park, the temperament of racial groups determined the success of assimilation and thus how successfully those groups would "take over and assimilate the characteristic features of an alien civilization."[7] Because "the materials for investigation were more accessible," the Negro acted as a kind of test case for determining how non-Western groups could assimilate into American society.

While Ellison may have regarded Park's use of racial temperament as pseudoscience, Park regarded this concept as the outcome of scholarly observation. After observing the religious practices of the remote Sea Island blacks off the coast of Georgia and South Carolina, Park thought that he had witnessed "the nearest approach to anything positively African."[8] From his study, Park argued that the racial temperament of the Negro "disposes" the Negro toward "external, physical things," rather than abstraction. The heritable quality of Negroes was their "congenial nature and social disposition."[9] For Park, racial temperament was an interactive element in social existence:

> [T]his racial temperament has selected out of the mass of cultural materials to which it had access, such technical, mechanical, and intellectual devices as met its needs at a particular period of its existence. It [racial temperament] has clothed and enriched itself with such new customs, habits, and cultural forms as it was able, or permitted to use. It has put into these relatively external things, moreover, such concrete meanings as its changing experience and its unchanging racial individuality demanded.[10]

With "racial temperament," Park inscribed the biological with a momentum, logic, and consciousness all its own. That momentum, logic, and consciousness, for Park, was always linked to tradition and culture.

As far as the temperament of African Americans was concerned, Park wrote,

> Everywhere and always it [the Negro's racial temperament] has been interested rather in expression than in action; interested in life itself rather than in its reconstruction or reformation. The Negro is, by natural disposition, neither an intellectual nor an idealist, like the Jew; nor a brooding introspective, like the East Indian; nor a pioneer and frontiersman, like the Anglo-Saxon. He is primarily an artist, loving life for its own sake. His metier is expression rather than action. He is, so to speak, the *lady* among the races.[11]

African Americans' racial temperament feminized them. Park could feminize the Negro only after establishing that other races were masculine. For instance, Park associated stereotypically masculine qualities with the Jew, the East Indian, and the Anglo-Saxon; they were masculine in that they were logical (the Jew), contemplative (the East Indian), and adventurous (the Anglo-Saxon). Hence, Park implied that masculine qualities predominated among the races. The Negro, however, was the exception.

Park's address and article were meant to inform strategies of Americanization; those strategies were of the utmost significance during the period of immigration and migration. American institutions like the school would work to discipline the gendered and sexual differences of U.S. minorities in an effort to make those groups conform to national ideals. For instance, in "Education in its Relation to the Conflict and Fusion of Cultures," an essay that also contains "Temperament, Tradition, and Nationality," Park wrote, "It would . . . seem quite as important that we should, through schools and in the course of the educational process, make ourselves acquainted with the heritages and backgrounds of the foreign peoples."[12] Hence, Park's feminization of blacks was part of a larger strategy to discipline nonwhite immigrants and migrants according to the properties of the abstract citizen-subject. The school was responsible for the management of the racial, national, gender, and ethnic differences suggested by migrant populations. Educational institutions would manage those differences in the name of national unity and for the purpose of the ethical development of the citizen.

Racialization, Feminization, and Nonheteronormativity: The Specter of Woodridge

For the reasons mentioned above, it is understandable why Ellison would be incensed by Park's feminization of African Americans. But it is even more interesting that in the unpublished chapter of *Invisible Man*, Ellison was aware that Park's feminization was not simply a racial discourse that produced gender particularity only. That awareness is embodied in the character of Woodridge. As a black queer character, Woodridge represents the very nonconformity that Americanization programs were supposed to correct and that canonical forms excluded. In the unpublished chapter and the published version of the novel, African American nonheteronormativity figures prominently as the difference that drives canonical exclusion and shapes racial discourse and identity. In addition, the differences between normativity and nonnormativity are outlined spatially. We see this clearly with Woodridge's apartment, both a space of prohibition and of nagging interest. Despite his noncanonical and nonheteronormative difference, Woodridge is at the heart of a quintessentially canonical institution—the university.

As a canonically driven institution, the Western university has historically worked to socialize subjects into the state.[13] In many ways the college featured in the beginning of *Invisible Man* stands as an institutional symbol that motivates African American students on the campus to transcend the sociology of their existence on their way to achieving national ideals of equality and recognition. In this way, it claims to incorporate all African Americans without regard for their racial difference. As one legend about the college says, its president, Dr. Bledsoe, came to the school barefoot, having crossed two states in search of education. The story has it that he was given a job feeding slop to the hogs and worked his way up to president. The students look upon this tale *both* as a sign of the intimidating loftiness of their leader, and as a symbol of the heights they must reach.[14] As the college washed away Dr. Bledsoe's backwardness in order to mold him into a modern subject, the college promises to divest its students of those differences that may interfere with their transformation into the epitome of Enlightenment normality.

Given the newness of emancipation and the students' racial and class backgrounds, such a transformation would naturally be fraught with tensions and contradictions. These tensions and contradictions are in fact expressed through the built environment of the college. At first, the college appears to be the picture of canonical architecture, suggesting greatness and authenticity. As the narrator states,

> It was a beautiful college. The buildings were old and covered with vines and roads gracefully winding, lined with hedges and wild roses that dazzled the eyes in the summer sun. Honeysuckle and purple wisteria hung heavy from the trees and white magnolias mixed with their scents in the bee-humming air. . . . How the grass turned green in the springtime and how the mocking birds fluttered their tails and sang, how the moon shone down on the buildings, how the bell in the chapel tower rang out the precious

short-lived hours; how the girls in bright summer dresses promenaded the grassy lawn.[15]

But the canonical authority that the college wishes to foster is disrupted by its proximity to the noncanonical and the nonnormative:

> Many times, here at night, I've closed my eyes and walked along the forbidden road that winds past the girls' dormitories, past the hall with the clock in the tower, its windows warmly aglow, on down past the small white Home Economics practice cottage, whiter still in the moonlight, and on down the road with its sloping and turning, paralleling the black power-house with its engines drinking earth-shaking rhythms in the dark, its windows red from the glow of the furnace, on to where the road became a bridge over a dry riverbed, tangled with brush and clinging vines; the bridge of rustic logs, made for trysting, but virginal and untested by lovers; on up the road, past the buildings, with the southern verandas half-a-city-block long, to the sudden forking, barren of buildings, birds, or grass, where the road turned off to the asylum.[16]

As the passage carries the reader headlong to the asylum, the college seems inextricably linked to this symbol of irrationality and abnormality. Indeed, Ellison seems to imagine the college as holding one point on a line while the asylum occupies the other point. Imagined thus, the line that connects the college and the asylum stands for the dialectical relationship between the canonical and the nonnormative as it is manifested in African American racial formations.

Here we may interpret the college's proximity to the asylum as an example of what Foucault calls the "'internal discourse of the institution'— the one it employed to address itself, and which circulated among those who made it function."[17] The internal discourse of the college was one constituted and driven by an unmentionable anxiety about nonnormativity. That anxiety is part of the built environment of historically black colleges and universities (HBCUs). As "the cultural products of a recently emancipated people," HBCUs attempted to mimic the canonical features of modern architecture and claim its ideals of normativity and humanity, but the racial specificity of African American oppression disrupted efforts to display canonical and normative status through architecture. For instance, instead of being located within the heart of rural towns, southern HBCUs were often built on marginalized property and could only be accessed through backways that were distant from main streets.[18] The marginalizations that were recorded onto the landscape of HBCUs were constant reminders of the unassimilability of African Americans into categories of citizenship and normality. The relationship between the college and the asylum, in the novel, stands as such a reminder. If the canonical is a mode of incorporation that promises to assimilate racial difference, then the nonnormative is precisely that which haunts racial difference and drives canonical exclusion.

The lost character named Woodridge haunts the college and exists as an internal reminder of the college's proximity to nonnormativity. As the college publicly declares its fitness for citizenship, mobility, and normativity, its walls babble about a teacher who young boys, like the main character, must studiously avoid. In this way, Woodridge stands as a metaphor for an internal discourse of nonheteronormativity within and around the college. Woodridge appears after the main character is banished from the university by the president, Dr. Bledsoe, for having ruined the visit of Mr. Norton, the white trustee. The protagonist wanders through the campus, ends up at the teacher's quarters, and finds himself at Woodridge's door. Through the trepidation that the main character feels about venturing to Woodridge's apartment, Ellison illustrates how heteronormativity operates as a mode of regulation and segregation that establishes homosexuality and other nonheteronormative articulations as subjective and material terrains that must never be crossed, but spaces that are always close at hand. The proximity of Woodridge's apartment to the more normative spaces at the college suggests that even as the college mandates a racial formation that conforms to heteronormativity, that formation can never elude nonheteronormative elements. Because of the proximity of the nonheteronormative, canonical incorporation is always unstable, always subject to unraveling. The sexual hierarchies that divide normalized sexuality from its deviant counterpart are written onto the material space of the college:

> [T]here were certain rumors whispered about Woodridge and though I admired his knowledge of books and parlimentary strategy, I had always avoided his quarters. But now I had to talk. I pounded the door desperately. . . . Woodridge was one of the younger teachers, who had come to the school after a brilliant career in an eastern university. But for some reason he was not considered as important as less inspiring teachers; and in spite of the fact that his debate team remained champions year after year. Woodridge was the teacher mentioned when there was a question of ideas and scholarship. He was the nearest symbol of the intellectual to be found on the campus. I was about to turn away when I heard his muffled, "Come in!" issue through the door.[19]

The protagonist enters the room, decorated with "prints of modern paintings" and a "spinet piano." Woodridge himself wears a "wine red dressing robe" and a "silk stocking . . . stretched over his head to keep his hair in place." Knowingly, he says to his visitor, "I've been expecting you to drop in for a long time. . . . I would offer you a drink. . . . But that's not allowed. I may corrupt you only in those ways for which I am paid" (164).

Throughout the chapter, Woodridge reassures the main character that he need not fear his homosexuality, even going so far as to say, "Relax, relax. . . . I don't hurt little boys." Woodridge then points to a statue of a Greek nude torso that sits on one end of a chest and to an "ugly primitive African statue" that sits on the other: "Relax like the white boy there, the Greek," he said. "You live too much like the other all the time. . . . You're forced into extreme positions, . . . distorted in the interest of a design." Woodridge's privileging of the Greek statue—the white boy—may appear to be his favoring of the European over the African. But we may also read Woodridge's gesture as pointing to the ways that the main character's heteronormative regulation is part of his racial regulation as an African American college student, all of which comprise the ways that he is "distorted in the interest of a design" (164, 165).

Woodridge is keenly aware that his young college student has crossed a boundary in coming to his apartment at night. He asks, "Haven't you heard that I was a dangerous, wicked man . . . dangerous to see in my room?" To which the narrator replies, "No, but I heard that you were the smartest teacher on the campus" (165). In part, this exchange represents the ways that Woodridge is marked as a figure of curiosity at the same time that he is marked "dangerous." As a university professor, he can be accessed for his intellectual prowess, but he can never be accessed in the privatized space of his apartment. Such access would signal sexual curiosity instead of intellectual interest.

Ironically enough, it is in the apartment that the protagonist can partake of the full range of Woodridge's insights about the regulations of the college, regulations motivated by the tenuously normative status of African American subjects. Only in this marginalized and nonheteronormative space can the narrator receive a naked critique of the techniques of domination that pervade the campus. Indeed, after the protagonist addresses Woodridge as "sir," Woodridge explodes with "Don't say *Sir* to me! . . . In this room you can be a human being. Slavery is ended. . . . This is the *Emancipation*" (166). Hence, Ellison positions Woodridge as witness to emancipation. By doing so, emancipation, rather than being the entrance of the African American into the normative claims and protections of citizenship, is rearticulated as identification with and triumph of the nonheteronormative. In Woodridge's room, the main character can claim an alternative humanity constituted outside of hierarchical arrangements that hark back to slavery and that make up the social relations on the university campus.

Ellison continues his critique of the regulatory mechanisms of the campus by having Woodridge draw attention to how the main character is interpellated by canonical texts and the narrative of equality upon which they are based. When the narrator asks Woodridge about Ralph Waldo Emerson, saying that one of the trustees had "asked him about [Emerson] and I thought maybe you'd tell me something about him so that when I drive him again I wouldn't seem so dumb." Woodridge responds,

> Emerson, huh? . . . I bet Emerson never dreamed of this. Or of me. . . .
> You're an *idealist* and a *slave*. That's why you are a good debator. You
> *believe in the stuff.* You believe in any and everything that you're *supposed*
> to believe in. My god! You're the *model student* of the college. . . . So you
> want to know about books. You would. I've noticed you going around
> reading and making speeches. You put a lot of time into it, don't you? . . .
> And you've been told that you'll succeed if only you work hard at it,
> haven't you? (166–67)

Woodridge strikes at the very heart of American education by frustrating its claims to national ideals of equality and its promise of upward mobility. He renders the features of canonical formation into techniques of regulation. As "model student" of the American educational system, the protagonist is, in fact, a "slave." As slave, he is operated by techniques of racial domination that are obscured through the language of liberal progress. Addressing that language as an instrument of racial domination, Woodridge suggests that institutions organized around that language—Americanization programs, schools, and universities—are sites that manage the racial difference rather than inspire critical agency among racialized nonwhite minorities. Institutions formed out of canonicity, as Woodridge states, cannot possibly imagine the critical differences of nonheteronormative subjects and social formations, differences that exist as the discursive and material rebuke of liberal claims.

While canonical formations cannot apprehend African American non-heteronormativity, those formations produce conditions for nonheteronormative emergence as they produce racial, gender, and sexual differences to articulate our relationship to the normative. Addressing the gendered perversion of Park's racialization of African Americans in "Temperament, Tradition, and Nationality," Woodridge asks the narrator, "You study sociology?"

"I did last year."
"Well your sociology textbook teaches that we comprise what it describes as the 'Lady of the races.' Do you remember that?"
"Of course. It's from Robert E. Park."
"You believe it, don't you?"

"I don't know. It's in the text book. . . . I suppose so."
"Then even if the rumours about me were true, it shouldn't cause any
surprise, should it? If you belong to the lady of the races, isn't it all right
to become a 'lady'? Then everything's O.K. All things are possible. A
man is automatically a woman. Come, now, debator, orator," he yelled
dramatically. (167)

For Woodridge, the logical extension of sociological discourse is an erotic
difference and variation that ground African American subject and social formations in queerness, in polymorphous perversity. In other words, sociology
suggests that African American racial difference allows for the possibility of
alternative gender and sexual formations. At the same time, Woodridge insists that explaining those formations in the canonical language of sociology
would reduce the complexity of those formations. In an outcry against canonical formations as they emerge in literature, sociology, and philosophy,
he says,

> I spit on all these books, these writers, these dreams, these insults! What do
> they know about life? Which of them knew this life I live? They built illu-
> sions against life and I accepted them. But now, here, drunk, in this place,
> at this time, this moment, I see and I know that it's all a fucking lie. This
> too is a part of reality and any book that fails to include it is *obscene*. (168,
> emphasis mine)

In addition, Woodridge implies that the violence of interpellation is the signal feature of canonically informed education. Talking to the narrator, Woodridge says,

> I dream at night that all the students I've taught in these eight years are
> lined up before me, against the bare wall of a long hall, their faces are
> turned toward me expectantly awake, and I move along gripping a sharp
> cabinet maker's gouge and as I come to each student I stop and as I pinch
> each lovingly by his unsuspecting cheek, I scoop out his eyes and drop
> them bleeding and gelatinous into a white cotton sack that hangs chained
> to my neck. No, don't turn your eyes away, it sounds terrible but that isn't
> all, see? It's worse than that. It's worse because none of the students seems
> to feel the pain. Not a solitary one. Some even laugh as their snot-like eyes
> pop out and drip into the bag. That's what's horrible, they laugh. Or they
> just smile. If only one of them could feel it and cry out in pain! Just one.
> Then I could stop: then I could teach them to see. Then I wouldn't have to
> dream that dream night after night. This is real, more real than anything
> you can get in the books. They don't dream of it, they don't imagine it;

and because they don't they helped create it. Tonight you're a lucky young
man. . . . Tonight drunk and disgusted I can tell you things I will be too
afraid to tell you tomorrow. (168–69)

Describing Ellison's theory of the American novel, John M. Reilly writes,
the "tentative and open form of the novel associates with democratic philosophy" and the novel's "morality confirms an identity between democracy
and fiction."[20] As Woodridge casts aspersion on the claims of democracy
by rejecting the promises of canonical formation, he calls for alternative
formulations of morality, democracy, and fiction—that is, formulations that
can challenge the interpellative agendas of literature, sociology, and liberal
democracy. Again, it is no small matter that an African American queer
subject demands resistance to interpellation. By doing so, Ellison suggests
that the queer of color subject can both trace the workings of interpellation
and inspire other subjects to defy its operation. While canonical formations
promise normalcy to the racialized nonwhite subject, the queer of color subject reminds us that such promises are techniques of discipline rather than
vehicles toward liberation. After ordering the protagonist to leave his room,
Woodridge imparts this moral to him: "This is no place to get lead in your
pencil, bullets in your gun, wad in your pocket, sense in your head. Our job
here is to take it out. Now get OUT! This is your diploma, and your gradua-
tion day address."[21]

In the published version of the novel, Ellison uses the nonheteronormative space of the brothel/bar called the Golden Day to expose the regulatory
features of race relations. After Norton's botched visit to the country, Norton
insists that the protagonist take him to get a drink. The nearest place is the
Golden Day. After a brawl in which Norton faints, he and the protagonist
are taken upstairs to be cared for by one of the black war veterans who pa-
tronize the place. Presumably unbalanced, the vet tells the protagonist his
own story. It is one that begins with the vet's own interpellation by the
medical establishment. As if he were rambling, he begins:

> It is an issue which I can confront only by evading it. An utterly stupid
> proposition, and these hands so lovingly trained to master a scalpel yearn
> to caress a trigger. I returned to save life and I was refused. . . . Ten men in
> masks drove me out from the city at midnight and beat me with whips for
> saving a human life. And I was forced to the utmost degradation because I
> possessed skilled hands and the belief that my knowledge could bring me
> dignity—not wealth, only dignity—and other men health![22]

Like the protagonist, the vet believed that he could purchase normalization
by yielding to disciplinary requirements.

Aware of the futility and danger of submitting to discipline, the vet says to the protagonist and Norton,

> "You see," he said turning to Mr. Norton, "he has eyes and ears and a good distended African nose, but he fails to understand the simple facts of life. *Understand*. Understand? It's worse than that. He registers with his senses but short-circuits his brain. Nothing has meaning. He takes it in but he doesn't digest it. Already he is—well, bless my soul! Behold! A walking zombie. Already he's learned to repress not only his emotions but his humanity. He's *invisible*, a walking *personification of the Negative*, the most *perfect achievement* of your dreams, sir! The *mechanical man*!"[23]

As the perfection of Mr. Norton's dreams of racial progress, the protagonist is the embodiment of the regulatory imperatives necessitated by canonical formation. As the vet says, he is "the personification of the Negative. . . . the mechanical man." To a large degree, this regulation causes his invisibility. As a college student, his entrance into the university is supposed to bring him recognition, freedom, and normalcy—all the rewards of a minoritized subject turned modern. Believing that it can attain modern agency through normalization, the university marginalizes and excludes other African American subjects because of class difference and disability, as well as gender/sexual nonconformity. These subjects represent the alienated image of the minoritized subject seeking modern confirmation. As the Invisible Man and the other inhabitants of the school work to demonstrate their modernity, they are constantly reminded that they are moored to these figures of African American deviancy. Hence, the student is led to Woodridge's door and to the Golden Day, just as the college is connected to the insane asylum. The vet, like Woodridge, symbolizes the nonheteronormative presence as that which reveals the fictions of disciplinarity, conformity, and canonization. Promising progress and recognition, they deliver regulation and invisibility.

The Canonization of African American Cultural Difference

Canonical formations outline trajectories for ethical subject formation; they specify what it means to be a human, a citizen, and a moral being. As champions of normativity, these formations can only be consummated through the regulation of nonheteronormative difference. As such, canonical formations used gender, sexual, and racial differences to constitute a "political economy of a will to knowledge."[24] Here, I refer to the ways in which racial subjects were produced and observed through canonical formations and ethically developed through citizenship only by submitting to heteronormative regulation. In opposition to the chapter on Woodridge,

Ellison's essays and parts of the published version of the novel endorse such a submission. More specifically, the essays often suppress the ambiguity and ambivalence of the published and unpublished texts by presenting the United States as an ethical and national ideal. Tracing American fiction to the nineteenth century and the literary emergence of the "Negro as the symbol of Man," Ellison locates the project of African American literature within this emergence. He argues,

> Negro writers and those of other minorities have their own task of contributing to the total image of the American by depicting the experience of their own groups. Certainly theirs is the task of defining Negro humanity, as this can no more be accomplished by others than freedom, which must be won again and again each day, can be conferred upon another. A people must define itself, and minorities have the responsibility of having their ideals and images recognized as part of the composite image which is that of the still forming American people.[25]

For Ellison, African American writers had to define African American humanity against the racial discourses produced, in part, by sociologists and institutionalized through the de facto and legal exclusions that characterized African American experience; such discursive and material practices violated the African American's "essence" as man and human being. For African American writers to define black humanity, Ellison assumes that those depictions would illustrate the complexity and heterogeneity of American life. In a lecture given in 1967, Ellison stated,

> Even today America remains an undiscovered country. . . . We are at once very unified, and at the same time very *diversified*. On many levels, we don't know who we are, and there are always moments of confrontation where we meet as absolute strangers. . . . Race is by no means the only thing that divides us in this still-undiscovered country. We're only a partially achieved nation, and I think this is good because it gives the writer of novels a role beyond that of entertainer. The novel's function permits him a maximum freedom to express his own vision of reality. It allows him to write out of his own group background and his own individual background. But the novel also places upon him a responsibility of reporting, imaginatively, of course, what is going on in his particular area of the American experience.[26]

Whereas the United States is only partially achieved, the novelist can fulfill national ideals of equality, unity, and diversity through aesthetic representations that champion those ideals. In doing so, African American and other minority novelists supplement the task of liberal democracy, by supplying in aesthetics what the unachieved country lacks in practice. In doing so, aesthetic culture becomes the means to perfect liberal capitalism.

For Ellison, the possibilities of canonical literature to incorporate and represent difference symbolized the nation's abilities to integrate difference as well. In a 1955 interview, he stated, "One function of serious literature is to deal with the moral core of a given society. Well, in the United States the Negro and his status have always stood for that moral concern. He symbolizes among other things the human and social possibility of equality."[27] In this way, literature "furnishes the domain of human freedom promised in theory by bourgeois states but belied in all but form by their practices."[28] By addressing literature as that cultural form that can deliver in aesthetics what the state will not render in practice, Ellison repeats liberalism's logic regarding aesthetic culture and political representation. Discussing this logic, David Lloyd argues,

> The aesthetic domain performs this function by virtue of the fact that, while bourgeois political theory postulates the essential identity of man, aesthetic works are held to furnish the representative instances of reconciliation which at once prefigure and produce an ethical subjectivity restored to identity with this universal human essence.[29]

Symbolizing the human and social possibility of equality, Ellison attempts to situate the African American within the grammar of liberal democracy and humanism, within the dominant national narrative of U.S. citizenship. As the symbol of democratic ideals, the African American is the figure from which the nation can develop ethically. The job of African American literature is to assist in that development by framing the African American as one image of the representative American and human. By doing so, African American literature adopts the ideals held sacred by major literature. Canonical literature assumes an ethical function both "by depicting the development of an identity to the point of identification with a more general humanity (the narrative of *Bildung*), and by eliciting the reader's similar identification with a character or a poetic subject."[30] Rather than African American culture symbolizing cultural and ethical lag, as it did with Park and other canonical sociologists, Ellison defines African American culture as the metaphor for that ethical and cultural development associated with American national identity.

If material conditions highlight the tenuous status of African American culture as a symbol of American norms and if aesthetic and epistemological canons work to reconcile such incongruities, we must cite Ellison's aestheticization of African American literature as a disciplinary strategy. While acknowledging that such a strategy was not without rewards—especially in a period in which racial exclusion was achieved by racializing U.S. minorities as the antitheses of American citizenship, those practices highlight the irreducible difference between African American culture and American identity. As Ellison implies, aesthetic rearticulation acknowledges the partial nature of liberal ideals and practices. Hence, the literary representation of African American culture as fully embodied American culture is at once an affirmation of liberal ideals and an acknowledgment that those ideals are never universalized for African Americans or for other subjects minoritized by racial difference.

The contradictions implied but concealed in Ellison's aestheticization of African American culture are illuminated through the novel's overarching metaphor of invisibility. Indeed, the meanings of invisibility are shaped by the historic exclusions around race, causing invisibility to be the trace of the African American's alienation from the rights and privileges of citizenship and from modern epistemologies of recognition and visibility that authorize those rights. As the narrator states, "Irresponsibility is part of my invisibility; any way you face it, it is a denial. But to whom can I be responsible, and why should I be, when you refuse to see me? And wait until I reveal how truly irresponsible I am. Responsibility rests upon *recognition,* and recognition is a form of *agreement.*"[31] Ellison, therefore, suggests that invisibility is not only antithetical to a logic of recognition and acceptance; it is antagonistic to that logic that helps to form the alliance between canonical formation, national identification, and ethical development under liberal capitalism. As invisibility is developed in antagonism to responsibility and acceptance, it does not represent an ontology of lack that seeks fulfillment through the recognition and visibility of citizenship. As Woodridge argues and as parts of the published version attest, canonical representation, recognition, and visibility depend on conformities produced and informed by the racially motivated regulations of gender and sexuality. As a narrative that dramatizes the regulatory outcomes of such demands, *Invisible Man* questions bourgeois identity's claims to depth and authenticity as the prizes of gender and sexual conformity, especially for subjects racialized as tenuously normative in the first place. In doing so, the novel also questions those reflexive modes—literature and sociology particularly—that base national affiliation on such conformity. Indeed, the vet and Woodridge summon a new epistemological orientation, one that calls for modes of political agency that are not based on visible compliance and conformity with modern formulations of normative development.

But the novel also retreats to the very logic of acceptance, responsibility, and identification that it rejects. Reflecting on the advice his grandfather gave him just before the grandfather's death, the narrator asks

> I'm still plagued by his deathbed advice. . . . Perhaps he hid his meaning
> deeper than I thought, perhaps his anger threw me off—I can't decide.
> Could he have meant—hell, he must have meant the principle, that we
> were to affirm the principle on which the country was built and not the
> men, or at least not the men who did the violence. . . . [Did] he mean that
> we had to take the *responsibility* for all of it, for the men as well as the
> principle, because no other fitted our needs? Not for the power or for
> vindication, but because we, with the given circumstance of our origin,
> could only thus find transcendence? Was it that we of all, we, most of all,
> had to affirm the principle, the plan in whose name we had been brutal-
> ized and sacrificed—not because we would always be weak nor because
> we were afraid or opportunistic, but because we were older than they, in
> the sense of what it took to live in the world with others and because they
> had exhausted in us, some—not much, but some—of the human greed and
> smallness, yes, and the fear and superstition that had kept them running?[32]

In other words, African Americans represent the kind of ethical maturity
needed to be responsible caretakers and stewards of liberal democratic ideals.
This passage exemplifies Ellison's argument in the essays that African American culture acts as a beacon of that ethical development needed for the perfection of liberal capitalism. To do so, African Americans must engage the very
logic of visibility, recognition, and acceptance that the novel problematizes.
On the other hand Woodridge and the vet call for a subject developed out of
an alternative ethic, one that does not comply with the ideological dictates
of the American citizen-subject and Enlightenment man. These dictates were
authorized by a language of responsibility, agreement, and visibility that excluded gender, sexual, and mental nonnormativity.

That perfection is achieved by promoting diversity, which—for Ellison—
corrects the nation-state's insistence on sameness and homogeneity. As the
narrator states,

> Whence all this passion toward conformity anyway?—diversity is the
> word. Let man keep his many parts and you'll have no tyrant states. Why,
> if they follow this conformity business they'll end up by forcing me, an in-
> visible man, to become white, which is not a color but a lack of one. Must
> I strive toward colorlessness? But seriously, and without snobbery, think
> of what the world would lose if that should happen. America is woven of
> many strands; I would recognize them and let it so remain. . . . Our fate is
> to become one, and yet many—This is not prophecy, but description.[33]

Like sameness, diversity arises out of liberal ideology and bears the contradictions of that ideology. Rather than resolving the inequality that character-

izes liberal capitalism, the discourse of diversity worked to conceal economic and social contradictions. As state and capital produced and utilized racial, gender, and erotic difference to exclude minoritized subjects from the rights and privileges of citizenship, the rhetoric of diversity concealed that use and production; hence, diversity was synonymous with an ideal of equality and fraternity during a period of racial transformation. As the narrator states, diversity was not prophecy but description. Wartime industry and postwar industrial expansion was responsible for expanding economic opportunities for Asian Americans, Chicanos, and African Americans. But the increased opportunities that these groups enjoyed did not thwart the onslaught of racial exclusion. Asian Americans were barred access to high-paying jobs in the manufacturing, craft, and construction sectors, and received less pay than whites doing equivalent work.[34] During this period, capitalist imperatives helped to produce plans for "urban renewal." In Los Angeles, for instance, urban renewal led to the creation of barrios by restricting Chicanos to East L.A.[35] Moreover, the wartime industry that promoted economic expansion also confined many Asian Americans, Chicanos, and African Americans to low-paying jobs.[36] In addition, the state used that labor as the motor for establishing hegemonic authority in Asia through war and economic imperialism. In sum, the "diversity" that the United States was experiencing indexed the contradictions of liberal capitalism instead of proving the state's ability to incorporate culturally and corporeally different subjects and social formations. By having the protagonist identify with diversity as a principle that solemnizes liberal democracy's interest in canonizing and assimilating difference, Ellison conceals how liberal epistemological, political, and economic formations have made regulation, inequality, misrecognition, and discipline the very terms of minority incorporation. This concealment is most powerfully figured in the very fact that Woodridge was exiled from the final version of the novel. In the essays that reflect on that final version, Ellison silences the very critiques that Woodridge and the vet are making.

As the essays and parts of *Invisible Man* insist on an ethical formation that complies with the national narrative of the United States, the texts align themselves with the discursive formations of Chicago School sociologists, despite Ellison's antipathy to sociology in general. As I stated in chapter 1, African American nonheteronormativity suggested a fundamental moral difference. For sociologists, that moral and ethical difference implied national difference and an incongruity between African American racial formation and American national identity. Like Chicago School sociologists, Ellison also uses ethical compliance to identify the stakes of national belonging. In contrast, Woodridge, as a nonheteronormative subject, refuses to reconcile with the nation and canonical formations by complying with gender and sexual ideals.

African American nonheteronormative formations imply an estrangement from *all* canonical formations. Therefore, we cannot reject the canonical features of one discipline only to imagine that another can integrate what the former excluded. To do so would be to "reproduce pluralist arguments of inclusion and rights"[37] that claim the state's perfection against glaring evidence of contradiction and exploitation. African American nonheteronormativity thus disrupts the idea that the literary and the sociological are discrete and discontinuous formations. Instead, we must assume that canonical sociology and canonical literature arise out of the same system of power, one that presents normativity and humanity as the gifts of state compliance and heteropatriarchal belonging.

The Science of Sexuality: African American Nonheteronormativity, Social Science, and the American State

Woodridge's rant provides important insights about the production of sexuality and racial difference as intertwining truths. He identifies canonical sociology and canonical literature as sites that presume notions of the human and the citizen and subsequently estrange African American racial and cultural difference from those notions. In his critique of sociology's production of racial knowledge about African Americans, Woodridge suggests a different account of the political economy of sexual knowledge, one that diverges from Foucault's assessment in *The History of Sexuality.* The specific history of African Americans' constitution as the objects of racial and sexual knowledge through canonical sociology has produced modes of deployment that cohere with and diverge from those outlined by Foucault.

In *The History of Sexuality,* Foucault relates the production of sexual knowledge to the act of confession. He writes,

> [N]ext to the testing rituals, next to the testimony of witnesses, and the learned *methods of observation and demonstration,* the confession became one of the West's most highly valued techniques of producing truth. We have since become a confessing society. . . .
>
> The confession was and still remains, the *general standard* governing the production of the true discourse of sex. . . . It is no longer a question simply of saying what was done—the sexual act—and how it was done; but of reconstructing, in and around the act, the thought that recapitulated it, the obsessions that accompanied it, the images, desires, modulations, and quality of the pleasure that animated it. . . .

. . . It was a time when the most singular pleasures were called upon to pronounce a discourse of truth concerning themselves, a discourse which had to model itself after that which spoke, not of sin and salvation, but of *bodies and life processes*—the *discourse of science*. It was enough to make one's voice tremble, for an improbable thing was then taking shape: a confessional science, a science which relied on a many-sided extortion, and took for its object what was unmentionable but admitted to nonetheless.[38]

As an example of the confession as the context for the production of a discourse concerning the truth of sexuality, we need only look to that infamous part of *Invisible Man,* the "Trueblood Incident." As the narrator says, Jim Trueblood was the name of a "sharecropper who had brought disgrace upon the black community."[39] The man's name comes up as the protagonist is assigned the task of giving Mr. Norton a tour. But Mr. Norton is much more interested in seeing the areas that surround the college and the protagonist is afraid that he will discover the shame that Trueblood has brought to all. Indeed, the protagonist soon tells Mr. Norton that Trueblood has not only impregnated his wife, but his daughter as well. Mr. Norton is horrified to learn this, crying out "No, no, no," but immediately begs to hear more. He catches up with Trueblood and tries to incite him to confession. Trueblood obliges. Indeed, he has become well practiced at telling the story of how he raped his daughter. Imagine his surprise when local white men wanted to hear about the story over and over again, giving him drink, tobacco, and other treats when he tells it. And as Trueblood says, "[Big] white folks, too, from the big school way cross the State . . . [ask] me lots 'bout what I thought 'bout things, and 'bout my folks and the kids, and wrote it all down in a book."[40] Even while the story pains him, Mr. Norton needs to hear it as well.

The Trueblood incident clearly illustrates the confession as a highly valued technique for producing truth. But the incident and the general production of racial discourses about African Americans possess elements that exceed Foucault's theorization of the production of sexual knowledge. To begin with, confession in this instance is a technique that has a particularly racialized angle. This angle denotes the ways in which the incitement to discourse confirmed and ensured the repetition of stereotype. In other words, it assisted the production of racial knowledge about African Americans. As Trueblood explains and as the protagonist knows, local whites, particularly, induce confession to undermine the college's quest for equivalence and normativity.

Yes, Trueblood is a "confessing animal,"[41] to use Foucault's language. But in the racist logic of the local whites and Mr. Norton, he *is* an animal whose confession proves that *they* are all animals. When figuring the clamor for knowledge about sexuality in the image of the confession, Foucault rightfully argues, "For the first time no doubt, a society has taken upon itself to solicit and hear the imparting of individual pleasures."[42] This incitement to discourse occasioned such personages as the nervous woman, the frigid wife, the indifferent mother, the impotent and sadistic husband, the hysterical girl, the "young homosexual who rejects marriage or neglects his wife," and so forth.[43] For Foucault, the confession yielded knowledge about perverse individuals. In the Trueblood incident, on the other hand, the confession was used not to produce knowledge about the perversities of individuals, but to construct an archive of the sexual grotesqueries that presumably belonged to a collective.

One cannot deny the power that the confession has had in defining the modern West's narrative of sexuality. But we need not overstate its authority. A model of sexuality based solely on the confession cannot address the racial specificity of epistemologies and methodologies in determining sexual "truth" and producing sexual discourse. Unlike psychoanalysis and the religious confessional before it, sociology attempted to diagnose social rather than psychological stability. As confessional models defined sexuality as the buried truth of interiority, sociology apprehended sexuality as the open truth of social practice. This agenda positioned culture as that domain that registers the stability of the social, a stability measured in terms of minority culture's ability to manage differences of race, class, and gender as they work to produce sexual variation. Confessional models, Foucault suggests, designated interiority as the truth of human subjectivity and imagined Western culture as that system of norms and practices that could ensure that the erratic and unstable features of consciousness did not contaminate social order. Sociology, on the other hand, used exteriority[44]—neighborhood, intimate arrangements, gender formations, and so forth—to articulate the sexual truth of racialized subjectivity. The moral and subjective life of African Americans, for example, became inextricably linked to such issues as the stability of neighborhood and the structural makeup of family. Hence, as pathology operated on a visible plateau, so did canonical sociology presume morality as the subjective counterpart to the material and social conditions that originated in African American life in the twentieth century. Minority culture, thus, stood as that figure of unpredictability in need of moral regulation by Western bourgeois culture.

We may interpret the Trueblood incident as an allegory of actual sociological encounters with rural blacks. During the period of African American migration, American sociologists and black middle-class elites articulated the positions of African Americans in rural agrarian economy versus the positions of African Americans in urban industrial economies as a difference of sexuality. Though sociology's interest in black folk culture was short-lived, several ethnographic studies were published in the 1920s. Sympathetic to a culture that they thought was dying out because of the approach of industrialization and urbanization, this literature constructed African American folk culture as outside modernity. Black middle-class persons responded to the sociological treatments of folk culture by arguing that sociologists were in fact "glamorizing crudity and immorality."[45] The glamorization of crudity and immorality referred to sexual matters that presumably circulated in public when they should have been confined to the private.

One such influential text was John Dollard's *Caste and Class in a Southern Town*. In this text, Dollard argued that African Americans gained sexual freedom from the sharecropping system. Released from traditional economic responsibilities because of their subordinated status as sharecroppers, Dollard argued that this exemption released lower-class blacks from heteronormative regulation. The absence of such regulation, for Dollard, had widespread communal reverberations in the form of "greater freedom of aggression and resentment within his own group." As he stated, that aggression was "linked to the weakness of the monogamous family among lower-class Negroes. . . . Seen from the standpoint of the white-caste mores, the lower-class Negro family is much less tightly organized to control impulse expression."[46] While relying on Freudian psychoanalysis to distinguish between the cultural subjectivities of lower-class blacks and whites, Dollard did so to explore a *sociological* interest in racial formations under southern agrarian economies. Rather than reproducing a psychoanalytic taxonomy, that sociological interest produced nonmonogamy as the emblem of southern black sexual perversion and variation. For sociologists like Dollard, culture had to act as a force of repression in order for African Americans to claim Western bourgeois status.

As cultural pathology was located within the terrain of the social and the visible, middle-class redemption was staged on that terrain as well. Black middle-class persons had to publicly demonstrate their compliance with heteropatriarchal cultural standards as a way of proving their distance from "obviously" pathological subjects and social relations and as a way of claiming access to state and civil society. As an example of such public demonstrations, we might only think of the flyer that the Chicago chapter of the National Urban League presented to new southern migrants. The pamphlet contained such mantras as "I AM AN AMERICAN CITIZEN. . . . I DESIRE to render CITIZEN service. . . . I DESIRE to help bring about a NEW ORDER OF LIVING in this community. . . . I WILL ATTEND to the neatness of my personal appearance on the street or when sitting in front doorways. . . . I WILL REFRAIN from wearing dust caps, bungalow aprons, house clothing and bedroom shoes out of doors. . . . I WILL ARRANGE MY TOILET within doors and not on the front of the porch. . . . I WILL REFRAIN from loud talking and objectionable deportment on street cars and in public places."[47] As African American cultural pathology was believed to be inscribed externally rather than residing internally, the discourse of black sexuality seemed to speak in every household and neighborhood, and on every black body. Black subjects seeking normalization responded to the hyperdiscursivity surrounding African American sexual practices with restrained and disciplined behavior.[48] The terms for black middle-class subject and social formation demanded that black middle-class persons and those seeking middle-class status would make themselves, as well as queer and working-class blacks, available for surveillance and do so in the name of recognition and normativity.

In many ways, the protagonist of *Invisible Man* symbolizes the attempt made by many African Americans to engage a bourgeois trajectory by displaying bourgeois practices and norms, presuming that they would then gain visibility and recognition from those institutions that define liberal culture. As the novel illustrates and as Woodridge and the vet attest, such appeals to visibility are—ironically—destined for an invisibility that challenges visibility's promise. As the Invisible Man himself argues, "You ache with the need to convince yourself that you do exist in the real world, that you're part of all the sound and anguish, and you strike out with your fists, you curse and you swear *to make them recognize you. And alas it's seldom successful.*"[49]

As sociology positioned itself as part of the state's reform agenda, its production of racial knowledge about African Americans as nonheteronormative subjects also mediated its relationship with the state. A whole set of methodologies was deployed to produce that exteriority as part of the racial knowledge about African Americans. The Chicago School sociologists and Jonathan Dollard expressly used ethnography to measure the effects of economic change on black racial formations in the urban North and the South. Statistics emerged as the apparatus for tallying African American cultural dysfunction for the good of liberal capitalist stability. Statistics became an invaluable tool not only for measuring demographic changes around African American migration, urbanization, and employment, but for producing knowledge about the importance of such changes. Pointing to statistics as a technology of race, Ellison made the following remarks in an interview conducted in 1961:

> Too many of us have accepted a statistical interpretation of our lives and thus much of that which makes us a source of moral strength to America goes unappreciated and undefined. . . . You can find sociological descriptions of the conditions under which they [African Americans] live but few indications of their morale.[50]

Let us locate statistical interpretation within the genealogy of sexuality, generally, and within the category "population" specifically. Foucault argues that the emergence of the category "population" represented "one of the great innovations in the technique of power in the eighteenth century."[51] Population was denoted as wealth, manpower, or labor capacity, population balanced between its own growth and the resources it commanded.[52] Elaborating his understanding of population, Foucault writes,

> Governments perceived that they were not dealing simply with subjects, or even with a "people," but with a "population," with its specific phenomena and its peculiar variables: birth and death rates, life expectancy, fertility, state of health, frequency of illnesses, patterns of diet and habitation. . . . At the heart of the economic and political problem of population was sex: it was necessary to analyze the birthrate, the age of marriage, the legitimate and illegitimate births, the precocity and frequency of sexual relations, the ways of making them fertile or sterile, the effects of unmarried life or of those prohibitions, the impact of contraceptive practices. . . . [53]

In the context of racial knowledge about African Americans, statistics was a way of gleaning sexual truths about that group. Statistics helped to present African Americans as a population for study and evaluation. The methodologies therein could help illuminate the gendered and sexual peculiarities of African American existence. Statistics helped to produce surveillance as one mode, alongside confession, for producing the truth of sexuality in Western society.

As sex was "sociologized," surveillance helped to constitute sexual knowledge in this way: sociological knowledge would be produced for the good of social order. With this effort in mind, canonical sociology would help transform observation into an epistemological and "objective" technique for the good of modern state power. This was a way of defining surveillance as a scientifically acceptable and socially necessary practice. It established the sociological onlooker as safely removed and insulated from the prurient practices of African American men, women, and children.

Sex was also sociologized through a postulate of a general and diffuse causality concerning social order. Housing and neighborhood conditions, illiteracy, and poverty became omens of gender and sexual pathologies that could topple the rational orders of cities and even the nation. Postulating sexuality as a general and diffuse causality provides an example of how "sexuality" came to mean much more than eros, sexual instincts, and practices, but came to signify a host of apparently "nonsexual" factors.

Another way in which sexuality was articulated as a sociological object was through the principle of the manifest (i.e., racialized) character of sexuality. Foucault discusses the ways in which sexuality was defined by a latency intrinsic to sexuality. In the case of African Americans and other nonwhite racial groups whose corporeal difference stands as the conduit for racial discourses, the body became the site upon which the racialized meanings of African American culture, in particular, and minority culture, in general, were legible. The nonwhite body, therefore, was not simply skin and bone, but the screen upon which images of neighborhoods, housing conditions, and sexual and gender practices could be seen.

Yet another way in which African American sexual formations were sociologized was through the interpretive status of the sociologist. African American subjects could not access the truth of sexuality, the truth of their sociality. Assessing that truth required the sociologist who could analyze the obscurity of the social. The manifest quality of African American culture, in other words, had to be deciphered by the sociologist. By making the social a sign that had to be deciphered for its racial, gender, and sexual truths, the twentieth century made it possible for racialized surveillance to operate as a scientific discourse.

Another feature of the sociologization of sex can be seen through the constitution of the gender and sexual idiosyncrasies of African American racial formation as that which could be resolved through policy. As African American gender and sexual practices were made into social phenomena, it then followed that those practices could be reformed through state intervention. African American gender and sexual practices were constituted as unstable fields that could have grave repercussions for the U.S. nation-state. The surveillance of African American gender and sexual practices would not only be a matter of knowledge, but of state as well. As the changes fashioned by industrialization, urbanization, and migration imply, capital provided the conditions by which African Americans and other nonwhite subjects would be placed under the gazes of state and epistemology.

Sociology has predominated as the epistemology from which we obtain sexual knowledge about African Americans. To do so, it has rallied methods of observation that cannot simply be accounted for in a model that privileges confession. The sexual formation of nonwhite subjects coheres with, but also departs from, the model presumed by Foucault's theory of confession. This departure makes it apparent why the critique of sexuality must be wedded to critiques of state and capital. The erotics of African American racial formation produce a taxonomy of perversions particular to that formation. Hence, we must reconsider explanations of sexuality that presume our emergence out of the same epistemological traditions, our subjection to the same taxonomy of perversions, and our production through the same methodologies. Acknowledging the place of surveillance in the construction of sexual truths about African Americans and possibly other nonwhite subjects means that we must also be willing to admit other standards for producing discourses of sexuality.

The Domain of Sexuality

Foucault opposed his theory of confession—which rendered sexuality into a domain of productivity, discourse, and knowledge—to the repressive hypothesis that had previously constituted sexuality in terms of silence. With this opposition Foucault implied another—the discursivity of sexuality versus the restrictiveness of capital. As he states,

> This discourse on modern sexual repression holds up well, owing no doubt to how easy it is to uphold. A solemn historical and political guarantee protects it. By placing the advent of the age of repression in the seventeenth century, after hundreds of years of open spaces and free expression, one adjusts it to coincide with the development of capitalism: it becomes an integral part of the bourgeois order. The minor chronicle of sex and its trials is transposed into the ceremonious history of the modes of production; its trifling aspect fades from view. A principle of explanation emerges after the fact: if sex is so rigorously repressed, this is because it is incompatible with a general and intensive work imperative.[54]

Foucault situates the repressive hypothesis within the theoretical procedures of marxism. As Foucault replaces the repressive hypothesis with an understanding of sexuality based on the incitement to discourse and the confessional model, he both neutralizes the repressive hypothesis *and* alienates the critique of sexuality from the critique of capital.

African American nonheteronormative formations suggest not only the repressive nature of capital—that capital regulates sexuality—but also the productive nature of capital—that it produces conditions for alternative gender and sexual arrangements, practices, and identities. African American nonheteronormative formations present capital as much more than the site of repression; it is the site of productivity as well, a site whose productivity becomes sociology's object of interest. A history of those formations must present the critique of sexuality as simultaneous with the critique of capitalist economic formations.

With regard to African American nonheteronormative formations, sociological methodologies helped formulate knowledge about the exteriors of African American life and then articulated African American nonheteronormative difference through that exteriority. While a confessional mode like psychoanalysis interpreted individual consciousness to determine how the mind economized sexual desire, canonical sociology analyzed the social conditions of African American life to determine how African American *culture* economized sexual desire. As Conrad Bentzen argued that social conditions on the South Side liberated its inhabitants and visitors from sexual repression, so Dollard argued that the caste system that relegated African Americans to the bottom rung in southern agrarian economies released blacks from the bounds of sexual propriety. By designating exteriority instead of interiority as the origin of regulation, sociology made African American culture part of modernity's visible economy and thereby cited the body and social conditions as the locus of being for African Americans. With an epistemological gesture of this sort, the nonheteronormative would not simply lurk within the cracks and crevices of consciousness, but would traverse up and down the neighborhood. We may think of the first half of *Invisible Man* as an allegory about the limits of black subjects deploying the strategies of citizenship—recognition and the performance of normativity—to drown out the cacophony of African American nonheteronormative difference.

Here are the unities that in the twentieth century formed specific mechanisms between knowledge and power that centered on African American sexual formations: the hysterization of black women's reproductivity. Take, for instance, the bodies of Matty Lou, Trueblood's daughter, and Mrs. Trueblood, "women who move with the weary, full-fronted motions of far-gone pregnancy."[55] The Trueblood women's bodies allegorize the ways in which black women's reproductive practices were taken to be signs of communal health or social disintegration. Matty Lou and Mrs. Trueblood's bodies refer just as much to the dilapidated conditions of their environments—slave quarters still being used years after emancipation—as they do to Mr. Trueblood's sexual aberrance.[56] Their pregnancies suggest not only the reproduction of children, but the reproduction of disorganized social relations. Sociological analyses of black women's reproductivity were constantly integrated into discussions about the social body. In sum, black women's reproductivity was analyzed not simply for medical reasons, but for social reasons as well.

A socialization of legal marriage and heteropatriarchal nuclearity also formed links between knowledge and power. As an example, Dollard's *Caste and Class* made marriage the linchpin between conjugal domesticity and citizen status. Dollard's text was part of a larger epistemic maneuver in which the sociologization of African American sexual and gender practices resulted in legalized heteropatriarchal domesticity becoming the symbol of ethical development and responsibility. In addition, another domain for sociology's effort to combine knowledge and power was by sociologizing nonconjugal and nonheteronormative pleasure. This move entailed designating nonheteronormative subjects and practices as sociological and therefore social problems.

The figures that emerge from this preoccupation are the African American homosexual, the black unwed mother, the African American family, and the heterosexual black man.

The history of African American sexuality thus must be written as a materialist history of discourses and as a discursive history of material practices. African American nonheteronormative formations function as a palimpsest in which the disparate genealogies of sociology, American citizenship, Western nation-state formation, aesthetic culture, and capital collide. The history of the deployment of African American nonheteronormativity can serve as an archaeology of sociology. Sociology made the production of racial knowledge about African Americans into a political economy of sexual knowledge in which blacks could be used to justify the extension and support of normative presumptions about American citizenship. If sociology was, in part, the supplicant of the American state, it helped to corroborate the expansion of state power by legitimating surveillance as a vital scientific and social endeavor. As we will see in the next chapter, during and after World War II, canonical sociology would proceed to crown the U.S. nation-state as the heir to Western rationality, sketching it against a discursively manufactured African American Other.

3

Nightmares of the Heteronormative: *Go Tell It on the Mountain* versus *An American Dilemma*

> Well, that winter in Switzerland, I was working on my first novel—I thought I would never be able to finish it—and I finally realized that one of the reasons that I couldn't fin-ish this novel was that I was ashamed of where I came from and where I had been. I was ashamed of the life in the Negro church, ashamed of my father, ashamed of the Blues, ashamed of Jazz, and, of course, ashamed of watermelon: all of these stereotypes that the country inflicts on Negroes, that we all eat watermelon or we all do nothing but sing the Blues. Well, I was afraid of all that; and I ran from it.
>
> When I say I was trying to *dig* back to the way I myself must have spoken when I was little, I realized that I had acquired so many affectations, had told myself so many lies, that I really had buried myself beneath a whole fantastic image of myself which wasn't mine, but white people's image of me.
>
> —James Baldwin

John Grimes, the protagonist of *Go Tell It on the Mountain,* is a poor black teenager struggling with homoerotic desires. Because of this strug-gle, he must negotiate the ways in which heterosexism, poverty, racism, and patriarchy converge in African American urban communities and are then rationalized within a liberal capitalist order that justifies racial segrega-tion in formal and informal ways. This struggle was set afoot long before John was born; it owes its origins to Western modernity. John's story allegorizes how canonical sociology helped to produce the discursive horizon that would antagonize black subjects because of their nonheteronormative difference. As part of the institutional reflexivity of modernity, sociology is entangled within the contentious relations between modern institutions and those who are subjected to them. Black diasporic cultures arise out of such antagonisms, and the cultural form that gave birth to John Grimes is part of diaspora's rebuttal.

To illustrate how those differences structure the compulsions and identifications under rationality and how they constitute a historic burden for black subjects, we may situate black queer writer James Baldwin's *Go Tell It on the Mountain* against Gunnar Myrdal's *An American Dilemma*. This contrast dramatizes the foundational relationships that link canonical sociology to African American culture. *An American Dilemma* and *Go Tell It on the Mountain*'s differing racial formations lead them to elaborate conflicting positions about the Enlightenment legacy and scientific objectivity. Indeed, Baldwin's novel responded self-consciously to sociological discourses articulated before and during the period of *An American Dilemma*'s influence. Using Baldwin's novel to explore the features of rationalization begs us to ask how canonical sociology idealized rationality through the intersections of race, gender, class, and sexuality. If the disciplinary strategies of state, capital, and canonical sociology compel an identification with the normative assumptions about citizenship and humanity, then rationality determines the governing logic that informs the ways that we understand and embody social order. As social order achieves normativity by suppressing intersections of race, class, gender, and sexuality, rationality must thus conceal the ways in which it is particularized by those differences. An *American Dilemma* attempted to do just that in a moment in which the United States depended on Western rationality to achieve liberal dominance.

Rationalization and Heteronormativity: To Discipline African American Nonheteronormative Sexualities

We may look to Max Weber to begin unpacking the components of rationality. In general, rationalization, as used by Weber, describes how "the specifically Western idea of reason is reified in a system of material and intellectual culture (economics, technology, 'way of life,' science, art), which is fully developed in industrial capitalism."[1] For that reification to take place, rationalization has to be a process of interpellation. As such, rationalization must strive to promote a logic of equivalence that each thing or person is formally identical with another and has the same relationship with the institutional and cultural products of liberal capitalism. That logic paves the way for the formation of a national citizenry supposedly united over different historical and material formations, formations that could possibly disrupt that unity.

Rationalization announced itself as a modern operation by regulating sexual expression through heteropatriarchal intimate relations. In "Religious Rejections of the World and Their Directions," Weber argues, "[O]riginally the relation of sex and religion was very intimate. Sexual intercourse was very frequently part of magic orgiasticism or was an unintended result of orgiastic excitement."[2] The division between sexuality and religion, Weber continues, only comes about with the emergence of a cultic priesthood that regulated sexuality through legally constituted marriage.[3] Modern regulatory apparatuses seized sexuality as the object of rationalization and control because—in the eyes of hegemonic rationality—sexuality is a fundamentally irrational force.[4] Erotic relations, according to Weber, are neither functional nor rational, and require legalized heterosexual marriage to regulate them. The rationality of marriage is defined in terms of "[procreating and rearing] . . . children and [furthering] one another in a state of grace."[5] This state of grace is expressed in the supposed complementary relationships of *the* heteropatriarchal household, an institution that claims to exhaust the identity of women, identifying their proper place within the private sphere, and theoretically shortchanges the identity of men, requiring the male patriarch to complete himself in the public sphere. This complementarity links heterosexual domesticity to those rationalizations of the liberal state and capital. Moreover, to associate sexuality with the irrational means that all other constructions of irrationality will inevitably evoke the sexual, be they racialized, gendered, or class-based constructions. To control that erotic impulse as part of a rationalizing regime, the body must be taken away from religious supervision and placed within the hands of Man. Thus, the theoretically privatized spaces of home and body must be controlled by Mankind if state and civil society are to be fully rationalized.

As a regulatory ideal, labor also finds common cause with the rationalizing functions of church and home. Indeed, labor, under liberal capitalism, functions as the antithesis and regulator of sexuality. As Weber says, "[Labor] is . . . the specific defense against all those temptations which Puritanism united under the name of the unclean life."[6] The potential expansiveness implied in the "unclean life" is offset by the sexually ascetic influence that heteronormative marriage enjoys, an influence "more far-reaching than monasticism," whose sexually ascetic labor differs from Puritanism only in degree but not in principle.[7] Modern rationality's juxtaposition of labor against sexuality accounts for the hegemonic formulation that developed the racialization of black subjects.

Weber's theory of rationalization is limited as an explanation of racial discourse and racial formation. As an interpellative process, Weber's notion of rationalization promotes a "fantasy of formal equivalence and identity."[8] As he writes, "[the development of economic rationalism] is . . . determined by the ability and disposition of men to adopt certain types of practical rational conduct."[9] In Weber's narrative, religion is one sphere that can articulate those differences that could prevent the adoption of rational conduct. As Weber imagines them, the religious differences that hinder rationalization are voluntary and extrinsic. Like converting from one faith to another, these differences can be discarded for ones more suitable for the purposes of rationalization. They are not fixed biological or cultural differences whose fixity positions them outside rationalizing processes. Weber's "main characters" are unhampered by the illegitimate particularities of race, class, gender, and sexuality, particularities from which others cannot resign. The Puritans of whom Weber writes are not at the mercy of discourses that render them illegitimate rational subjects from the start. Their material and corporeal difference does not disqualify them from becoming rational subjects. Because of Weber's failure to address exclusion, we must articulate a theory of rationality that accounts for processes of marginalization, disfranchisement, and enslavement. Black subjects, on the other hand, have historically been located outside the idealized and normative properties of rationality. Indeed, black nonheteronormative formations present histories in which black sexual and gender practices and identities refute the universalizing claims of Western rationalization.

For instance, black slaves in North America engaged in a range of sexual practices and elaborated a variety of family structures.[10] In Cuba, for instance, male Afro-Cuban slaves developed "exclusively male families" in which male "wives," who tended the lands allocated to Cuban slaves, turned their produce over to their "husbands," who then sold it in the local market. One former slave, Esteban Montejo, observed in his book, *The Autobiography of a Runaway Slave,* that though such families may have been looked down upon by older male slaves, there was no pejorative for homosexual activity in the slave community. As Montejo stated, it was only after the abolition of slavery in Cuba that the "term ['effeminate'] came into use."[11] Challenging heteropatriarchal bias in family models, a prejudice that seemed to accompany formal emancipation, Montejo wrote, "To tell the truth, it [homosexuality] never bothered me. I am of the opinion that a man can stick his arse where he wants."[12] Indeed, Montejo suggests that black homosexual and black heterosexual practices, at least during slavery, enjoyed a proximity that did not necessitate one working toward the eradication of the other.

Likewise, in the United States slave emancipation enacted a demand for sexual regulation and the abolition of nonheteronormative practices. In fact, the issue of African American nonheteronormativity was foremost on the agenda of the American Freedman's Inquiry Commission, created in 1863 as part of the Freedman's Bureau's efforts to determine the state's relationship to newly emancipated slaves. Targeting the nonmonogamous and fluid intimate arrangements elaborated by slaves as evidence of their ineligibility for citizenship, the commission's reports to the secretary of war express an anxiety about the nonheteronormative practices of African Americans, coding those practices as proof of the "uncivilized, degraded, undisciplined, and . . . wholly unchristian ways" of the slaves.[13] As the bureau attempted to rationalize African American sexuality by imposing heterosexual marriage upon the freedman through the rule of law and as a condition for citizenship, the racialization of blacks as pathologically nonheteronormative tightened the link between citizenship and a racialized heteronormativity. Those newly freed African Americans who rejected marriage and monogamy were imprisoned and/or denied pension payments.

Future material contradictions could be displaced onto African American intimate relations as the state regulated heterosexual marriage, making the husband legally responsible for the function and care of the household.[14] By doing so, the state could shift the care of freed slaves from the state and former slavemasters. Within a national context that has historically constructed the heteropatriarchal household as a site that can absorb and withstand material catastrophes, African American poverty was often explained by reverting back to the question of African American intimate relations and denying the irresolvability and historicity of state and capital's own exploitative practices.

In a state in which material strata is differentiated along racial lines, that difference contradicts the rational ideals of liberal capitalism. As racial differences in how people make a living affected domestic life, producing increasingly diverse forms of family, family became an index of those differences.[15] Subsequently, the family became the site of material and ideological contradictions. In such a context, white heteropatriarchal middle-class families became the standard against which other families were judged.[16] In fact, between 1880 and 1925 white labor, using the rhetoric of the "American Standard of Living," demanded the protections of state and capital for the explicit purposes of perfecting and representing the heteropatriarchal family.[17] That demand for a racialized heteronormativity released polymorphous exclusions targeting women, people of color, and gays and lesbians at the same time that it became a regulatory regime, working to inspire conformity among women, people of color, and homosexuals.

In this context, African American familial forms and gender relations were regarded as perversions of the American family ideal. To resituate the authority of those ideals, questions concerning material exclusion—as they pertain to African Americans—were displaced onto African American sexual and familial practices, conceptualizing African American racial difference as a violation of the heteronormative demands that underlie liberal values. Presuming African American violation of those demands became the justification for subordinating African Americans.

As figures of nonheteronormative perversions, straight African Americans were reproductive rather than *productive*, heterosexual but never *heteronormative*. In other words, African American racialization expresses modern rationality's opposition between labor and sexuality. This construction of African American sexuality as wild, unstable, and undomesticated locates African American sexuality within the irrational, and therefore outside the bounds of the citizenship machinery. Though African American homosexuality, unlike its heterosexual counterpart, symbolized a rejection of heterosexuality, neither could claim heteronormativity. The racialized eroticization of black heterosexuals and homosexuals outside the rationalized (i.e., heteronormative) household symbolically aligned black straight and gay persons. A taxonomy of black nonheteronormativity, especially as it was imagined in the postwar era, is instructive: common law marriages, out-of-wedlock births, lodgers, single-headed families, nonmonogamous sexual relationships, unmarried persons, and homosexual persons and relationships. Without equating the items in that taxonomy and thereby eliding their various meanings, all are related because they fail to conform to a heteropatriarchal household legalized through marriage.

The heteronormative gained even more primacy with the advent of industrialization in the twentieth century. As Angela Davis argues, "In the context of the consolidation of industrial capitalism, the sphere of personal love and domestic life in mainstream American culture came to be increasingly idealized as the arena in which happiness was sought."[18] This idealization made African American nonheteronormative sexual relations all the more scandalous, all the more ripe for sociological investigation. Such was the scene within which *An American Dilemma* made its entrance.

An American Dilemma and the American Creed: Evoking the Nonheteronormative

The imperatives of a war economy positioned against the rise of fascism in Germany were shaped by and resulted in the international hegemony of liberal ideology.[19] As part of this hegemonic operation, American capital solicited African Americans as workers in wartime industry, inspiring black southerners to migrate north. As capital turned its eye toward African Americans, concentrating blacks in the industrialized North, this liberal ethos became the context for addressing African American inequality and racial domination: the Democratic party courted the African American vote, emphasizing the gains that blacks had won under the New Deal. Eleanor Roosevelt waged a personal campaign against lynching and racial discrimination. As chapter 1 illustrated through the rise of the Chicago School of Sociology, a new liberal social science was emerging. This liberal social science addressed culture rather than biology as the site of human difference,[20] using this new orientation to challenge "scientific racism and rejecting notions of innate black inferiority."[21] Gunnar Myrdal's classic text *An American Dilemma* was part of this challenge. But by rejecting biology as the domain of difference in favor of culture, Myrdal—rather than neutralizing racism—merely articulated racial knowledge through enunciations of African American cultural difference:

> Negroes have been segregated, and they have developed, or there have been provided for them, separate institutions in many spheres of life, as, for instance, in religion and education. Segregation and discrimination have also in other ways hampered assimilation. Particularly they have steered acculturation so that Negroes have acquired the norms of lower class people in America. . . .
>
> Also not to be taken in a doctrinal sense is the observation that peculiarities in the Negro community may be characterized as social pathology. As a reaction to adverse and degrading living conditions, the Negroes' culture is taking on some characteristics which are not given a high evaluation in the larger American culture.[22]

This articulation inscribed the racial difference of African American culture as one that rotated around the centrality of the nonheteronormative.

From the correspondence between officers in the Carnegie Corporation, it is clear that from its inception, *An American Dilemma* was inspired by heteronormative anxieties that constructed African Americans as figures of nonheteronormativity who could potentially throw the American social order into chaos. Understanding those anxieties and the material conditions that occasioned them requires us to place the book within the context of an ideology of pluralism formalized by American law and structured by capital's effect. That difference was foremost on the minds of white elites. Carnegie Corporation board trustee Newton Baker, who began to formulate plans for *An American Dilemma* in October 1935, expressed concerns about the possible danger of racial strife in public housing projects in Cleveland, Ohio. That strife was the outcome of unemployment, ghettoization, and the economic exploitation of northern African Americans who had migrated from the South—away from a collapsing agrarian economy—in hopes of better jobs and higher wages. These migrants eventually faced the reality of black unemployment and poverty. The ghettoes into which they settled were increasingly gaining a national reputation as breeding grounds for social instability in the form of crime and female-headed households. The crime and poverty that developed in inner-city neighborhoods was thus narrated as an instability rooted in nonheteronormative intimate relations among blacks, relations whose alleged potential to generate social instability had national implications.

Though industrialization and ghettoization encouraged nonheteronormative intimate arrangements among African Americans, for Baker, African American nonheteronormativity preceded those processes. In a letter he wrote to Frederick Keppel, president of the Carnegie Corporation, Baker located his charitable nature toward blacks within sexualized constructions of black savagery, praising "white people in this country who received the slaves from slave ships and undertook to make *useful laborers* of them." He continues by asking Keppel to consider "[h]ow many white civilizations could have dared to receive so many *wild savages,* who were practically *uncaged animals,* and spread them around over their farms in contact with their own families passes human comprehension."[23] Situating efforts to civilize African Americans within an economy constituted by the productive needs of chattel slavery, Baker, in fact, identifies the capitalist relations of production as the mode through which African Americans are civilized, as the key that can release blacks from their "wild" and "savage" habits. For Baker, African Americans had to be introduced into a process of rationalization that made their conversion from savages to rational subjects inseparable from the needs of capital. *An American Dilemma,* Baker implies, would extend a civilizing mission that began in slavery.

Myrdal also juxtaposed the rationality of American identity with the irrationality of the Negro "problem." In the introduction to *An American Dilemma,* he wrote,

> Compared with members of other nations of Western civilization, the ordinary American is a rationalistic being, and there are close relations between his moralism and his rationalism. Even romanticism, transcendentalism, and mysticism tend to be, in the American culture, rational, pragmatic and optimistic. (xlii)

In Myrdal's narrative of American identity and state formation, rationalization achieves its peak within the United States. Indeed, for Myrdal, rationality and a rationalized moralism are "the essentials of the American ethos," as well as the "glory of the nation." For Myrdal, the Negro problem is a force that utterly confounds the rational values upon which the American social order is founded (xlii).

As Myrdal attests, identifying with rationalisms is part of the initiation into American citizenship, uniting citizens across the particularities of race, ethnicity, class, and gender (3). As that force that binds the "disparate" elements of the American nation, the "American Creed" attempts to regulate the heterogeneity that makes up the national body and the particularisms that threaten national unity. In this regulatory capacity, the American Creed is the mantle of rationality. For Myrdal, the creed—understood here as the ideological basis for the rationalization of American culture—is also the banner of Enlightenment ideals and values:

> The American Creed is a humanistic liberalism developing out of the epoch of Enlightenment when America received its national consciousness and its political structure. . . . The enticing flavor of the eighteenth century, so dear to every intellectual and rationalist, has not been lost on the long journey up to the present time. . . .
>
> For practical purposes the main norms of the American Creed as usually pronounced are centered in the belief in equality and in the rights of liberty. In the Declaration of Independence—as in the earlier Virginia Bill of Rights—equality was given the supreme rank and the rights to liberty are posited as derived from equality. (8)

Claiming American citizenship means claiming the Enlightenment as well. Writing about the appropriateness of liberal democratic ideals in setting the parameters for the study of the Negro problem, Myrdal wrote, "For the study of a national problem which cuts so sharply through the whole body politic as does the Negro problem, no other set of valuations could serve as adequately as the norm for an incisive formulation of our value premises as can the American Creed" (23). Indeed, that creed exposes the Negro problem as a contradiction between liberal democratic ideals and exclusionary practices. For Myrdal, the Negro problem is an "anachronism," "a century-long lag of public morals." The solution to it can be found in the liberal ideals already solemnized in the American constitution and by American national culture, which together constitute the American Creed (24). Myrdal implies that the American Creed rejects the racial exclusions suffered by African Americans. As Myrdal says, the issue of exclusions was "settled a long time ago." With this, Myrdal implies that liberal democratic capitalism and its attending ideology represented the perfect system or the epitome of human progress.

But formulating liberalism as the culmination of human progress ignores the ways that liberalism not only condoned exclusions within the borders of the democratic capitalist state, but required those exclusions. Myrdal, therefore, cannot grasp how the American Creed, as a liberal expression grounded in universalist principles, was sustained by engaging and producing exclusions based on particularities of race, gender, class, and sexuality. Those exclusions, for African Americans, were explained as consequences of their own nonheteronormativity. Thus, African Americans enter Myrdal's framework as the antithesis of heteronormative American identity and thus as the antithesis of Enlightenment rationality. In a section entitled "The Negro Community as a Pathological Form of an American Community," Myrdal argues,

> In practically all its divergences, American Negro culture is not something independent of general American culture. It is a distorted development, or a pathological condition, of the general American culture. (928)

As evidence of the African American's cultural pathology, Myrdal cites many vices as proof of the irrationality of African American culture. Two of those themes, in particular, highlight the significance of nonheteronormativity in the inscription of African Americans as culturally pathological. Those themes are "the instability of the Negro family" and "the emotionalism of the Negro church."

Although Myrdal concedes that the emotionalism of the black church is greatly exaggerated and was, in part, derived from the Great Revival of 1800 that deployed emotional forms of religion to convert whites and blacks alike, nonetheless he argues that emotionalism differentiated black congregations from white congregations, who eventually discarded emotionalism for a more "rational" and subdued worship style. Historically, the emotionalism of black church denominations like the Holiness, Pentecostal, and Apostolic churches originated from black Christians' departure from "mainline black denominational churches."[24]

As several scholars have noted, those styles—particularly for Pentecostals—are deeply connected to Haitian voudou and traditional African religions, which are characterized by spirit possession, a phenomenon that a secular and rationalizing ethos often relegates to the realm of magic. In addition to exploring the influence of African religious traditions on African American worship styles, recent scholarship has also suggested that African Americans have historically approached the Bible in ways that diverge from traditional (i.e., white) Protestant readings and interpretations. As the theologian Theophus Smith claims, African Americans have read the Bible as a kind of "magical formulary for African Americans, a book of ritual prescriptions for reenvisioning and, therein, transforming history and culture."[25]

For Smith, such revisions and transformations are inseparable from the emotional and ecstatic responses that are a part of many African American religious practices.

Though it is difficult at times to determine why emotionalism is a problem for Myrdal (other than because it sets the black churchgoers apart from churchgoing whites), the disturbance seems to reside in the fact that the persistence of emotionalism among blacks suggests that blacks are not progressing toward some developmental ideal symbolized by rationalized—and therefore, nondemonstrative—worship forms. According to Myrdal, this developmental retardation evoked for many whites the specter of unregulated nonheteronormativity. For instance, Myrdal states that whites often rationalized African American subordination by "[seizing] upon the fact of religious emotionalism and [ascribing] it to 'animal nature' and even to 'excessive sexuality.'"[26] African American religion—when narrated by white racists—harkened to a sexuality impervious to regulation and, in fact, summons the developmental narrative of premodern religions' magical orgiasticism. Associating African American religious emotionalism with bestial sexuality located African Americans within premodern time, placing them within the time of unregulated sexuality, before the emergence of modern rationalities. The conflation of sexuality and religion that is obtained in the category of the "traditional" is thus ascribed to the bodies of African Americans, making sexuality an integral feature in the racialization of African Americans and responsible for the exclusions that shaped African American existence during legalized segregation.

Lurking behind Myrdal's own anxieties about emotionalism within African American religious practices is an anxiety about how African American religion is insufficiently rationalized and how that irrationality cannot possibly be a source of regulatory agency. The emotionalism of African American religion, whether or not it harkened to an unregulated sexuality, contradicted the "traits held in esteem by the dominant white Americans," and located blacks outside the properties of the rational citizen-subject. Anxieties about the supposed undomesticated quality of African American sexuality could be seen in Myrdal's anxieties about the disorganized African American family. For Myrdal the so-called "disorganization" of African American families is defined in terms of whether the family is constituted through legal marriage and whether the family conforms to the parameters of the nuclear family model idealized in whiteness. In fact, in 1930, 13 percent of black families in the United States were composed of unattached individuals who had left common-law marriages. During that same period, 30 percent of black families were made up of single-headed households, compared to 20 percent among whites. In 1930 African Americans were eight times more likely to have had children out of wedlock than whites. Myrdal also identifies lodgers as a factor that contributes to African American family disorganization. Almost 30 percent of African Americans in the North reported that they were lodging people not part of the immediate nuclear family in their homes. This figure Myrdal compares to 10 percent among northern whites. In the South, 20 percent of black families in urban areas reported having lodgers, compared to 11 percent for whites.[27] Common law marriage, out-of-wedlock births, lodgers, single-headed families, and unattached individuals are all indicators of African American disorganization defined in terms of its distance from heterosexual and nuclear intimate arrangements that are rationalized through American law and cultural norms that valorize heterosexual monogamy and patriarchal domesticity.

An American Dilemma was finished in 1942 and published in 1944. During this period and immediately following it, capital and white labor used sexualized racial divisions for the productive process, using fears of bodily taboos and transgressions to preserve a segregated workforce. In the 1940s African Americans were racialized as wholly sexual beings whose sexuality deviated from the model of rational heterosexual expressions and domestic forms. The subordination of African Americans during and after World War II was enabled by the rationalization of a "series of stereotypes and beliefs that made their conditions appear logical and natural."[28] Discussing the authority of those racial discourses that were rationalized during World War II and the resulting African American political projects positioned against them, Eileen Boris argues that African American struggles against economic and political disfranchisement were always waged against "a discourse that displaced demands for economic equity into openings for sexual intimacy."[29] Indeed, when the state attempted to address African American occupational segregation by forming the Committee on Fair Employment Practices (FEPC) in June 1941, unionists, politicians, and white workers alike objected to the FEPC on the grounds that it would bring blacks and whites, particularly black men and white women, into close proximity with one another.[30] Rather than an integrated shop floor being the site of productive labor, for white racists it was the site of potential sexual chaos. For those whites, an integrated labor force violated their understanding of a rationally functioning economy. Such an economy could not accommodate "social equality," especially since that equality summoned images of blacks driven by uncontrollable sexual desires. The idea of a depraved African American sexuality promoted productive relations based on "racialized gender."

Those boundaries were placed at the center of contention as increased productivity inaugurated by the war economy inspired African Americans to fill jobs in northern industries. Southern migrants stepped into northern and midwestern cities hoping for job security, only to find those hopes dashed by the rude fact that only a few blacks had gained access to industrial jobs and training programs. In fact, in March 1942, most blacks were placed in low-wage and low-skilled positions and only made up 2.5 to 3 percent of all wartime workers.[31]

Moreover, capital during World War II required an exploitable labor force whose nonheteronormative racial difference could be manipulated for the goal of accumulation.[32] Black demands for economic justice were characterized by whites as petitions for black men's sexual access to white women. The U.S. Cartridge Company assigned blacks and whites the task of making different types of ammunition so that the company could bypass the FEPC mandate of "'equal pay for equal work' by claiming different work," and keep white women, in particular, from having to work next to black men.[33] A rationally organized labor force was one in which labor was produced through differences of race and gender, differences always conceived within a racialized heteronormative imaginary.

Though *An American Dilemma* decried African American exclusion as a violation of the American Creed, the text rationalized it nonetheless by constructing African American culture as the antithesis of that creed. The assumption that the American Creed presumes an agent capable of rational action and judgment led Myrdal to recommend voting rights only to those black southerners who hailed from the "higher strata of the Negro population," and to "push the movement down to the lowest groups gradually."[34] In this schema, whites were presumed capable of determining which African Americans were fit for rational assimilation.

For *An American Dilemma,* the American Creed was the principle by which knowledge of rationality and irrationality was determined. Though the notion of the American Creed claims to be a program for universal application, it—in fact—articulated African American cultural difference as a real and observable impediment to that application, an impediment whose racial and sexual burden of irrationality could only be attenuated through middle-class formation. As the terms by which voting rights might be extended and as a measure of the fitness of designated racial and cultural groups for liberal capitalism, the creed determined the differential application of rights. The rationality of such discrimination could be taken for granted since culture—and not biology—was now regarded as the location of human difference. Hence, whites were regarded as culturally appropriate for rational adjudication, whereas African Americans' potential for rational agency was indeterminate at best. Indeed, the indeterminacy of African American rationality led Myrdal to advocate a gradualist approach to African American enfranchisement.

Within the demand for the gradual extension of liberal democratic principles to the lives of African Americans is a plea for African Americans to internalize those principles and make them the basis for conforming to American culture. Again, this demand was informed by Myrdal's belief in African American cultural pathology. He wrote that the poorest African Americans were incapable of conforming to the American Creed and were "beyond salvage by any social program." The text is most apparent in its regulatory function when it argues that in the South there were "a greater number of Negroes so destitute . . . that it would be better that they did not procreate."[35]

In its construction of African Americans as culturally pathological and its reliance on heteronormativity to delineate those pathologies, *An American Dilemma* colluded with the exclusionary practices of state, capital, and labor. Those practices relied on a racially defined heteronormativity to prohibit African Americans from claiming the rights and privileges of state and civil society. Such exclusionary practices inspired an array of critical interventions from blacks within and outside the United States. One such critic was the writer James Arthur Baldwin.

Baldwin, Myrdal, and the Two-Faced Visage of Political Modernity

In response to the changes in African American status because of migration, urbanization, and industrialization,[36] Robert Park, in 1928, located migration within rationalizing processes that dispose of the traditional, arguing that "[migration] involves, at the very least, change of residence and the breaking of home ties."[37] For Park, migration, driven by the expansion of commerce and communication, culminates in the national unification of persons from diverse ethnic, cultural, and historical backgrounds. Understood as a rationalizing process, migration leads to enlightenment and emancipation.[38] To Park, rational organization is obstructed by those groups (like blacks and Japanese) whose corporeal difference prevented assimilation and contradicted the profile of the rational individual through which the abstract citizen-subject is enunciated.[39] Arising out of a history of exclusion and denial, Baldwin's writings help to illustrate black people's contradictory relationship to rationalizing forces.

Reflecting on the "dilemma" of assimilation—that is, the psychic costs of conformity incurred by African Americans—James Baldwin said,

> [T]hat is one of the great dilemmas, one of the great psychological hazards, of being an American negro. In fact, it is much more than that. I've seen a great many people go under because of this dilemma. Every Negro in America is in one way or another menaced by it. One is born in a white country, a white Protestant Puritan country, where one was once a slave,

where all the standards and all the images. . . . when you open your eyes
on the world, everything you see: none of it applies to you.[40]

Next to Baldwin's depiction of assimilation as materially and psychologically disastrous, Myrdal's demand that African Americans conform to the ideals valued by white Americans seems, at best, shortsighted. Within Baldwin's statements is an implicit critique of the processes of rationalization, whose intended aim is to assimilate African Americans into American society. Rationalization is shorn of its promise of resolution and its benevolent tone and instead is constructed as a futile and deadly undertaking.

Baldwin was not the only one to confront the Enlightenment vision and its exclusions. This confrontation was waged within and outside the United States by blacks who were stung by the exclusionary practices of Western nation-states. Indeed an international Pan-Africanist movement emerged in Britain and the United States, in large part because of Italy's invasion of Ethiopia in 1935. The intellectuals and organizations that constituted that movement launched some of the most resounding critiques of imperialist and colonialist practices and their effects on blacks all over the globe. In fact, in 1936 the Trinidadian intellectual C. L. R. James wrote his essay, "Abyssinia and the Imperialists," in which he argued that the colonization of Ethiopia by Italy was part of a global imperialist venture that identified "Africans and people of African descent" as ripe for capitalist exploitation. That exploitation challenged the veracity of the Enlightenment vision. As James understood, that exploitation was couched within the rationalizing discourse of state and capital and discussed in terms of "*developing the country and raising the standard of civilisation.*"[41] James was also aware that the economic exploitation of colonized blacks required legitimation and rationalization. The imperialist had to convince the "exploited races" that they were inferior to the colonizer and thereby reinforce "the power of arms by democratizing the mentality of those whom he uses for his purposes both at home and abroad."[42]

If the notion of abstract labor, upon which the capitalist system is founded, is a way of defining and imagining the resources of the worker's body, then the inferiorization of blacks was a means of inflecting and shaping the disciplinary and rationalizing modes of capitalist expansion. Within the context of colonialism and legalized segregation, the corporealization of black bodies as physicalities divested of self-generating rationality imagined physical labor as the only real resource that the racialized black subject could offer. As such, black labor had to be constantly regulated, disciplined, and rationalized. As James implies, this inferiorization of blacks was part of capital's structure, rather than the result of aberrant incidents in capital's history. As the period that witnessed the emergence of liberal politics within the United States and abroad, the ascendancy of culturalist social science, the expansion of economic imperialism, and the growth of critiques against the colonization and subjugation of blacks throughout the world, the post–World War II era was a period in which the contradictions of state and capital erupted into challenges to the Enlightenment vision, rupturing its grip on such concepts as "citizenship," "the West," "justice," "assimilation," and "rationality."

Rather than being an "objective" observer removed from the American racial scene, Myrdal was formed within and laid claim to a political modernity that invented race as one of its central concepts. Myrdal subscribed to a script that had its own particular enactment within the United States, but was composed within the Enlightenment. To assume that Myrdal was an objective observer because of his Swedish nationality denies race's genealogy within the modern Western nation-state and turns race simply into an "American Dilemma."

Baldwin, on the other hand, addressed America as an example of the exclusions rationalized into Western political and economic culture. And just as An American Dilemma belongs to an imagined community bounded by the privileges promised in Enlightenment ideals and materialized in the racialized and gendered practices of state and capital, Baldwin's work emerges out of a diasporic community constituted through the displacements, exclusions, and contradictions engendered by modern political, academic, and economic institutions.

Discussing the critiques that flower within the imagined terrain of the Black Diaspora, critiques born of the material and discursive exclusions that render blacks as "people in, but not necessarily of, the modern western world," Paul Gilroy argues that the diaspora's "intellectuals, and activists, writers, speakers, poets, and artists repeatedly articulate a desire to escape the restrictive bonds of ethnicity, national identification, and sometimes even 'race' itself."[43] Gilroy's conception of African American artistic and critical work as engaging with the Enlightenment legacy and elaborating epistemological and aesthetic modes that counter that legacy allows us to contextualize Baldwin's first novel.

The exclusions of the Enlightenment informed Go Tell It on the Mountain. In an interview about the book, Baldwin argued that "we cannot think of ourselves as belonging to a golden age or even a Renaissance." Baldwin continued by insisting on the importance of "destroying" the foundational myths of the West and "[of discovering] who [the founding fathers] really were, why they came here and what they did."[44] This task was unavoidable, according to Baldwin, because of the relationship that all national subjects

have to political modernity. As he said, "[W]e are the issue of those beginnings, and until we excavate our history, we will never know who we
are."[45] In his call for a new narrative that would destroy the myth of the
"Far West" and the American founding fathers, Baldwin suggests a new
historiography, one not governed by the myths of the Enlightenment—those
fictions of progress, universal access, and universal identity that disavow
particularities even as they articulate them. Baldwin's own position as a subject who is racialized as black triggered an estrangement from the Enlightenment that became the site within which new epistemologies, new historiog-
raphies, and new aesthetics were yearned for and elaborated. The critiques
that inhere within these new critical modes address both the international
context of the Enlightenment and the national formations that it inspired,
making the diaspora the sphere within which simultaneous estrangements
are developed.

Baldwin's work also engages sociology as a rational reflexive mode that
attempted to record African American culture. Because of sociology's historic
position as a definer of African American existence and due to *An American
Dilemma*'s role in defining sociology after World War II, African American
literature had to engage sociology. In "Everybody's Protest Novel," a 1949
essay about how the naturalist fiction of the protest novel appropriates canonical sociology's image of African American culture, Baldwin wrote,

> [L]iterature and sociology are not one and the same; it is impossible to
> discuss them as if they were. Our passion for categorization, life neatly
> fitted into pegs, has led to an unforeseen, paradoxical distress; confusion, a
> breakdown of meaning. Those categories which were meant to define and
> control the world for us have boomeranged us into chaos; in which limbo
> we whirl, clutching the straws of our definitions. The "protest" novel,
> so far from being disturbing, is an accepted and comforting aspect of the
> American scene, ramifying that framework we believe to be so necessary.[46]

The essay's critique of the protest novel was a simultaneous interrogation of
canonical sociology, one that attempted to name the ways in which sociology
invests in rational reflection ostensibly to record, but actually to construct,
African American culture as the site of irrationality, and how that articulation is appropriated in literary domains. Continuing this critique in a 1951
article, "Many Thousands Gone," Baldwin wrote,

> The Negro in America, gloomily referred to as that shadow which lies
> athwart our national life, is far more than that. He is a series of shadows,
> self-created, intertwining, which now we helplessly battle. One may say
> that the Negro in America does not really exist except in the darkness of

our minds. This is why his history and progress, his relationship to all other Americans, has been kept in the social arena. He is a social and not a personal or a human problem; to think of him is to think of statistics, slums, rapes, injustices, remote violence; it is to be confronted with an endless cataloguing of losses, gains, skirmishes; it is to feel virtuous, outraged, helpless, as though his continuing status among us were somehow analogous to disease—cancer, perhaps, or tuberculosis—which must be checked, even though it cannot be cured. . . . If he breaks our sociological and sentimental image of him we are panic-stricken and we feel ourselves betrayed.[47]

Like "Everybody's Protest Novel," "Many Thousands Gone" targets sociology as that culprit that produces knowledge about African American culture and imbues it with pathologies and irrationalities. The intersection of a culturalist social science that was confirmed in the post–World War II era and an African American literary naturalism that was enthroned during the 1930s is the birthplace of that knowledge, as well as the essay's implicit historical reference.

The essays illustrate how sociological constructions of African Americans were grounded in an anxiety about African American sexuality. Addressing this anxiety to explain the rhetorical moves of the sociologically informed protest novel and Harriet Beecher Stowe's *Uncle Tom's Cabin,* Baldwin wrote that "here, black equates with evil and white with grace."[48] Baldwin describes Stowe's novel, illustrating how at its center is an anxiety about the nonheteronormative meanings of blackness. For this reason, he writes, Stowe must "cover [the black characters'] intimidating nakedness, robe them in white, the garments of salvation; only thus could she herself be delivered from ever-present sin, only thus could she bury, as St. Paul demanded, 'the carnal man, the man of the flesh.'" According to Baldwin, Stowe uses salvation to wash the black characters of their nonheteronormative stain.

Faced with a symbolic economy that idealizes the normativity of white heterosexuality and which in turn imposes purity/goodness and uncleanliness/badness onto white and black bodies, respectively, the only way in which blacks can attain heteronormative status is by "[assimilating] into American culture, [acquiring] the traits held in esteem by the dominant white Americans," to use Myrdal's words.[49] But assimilation, as it was configured in the symbolic economy of legalized segregation, was founded on unceasing regulation of African American sexuality. Driven by the eroticized racialization of the African American as outside heteronormative boundaries, assimilation—as the essay attests—is charged with erotic import.

Baldwin's essays consistently opposed African American cultural practices to the epistemologies that sociology presumed would help it understand and know African American identity and experiences, epistemologies that actually ended up making the meaning of African American culture inseparable from its eroticization. The novelist's task, for Baldwin, was not to extinguish the sexual and its nonheteronormative expressions from African American representation, but to problematize its irrationalization and ensuing regulation. In "Preservation of Innocence," an article that problematized representations of homosexuality in American literature and a text that Baldwin intended as the companion piece to "Everybody's Protest Novel," Baldwin argues, "A novel insistently demands the presence and passion of human beings, who cannot ever be labeled."[50] Just as "Everybody's Protest Novel" critiqued how sociological categories confound African American representation, "Preservation of Innocence" makes a similar critique of how "labels," as rational and rationalized categories, only partially represent homoerotic experience. If the rational is defined by the legitimation of marriage and heteronormativity, as Weber suggests, then the nonheteronormative constantly slips out of the comprehension of the rationalizing processes of Western science, excluding the nonheteronormative subject from the imaginative possibilities of rational modes of reflection. Indeed, for Baldwin's novel the nonheteronormative figures of the homosexual and the Negro were impossible subjects for the sociological imagination. But where sociology ended, *Go Tell It on the Mountain* tried to begin.

Go Tell It on the Mountain and the Critique of Heteronormativity

In *The Protestant Ethic and the Spirit of Capitalism,* Weber outlines the personal endowments of that subject who can "[penetrate] economic life with the rational spirit," writing that "they were men who had grown up in the hard school of life, calculating and daring at the same time, above all temperate and reliable, shrewd and completely devoted to their business, with strictly bourgeois opinions and principles."[51] As Weber attests, the rational subject is daring, calculating, temperate, shrewd, and devoted. It is a subject who embodies bourgeois opinions and principles and one who enjoys access to the rights and privileges of state and civil society. This is the subject who can subscribe to and fulfill rationalization.

It is not, however, the subject who is racialized as pathological because of some real or imagined nonheteronormativity. Those subjects whose social differences mark them as outside the rational and place them within the margins of political and economic spheres represent the underside of rationalization, that location left untheorized by Weber but narrativized by Baldwin. Because of its attention to the material and corporeal differences that are used to enact the racial exclusions that help constitute rationalizing processes, *Go Tell It on the Mountain* can productively be understood as the Other('s) *Protestant Ethic.*

Go Tell It on the Mountain was first published in 1952. That year, according to Bernard Bell, was the beginning of two parallel movements that spanned ten years: "a movement away from naturalism and . . . a movement toward the rediscovery and revitalization of myth, legend, and ritual as appropriate sign systems for expressing the double-consciousness, socialized ambivalence, and double vision of the modern black experience."[52] That took place in a climate that highlighted the injustices of racial exclusions. As such, this movement is the aesthetic trace of the migrations that took place in the 1930s and 1940s and was the artistic means of "[coming] to terms with the massive dislocation of black peoples following migration."[53] As has been illustrated, that dislocation promoted anxieties about the nonheteronormative status and inscription of African American sexuality. *Go Tell It on the Mountain* arose out of the sexual anxieties generated by African American migration and northern urbanization.

The novel is set in the "sexually historic" space of Harlem, New York.[54] Specifically, it is the Harlem of the 1920s and 1930s to which the novel refers, a region in which nonheteronormative intimate relations and identities could grow. This was the Harlem known for its racially mixed speakeasies and nightclubs frequented by straight and queer persons. Because of the structural changes resulting from migration and industrialization in the post–World War I era, Harlem became, along with Greenwich Village, one of the sexual satellites of New York City. In 1927, the New York Vice Commission reported "the existence of black/white homosexual institutions in Harlem."[55] White law enforcement officials worked to confine the prostitution, gambling, and drug and alcohol use to black neighborhoods, moving them away from the "respectable" neighborhoods of whites. Those efforts to confine vice to black neighborhoods provided white entrepreneurs with profit and capital and provided white consumers with access to commodities whose pleasures and values were rooted in Harlem's racial specificity. The racialization of Harlem as an unregulated nonheteronormative urban space allowed white New Yorkers to descend upon Harlem like "hunters . . . in the heart of darkness."[56] For those whites, the material conditions that located Harlem outside the proper boundaries of the heteropatriarchal household authorized Harlem's racialization as a "psychic space that had survived the psychic fetters of Puritanism" and in turn encouraged whites to access the delights of the nonheteronormative.[57]

In fact, the novel begins by taking nonheteronormativity head on. For years, the narrator informs us, the main character John Grimes had believed that he would be a preacher, "just like his father." The idea was spoken so often that it had become commonplace. Not until his fourteenth birthday was the idea of being a preacher spoiled for good. And then it was "too late." The reader learns that what makes the dream impossible is the sin that John had committed "with his hands" and the very homoerotic images that he had conjured while engaging in the "sinful" act.

> He had sinned. In spite of the saints, his mother and his father, the warn-
> ings he had heard from his earliest beginnings, he had sinned with his
> hands a sin that was hard to forgive. In the school lavatory, alone, thinking
> of the boys, older, bigger, braver, who made bets with each other as to
> whose urine could arch higher, he had watched in himself a transformation
> of which he would never dare to speak.[58]

Though certain forms of ecstatic worship by African Americans often excited the body in ways that resembled sexual climax, it is important to note the regulatory function of African American Christian denominations. In part 1 of the novel, "The Seventh Day," the narrator addresses the ways in which a rationalized religious ethic drives a wedge between the religious and the sexual. Operating under this ethic, the Grimes family divides Harlem into saints—represented by black churchgoers, particularly members of the Grimeses' church, the Temple of the Fire Baptized—and those who are sinners—represented by people who live their lives on the streets, namely prostitutes and their customers—those figures of nonheteronormativity whose lives appear to be unregulated by heteropatriarchal domesticity.

Indeed, the Temple of the Fire Baptized, as a historical institution, originated from the Holiness/Pentecostal movement, which emerged before the turn of the twentieth century, promoting the doctrine of sanctification. That doctrine emphasized "personal holiness," fostering an "ascetic ethic forbidding the use of alcohol, tobacco, and other addictive substances, gambling, secular dancing, and the wearing of immodest apparel."[59] As an ascetic ethic, Pentecostal sanctification targets the body and sexuality as objects of regulation. Such regulation renders the body and sexuality as the locus of corruptions that threaten religious sanctity. In the novel, the duality between sexuality and religiosity works to "[make] sex and sin synonymous" and compels the members of the Fire Baptized to look to the church as a haven from a sinful world.[60]

As the predominantly black space of Harlem takes on very sexualized meanings, the Grimes family struggles with the fact that their religiosity will not insulate them from those meanings after all. Describing the kitchen, the narrator states,

The room was narrow and dirty; nothing could alter its dimensions, no labor could ever make it clean. Dirt was in the walls and the floorboards, and triumphed beneath the sink where roaches spawned; was in the fine ridges of the pots and pans, scoured daily, burnt black on the bottom, hanging above the stove; was in the wall against which they hung, and revealed itself where the paint had cracked and leaned outward in stiff squares and fragments, the paper-thin underside webbed with black. Dirt was in every corner, angle, crevice of the monstrous stove, and lived behind it in delirious communion with the corrupted wall. Dirt was in the base-board that John scrubbed every Saturday, and roughened the cupboard shelves that held the cracked and gleaming dishes. Under this dark weight the walls leaned, under it the ceiling, with a great crack like lightning in its center, sagged. The windows gleamed like beaten gold or silver, but now John saw, in the yellow light how fine dust veiled their doubtful glory. Dirt crawled in the gray mop hung out of the windows to dry. John thought with shame and horror, yet in angry hardness of heart: *He who is filthy, let him be filthy still.*[61]

In *Domesticity and Dirt: Housewives and Domestic Servants in the United States, 1920–1945*, Phyllis Palmer writes that "sex, dirt, housework, and bad-ness in women are linked in Western unconsciousness," and that the home is reified as that space that both confirms sexual purity through the act of cleaning *and* threatens to "taint the character of the woman who [works in the home] because of the close association between dirt and sex in Western culture."[62] The close association between dirt and sex is the modern asso-ciation between sin and sex that is consummated through the rationaliza-tion of the heteropatriarchal household. Because that household has histori-cally been idealized and embodied in the white, middle-class, heterosexual home, the "dirt" symbolizes the ever-present and constantly regenerating racial, class, gender, and sexual differences that require heteronormative regulation. That rationalization justifies its operation in that household by regulating sexuality through heteropatriarchal arrangements, trying to steer the sexual away from the sinful and the dirty. As subjects interpellated by rationalization's dubious universality and its racialization of blacks as non-Western and therefore sexually unregulated, the Grimes family cleans up, but apparently to no avail.

The "filth" that overwhelmed the Grimes family and threatened to inhab-it their very pores was not particular to their household. In fact, it referred to the dirtiness outside their home, the filth that walked along the street and "did its business" in the alleyways. The dirt that the Grimeses believe they embody represents the hegemonic meanings that are imposed on Harlem as an urban space. In other words, the Grimeses and the other Harlemites function as metonyms for the so-called "cultural pathologies" of Harlem the community. Indeed, the passage refers to the process by which racialization has inscribed the bodies of African Americans with the hegemonic meanings of African American cultural and institutional practices.

The association between dirt and sex is played out in the aforementioned passage and no doubt implicates Elizabeth—John's mother—in the precarious balance between sexual pristineness and impurity. But the interesting difference in Palmer's explanation and the aforementioned scene is how John is seized by the sexualized dualism of dirtiness/cleanliness as well. The model of the "home" that the United States offers locates John outside of the heteropatriarchal ideologies presumed within that category. For the rationalized heteropatriarchal home was defined over and against the very nonheteronormative irrationalities believed to define African American sexuality, whether straight or gay.[63] By taking a queer African American teenager as its protagonist, the novel "interrogates processes of group and self-formation" from the experience of those who are excluded from the rationalized heteropatriarchal home.[64]

The heteronormative household was practically a "material impossibility" for people of color as the U.S. "family wage" in the early twentieth century defined the American home as white, heterosexual, and American, and thereby excluded people of color on the grounds that they were incapable of, or uninterested in, constituting heteronormative families and adopting their regulatory demands.[65] Despite the progressive nature of the demand, the family wage helped to reconstitute the heteropatriarchal family in the face of wage-earning single mothers who threatened this household. Welfare advocates during the period supported the family wage as part of "the American tradition that men support their families, the wives throughout life and the children at least until the fourteenth birthday."[66] In addition, the Federal Housing Act of 1934, while making housing available to millions of Americans, excluded communities of color through explicitly racist lending practices. After World War II, urban renewal programs resulted in suburban communities being the sites for the development of white identity and relegated African Americans to the inner city,[67] necessitating the development of nonheteronormative familial forms. The racial discourses that constructed those familial forms as "pathological" and "dirty"—as outside the logic of rationalization—displaced the material contradictions out of which those families arose onto the families themselves, making African American intimate relations the site of material struggle.

The rationalization of racial discourses that located people of color outside heteronormative bounds was inflected by practices of segregation and helped generate them, as well. For instance, because of the claims of racist southern politicians during the 1940s, claims that blacks had "a peculiar body odor; that it is unpleasant to remain in close proximity to them," managers circulated manuals that challenged those claims to their white employees. Because of the presumption that blacks had high rates of syphilis, a hospital in Oakland, California, refused to hire black women as dietitians because "Negroes couldn't pass Wasserman tests."[68] Indeed, the idea of a destructively nonheteronormative black sexuality was the ideological basis for segregated public facilities for blacks and whites, as the conflict over toilets and bathrooms as sites of racial struggle attests.

Go Tell It on the Mountain narrates how the construction of blacks as nonheteronormative impacted the psyche of African Americans. This impact could have only taken place because of a material context that relied on racial discourses of nonheteronormativity to constitute the exclusionary practices of state, capital, and labor. We may read the scene in the kitchen, indeed the entire novel, as a cautionary tale about the costs incurred by minoritized subjects, in general, and African Americans, in particular, for answering the call to rationalized heteronormative subjection. As this scene illustrates, rationalization seduces racialized ethnic minorities by promising to confirm them as fully rationalized heteronormative subjects and then reneges on that promise by constructing those subjects as irresolvably different.

In part 2 of the novel, "The Prayers of the Saints," the narrator follows John's regulation by household and church with similar narratives that address the sexual struggles and negotiations of his aunt Florence, his father Gabriel, and his mother Elizabeth. We learn of Florence's quest for self-discovery outside the boundaries of the heteropatriarchal household, which threatens to regulate her professionally and domesticate her sexually. Describing the regulatory regime that constituted Florence's childhood, the narrator says,

> There was only one future in that house, and it was Gabriel's—to which, since Gabriel was a manchild, all else must be sacrificed. Her mother did not, indeed, think of it as sacrifice, but as logic: Florence was a girl, and would by and by be married, and have children of her own, and all the duties of a woman; and this being so, her life in the cabin was the best possible preparation for her future life.[69]

Florence's mother prays that her daughter will not be raped by white men, as were Florence's friend and Gabriel's soon-to-be first wife, Deborah. For Florence's mother, the heteropatriarchal household can possibly provide her daughter protection. Indeed, while Florence is working as a maid, her white male boss makes sexual advances toward her, prompting Florence to finally

migrate northward. In this regard, Florence as a fictional character dramatizes the actual migration of African American women to urban areas in the
North, many of whom migrated to avoid inevitable economic and sexual
exploitation as domestics. Florence's decision to move north is significant in
that she chooses that as an option, rather than trying to find protection as a
wife. Florence is, in fact, rejecting the regulatory regimes of the heteropatriarchal household *and* the sexual subordination that racializes her as outside
the normative boundaries of the rationalized household and as part of the
sphere of unregulated natural desire.

The home and the church figure as sites of sexual regulation in Gabriel's
narrative as well. Gabriel is the unrepentant sinner, the wretch undone. He
spends his days as a young man drinking and womanizing. After having
sex with an unnamed woman, Gabriel has a conversion experience that results in him preaching and marrying Deborah. "And this was the beginning
of his life as a man." Gabriel is interpellated by the patriarchal ideology
of the household, longing for the barren Deborah to give him a "royal
line." Because Deborah cannot fulfill her reproductive or sexual obliga-
tions, Gabriel eventually has an affair with the sexually seductive Esther.
Throughout the chapter on Gabriel, we see him struggling with the dictates
and regulations that religion and household put on his sexual desires.

The regulatory regimes of church and household conspire against Elizabeth's sexual possibilities as well. As a young girl, Elizabeth's pious mater-
nal aunt snatched her from her father's house, which the aunt said was a
"stable" frequented by "low, common niggers" who "sometimes brought
their women." Despite the fact that it is in the seemingly unbourgeois and
unregulated space of her father's house that Elizabeth actually feels love,
her aunt tries to force her into a highly regulated, repressive, and depress-
ing religious and domestic orientation. Reflecting on the rationalizing and
regulatory regimen that her aunt tried to impose, Elizabeth realizes that love
"was a freedom . . . and had nothing to do with the prisons, churches, laws,
rewards, and punishments that so positively cluttered the landscape of her
aunt's mind" (156). But eventually Elizabeth falls back on the regulatory
demands of the church and the household, as she struggles with the sin that
she's committed in having sex with her erudite lover Richard and conceiving
John out of wedlock. In a case of mistaken identity, Richard is accused of
being a part of a gang of black boys that had just assaulted a storeowner.
"But I wasn't there! Look at me, goddammit—I wasn't there," Richard says.
The store owner replies, "You black bastards . . . you're all the same" (171).
After refusing to sign a confession, Richard is beaten by the police officers.
Despite being eventually acquitted of the crime, Richard loses hope that he

can find justice and recognition in the world and cuts his wrists with a razor. After Richard commits suicide, Elizabeth marries Gabriel, who promises to love her and her "nameless" son.

Because the chapter on John's rebirth follows Elizabeth's prayer, we may say that this rebirth is, in part, the result of Elizabeth's prayer and refers to Elizabeth's understanding that freely chosen love is an index of personal freedom. In this context, the novel begins to rearticulate the meaning of African American nonheteronormativity via a reinterpretation of Christian salvation. In a scene at the Temple of the Fire Baptized in which John is caught in the grip of the Holy Ghost, he is made to confront his self-loathing and the normative interpretations of blackness and homoerotic longing:

> Then there began to flood John's soul the waters of despair. Love is as strong as death, as deep as the grave. But love, which had, perhaps, like a benevolent monarch, swelled the population of his neighboring kingdom, Death, had not himself descended: they owed him no allegiance here. Here there was no speech or language, and there was no love; no one to say: You are beautiful, John; no one to forgive him, no matter what his sin; no one to heal him, and lift him up. (200)

Suggesting that death is the absence of redemption and self-affirmation, the novel constructs love as the presence of that redemption and self-affirmation. Indeed, he implies that love articulates a notion of blackness and homoerotic desire that end in John's own self-affirmation. As such, *Go Tell It on the Mountain* rearticulates the meaning of love, removing it from the romantic ideology of the heteropatriarchal household and the heterosexist church and placing it outside the framework of rational heteronormative regulation. In fact, John's newfound wholeness is consecrated by his Sunday School teacher, Elisha, who gives John a "holy kiss" and by the rising sun that "[falls] over Elisha like a golden robe, and struck John's forehead, where Elisha had kissed him, like a seal forever" (233). In opposition to the rationalization of sexuality, the novel registers the values accorded to nonheteronormative intimate relations as the index of freedom and sanctification.

Just as African American sexuality has been historically linked to the possibility for freedom in the economic and political realms,[70] the novel uses John's rebirth into nonheteronormative affirmation to reconceptualize Harlem as a racialized space. The text not only challenges those dichotomies as they are expressed in John's life, but frustrates the way in which the dualities between sacred and secular, religious and nonheteronormative inform how Harlem is regarded. After John's salvation, Harlem ceases to embody secularity and pathology. Baldwin writes,

Now the storm was over. And the avenue, like any landscape that had en-
dured a storm, lay changed under Heaven, exhausted and clean, and new.
Not again, forever, could it return to the avenue it once had been.[71]

Go Tell It on the Mountain expresses the interest of the 1950s' African
American novel in ritual, but the text also dramatizes the "conjurational" nature of African American religious practices. We may understand conjure as
a "metaphor that circumscribes black people's ritual, figural, and therapeutic
transformations of culture."[72] In addition to giving birth to new cultural articulations, conjure as "aesthetic, ecstatic, and ritual performances" denotes
identity transvaluations as well.[73] The novel deploys the "pharmacoepic
traditions" of African American aesthetic and ritual performances to affirm
African American nonheteronormative racial, sexual, and social formations.
    The racializing discourses that constructed the nonheteronormative as
pathological and ascribed that meaning onto black bodies and poor black
communities are undermined as Harlem is rearticulated in the moment of
salvation as a sacred space. Thus, John's own particular "salvation" extends
to the larger community itself, calling for a "politics of identification" that
asks what new subjectivities and social relations arise from nonheteronormative spaces. Unlike *An American Dilemma, Go Tell It on the Mountain* reimagines and reclaims the nonheteronormative because of the regulatory and exclusionary impulses inscribed within *the* heteronormative. For
Go Tell It on the Mountain, as opposed to *An American Dilemma,* the task
is not to accept the hegemonic meanings of the nonheteronormative and
therefore to pine for heteronormative ideals, but to claim the nonheteronormative as the location for new and emergent identifications and social
relations. The rearticulation of queer identity posits a new valuation of
black inner-city communities as sites of a regenerative nonheteronormativity, establishing a link between reconfigurations of African American queer
identity and African American culture. What Myrdal defines as pathological
is now rearticulated as the basis of restoration and healing.
    Situated next to *An American Dilemma,* this reading of *Go Tell It on the
Mountain* places the heteronormative outlines of the discourse of cultural
pathology in bold relief. Rather than resolving African American disfranchisement and lifting African Americans out of some alleged cultural degeneracy, the rational ideals encoded within the American Creed become the site
of an irresolvable tension and contradiction.
    Go Tell It on the Mountain, as an allegory of rationalization's exclusion-
ary practices and production of difference, assumes rationalization as a contradictory process that on the one hand, interpellates African Americans as
citizens through a discourse of universality, and on the other hand, excludes

them because of their material and symbolic nonheteronormativity. The characters in the novel struggle with the fact that the meanings imposed on African American bodies and culture delegitimate rational conduct even as they engage in it. Imagined in this way, *Go Tell It on the Mountain* critiques rationalization as a contradictory material and discursive process.

An American Dilemma produced a discourse of pathology that referenced the rationalizing practices of the United States during the post–World War II era, practices that would disfranchise African Americans. *Go Tell It on the Mountain,* as an African American cultural form, indexed those practices and hailed diasporic movements that contested the exclusions and regulations of Western nation-states. At the same time, the novel also mimicked those exclusions. While the novel initially imagines Florence, for instance, as a questing female, it cannot sustain that narrative and repositions Florence within a quest for heteropatriarchal domesticity, yearning for her husband, Frank, to be the "husband she had traveled so far to find."[74] A narrative that originally cast Florence's migration as a desire to circumvent the restrictions of patriarchy was later narrated as a tale of patriarchal longing. A sustained retelling of black female subjectivity, one that refused heteropatriarchal confirmation, would have to take place in other venues. This retelling would connect sociological discourses to changes within the economy. Indeed, the discourse of pathology would adapt to a new phase of liberal capital. The discourse would be refined and applied to surplus populations composed of black women especially, but women of color generally. This phase would expose the limits of national liberation and solicit other modes of political engagement.

4

Something Else to Be: *Sula,*
The Moynihan Report, and the Negations
of Black Lesbian Feminism

> In a society where the good is defined in terms of profit rather
> than in terms of human need, there must always be some
> group of people who, through systemized oppression, can be
> made to feel surplus, to occupy the place of the dehumanized
> inferior. Within this society, that group is made up of Black
> and Third World people, working-class people, older people,
> and women.
>
> —Audre Lorde, *Sister Outsider*

> When we talk about "Dykes against Racism Everywhere"
> and "Black and White Men Together," . . . when we see the
> coalition of black community organizations in the Boston
> area that got together to protest the wholesale murder of
> black women in 1978 and '79, we are talking about real
> coalitions. We must recognize that we need each other. . . .
> There are no more single issues.
>
> —Audre Lorde, *Black Women Writers at Work*

When Audre Lorde expressed these words she was naming something,
some new mode of exploitation, some recent set of conditions that could
yield unexpected ways of intervening and could make space for something
else to be. In another instance, describing the fundamental materiality of
discourse, she observed, "[W]e have all been raised in a society where those

110

distortions were endemic within our living. . . . [We] do not develop tools for using human difference as a springboard for creative change within our lives. We speak not of human difference, but of human deviance."[1] Speaking at Amherst College in April 1980, Lorde was referring to the discursive and material formations that came to characterize the 1960s, the 1970s, and the 1980s—the pathologization of difference, the displacement of those pathologies onto surplus populations, and the political and cultural challenges to such conservative formations.

Attempting to apprehend Lorde's importance and the significance of other women of color feminists, Chela Sandoval writes in *Methodology of the Oppressed,* "The social movement that was 'U.S. third world feminism' has yet to be fully understood by social theorists. This social movement developed an original form of historical consciousness, the very structure of which lay outside the conditions of possibility that regulated the praxes of 1960s, 1970s, and 1980s U.S. social movements."[2] Sandoval's argument about the importance of U.S. third world or women of color feminism can be elaborated by exploring women of color feminism's interest in "difference" and "coalition" as they were theorized by black lesbian feminists. Women of color and black lesbian feminist theorizations of coalition and difference marked the constitution of a heterogeneous labor force diversified in terms of ethnicity, nation, race, sexuality, and gender. These feminist formations can be located within the wake of Daniel Patrick Moynihan's 1965 text, *The Negro Family: A Case for National Action* (popularly known as the Moynihan Report). We may also situate women of color feminism within the limitations of national liberation movements and at the cusp of global capital's commodification of third world and immigrant labor. Moynihan's text helped authorize a hegemonic discourse about black matriarchy and enabled a nationalist discourse that understood nonheteronormative racial difference as deviant. Moreover, the discourse of black matriarchy justified and promoted the regulatory practices of the state and the exploitative practices of global capital as the U.S. nation-state began to absorb women of color labor from the United States and the third world as part of capital's new regimes of exploitation. As black nationalist movements often intersected with sociological discourses and state aims by demanding the gendered and sexual regulation of African American nonheteronormative formations, black lesbian feminists gravitated toward culture as a means of formulating a political alternative to heteropatriarchal and nationalist constructions of nonheteronormative difference as deviance. For example, Toni Morrison's *Sula* offered black lesbian feminists an opportunity to formulate a politics that could negate the gender, racial, and sexual regulations of nationalist formations. In sum, black lesbian intellectual and political practices became the trace of heterogeneous social formations within capital's new global phase.

To Periodize Women of Color Feminism

We can place women of color feminism's emergence after the period that Immanuel Wallerstein dubs the "second apotheosis of liberalism," that is, from 1945 to 1970, when liberal ideology seemed to have flourished global-ly. The second apotheosis represented the moment in which Western nations were presumably turning away from their past oppressions and national liberation movements were coming to power throughout the third world.[3] During this period, the United States was achieving superpower status par-tially on the basis of an apparent commitment to civil rights. The world would also witness the historic passage of the Civil Rights Act of 1964, which banned discrimination against blacks and other minorities. In 1966, the National Organization of Women would be founded, thus inaugurating the second wave of the women's movement.[4] This seeming concern for the liberation of subjugated populations, however, did not go unchallenged. Indeed, as Wallerstein states, an "annunciatory and denunciatory world revolution" took place in 1968 in which

> students and their allies in the Western countries, the Communist Bloc, and the peripheral zones were charging that liberal ideology . . . consisted of a set of fraudulent promises and that the reality for the great majority of the world's population was largely negative.[5]

Although it formally started in 1966, we may say that the Black Panther Party (BPP) was part of the global challenge that culminated in 1968. We may situate the BPP within other national liberation movements, as the party un-derstood itself to be part of an international and Marxist-Leninist revolution against white supremacy. The Black Power movement and the BPP responded to the presumption that the Voting Rights Act of 1966 represented the con-summation of civil rights and emancipation, noting the ways in which civil rights reform worked to preserve a fundamentally racist legal and economic system, rather than to abolish it. In addition to being the period that oc-casioned the emergence of rights-based movements, like the civil rights and women's movements, the second apotheosis gave birth to revolutionary nationalist organizations such as the Black Panther Party and its denounce-ments of liberal capitalism. As it challenged the civil rights establishment, the BPP also trained its critique on black cultural nationalist organizations and figures. For the BPP, the cultural nationalism of Haitian dictator Papa Doc Duvalier and Maulana Karenga, the leader of the cultural nationalist organization called Us for us black people, represented the obfuscating practices of liberal ideology. The BPP's Minister of Defense and chief theorist, Huey Newton, argued that Papa Doc and Karenga, like all cultural nationalists, displaced material enfranchisement onto a nostalgic longing for African culture, presuming that "African culture will automatically bring political freedom."[6] Rather than revolting against capitalism, the BPP argued, cultural nationalism only worked to facilitate capitalism and capitalist oppression.

Despite its critiques of civil rights, black cultural nationalism, and U.S. nationalism, black revolutionary nationalism shared some very important affinities with its antagonists. Those affinities had to do with revolutionary nationalism's investments in heteropatriarchy, investments that were consistent with U.S. nationalism, cultural nationalism, and the civil rights movement's beliefs in heteropatriarchal discourses and practices. We may determine the ways that national liberation struggles promoted the gendered and sexual regulations of liberal ideology by looking at how those struggles theorized culture. Revolutionary nationalism's often normative theorization of culture was derived from a normative interpretation of capitalist exploitation. For instance, revolutionary theorist Amilcar Cabral makes the following argument in "National Liberation and Culture":

> The principal characteristic, common to every kind of imperialist domination, is the negation of the historical process of the dominated people by means of violently usurping the free operation of the process of development of the productive forces. . . .
>
> . . . Like history, or because it is history, culture has as its material base the level of the productive forces and the mode of production. Culture plunges its roots into the physical reality of the environmental humus in which it develops, and it reflects the organic nature of the society, which may be more or less influenced by external factors.[7]

Because culture is rooted in the material environment, for Cabral it reflects the changes that imperialism brings to that environment. As imperialism diminishes the subjugated people's historical agency, culture reflects this diminution.

For Cabral, national liberation rescues and utilizes the generative aspects of culture for the good of emancipation and for the destruction of imperialist domination. Indeed, imperialism defiles and corrupts culture, necessitating national liberation's restorative aims. Cabral writes,

> In order for culture to play the important role which falls to it in the framework of the liberation movement, the movement must be able to preserve the positive values of every well-defined social group, of every

category, and to achieve the confluence of these values in the service of the struggle, giving it a new direction—the national dimension.[8]

National liberation engages culture through selection and discrimination, separating the negative aspects of culture to "preserve the positive values" of the group and to assemble these values for nationalist struggle. In its engagement with culture, national liberation betrays a normative bias.

More specifically, national liberation induces culture to compel action designed to regain normativity. In *The Wretched of the Earth*, Frantz Fanon theorizes this relationship between culture and revolutionary action:

> We believe that the conscious and organized undertaking by a colonized people to re-establish the sovereignty of that nation constitutes the most complete and obvious cultural manifestation that exists. . . . After the conflict there is not only the disappearance of colonialism but also the disappearance of the colonized man.[9]

Culture becomes the impetus toward revolutionary agency and the moral justification for heteropatriarchal uplift. For Fanon and Cabral, culture identifies the exploitations of colonialism as disruptions to heteropatriarchy *and* inspires the restoration of that which colonialism, in its castrating maneuvers, had destroyed. If morality is that which justifies forms of agency,[10] then for national liberation, culture was the moral lever that could determine revolutionary practice. Through national liberation's narrative of exploitation and revolutionary action, historical materialism passed its normative logic of heteropatriarchal retrieval.

We can see the BPP's lineage within the normative formulations of historical materialism and national liberation through the party's narrative of racial exploitation as well. Using the master/slave dialectic to formulate a gendered and eroticized narrative of the racial oppression of African Americans, Newton states,

> The historical relationship between black and white here in America has been the relationship between the slave and the master; the master being the mind and the slave the body. The slave would carry out the orders that the mind demanded him to carry out. By doing this the master took the manhood from the slave because he stripped him of a mind. He stripped black people of their mind. In the process the slave-master stripped himself of a body.
> . . . The white man cannot gain his manhood, cannot unite with the body because the body is black. The body is symbolic of slavery and strength. It's a biological thing as he views it. The slave is in a much better situation because his not being a full man has always been viewed psycho-

logically. And it's always easier to make a psychological transition than a biological one. If he can only recapture his mind, recapture his balls, then he will lose all fear and will be free to determine his destiny.[11]

This passage speaks the normative grammar of national liberation, figuring the history of racial exploitation through a narrative of castration and gender distortion and casting revolutionary agency as heteropatriarchal reclamation. While national liberation movements contested the authority of hegemonic nations, those movements reinvested in liberal ideology by grounding agency within the normative assumptions of nation-states, thereby expressing the normative elements of that historic juncture. As Fanon argues, "Far from keeping aloof from other nations, therefore, it is national liberation which leads the nation to play its part on the stage of history. It is at the heart of national consciousness that international consciousness lives and grows."[12] With national liberation, the oppositional bears the stamp of the normative.

We may revise Wallerstein's argument to say that the second apotheosis denotes the triumph of liberal ideology through racial and class exclusion and through the expansion of normative gender and sexual regimes. And if national liberation understood culture and agency as the moral justification for and reclamation of gender and sexual normativity, then national liberation enabled the normative itinerary of the second apotheosis. The second apotheosis of liberalism defines the entrenchment of liberal ideology even through the denunciatory strategies and discourses of national liberation movements and rights-based struggles. In the context of the United States, the women's movement became hegemonic as it engaged in racial and class exclusions, thereby normalizing white citizenship; the civil rights movement complied with liberal exclusions through its sexist ideologies and practices, thereby normalizing heteropatriarchal citizenship. A national liberation movement like the Black Panther Party inserted itself into hegemonic waters as it normalized heteropatriarchal culture and revolutionary agency. Hence, despite its antagonisms to liberal ideology, it—like the civil rights and women's movements—facilitated liberalism's triumph.

To understand the second apotheosis as a contradictory occurrence, that is, as a moment that posited the triumph of liberalism as the triumph of normativity, a moment in which even its antagonists enabled that triumph, we must mine the history of women of color feminism. These cultural, political, social, and epistemological formations challenged the second apotheosis of liberalism and its normative hues among anti-imperialist critics and movements. In doing so, women of color feminism attempted to dislodge interpretations of racial domination from the normative grip of liberal capitalism.

For example, in Frances Beale's essay for the first black feminist anthology, *The Black Woman,* the former member of the Student Nonviolent Coordinating Committee (SNCC) and founder of the Third World Women's Alliance pointed to an emergent affinity between minority and liberal nationalism. She wrote,

> America has defined the roles to which each individual should subscribe. It has defined "manhood" in terms of its own interests and "femininity" likewise. Therefore, an individual who has a good job, makes a lot of money, and drives a Cadillac is a real "man," and conversely, an individual who is lacking in these "qualities" is less of a man.[13]

Liberal ideology, Beale implies, interpellates subjects by hailing them as normative "man" and "woman." In doing so, she addresses the unforeseen convergence between black power, civil rights, and U.S. nationalism. That convergence took place over the mutual investments that these forms of nationalism had in gender and sexual subordination. When black women joined the Black Panther Party during the Free Huey Newton campaign of 1967, many of them discovered that fighting for national liberation entailed subjecting themselves to gender and sexual regulation.[14]

The history of black feminist formations underlines the contradictions of national liberation and identifies the ways in which relations of power were immanent within those struggles. In their book *Empire,* Michael Hardt and Antonio Negri argue that national liberation's adoption of the state form as the most rational organization of society poisoned anti-imperialist and anticolonial struggles.[15] While the state form further enacts systems of control, it is important not to figure the contradictions of national liberation simply through a figure of exteriority like the state apparatus. Indeed, the history of gender and sexual regulations within national liberation illustrates how the attainment of the state apparatus was not the only "poison" that compromised national liberation. More important, the history of those regulations suggests that the poison was *internal* to national liberation. The normalization of culture and agency contaminated national liberation from within those movements and before the attainment of the state. Insisting on the memory of gender and sexual regulations means that relations of power emanated from national liberation.

In contrast, women of color feminists attempted to devise notions of culture and agency that would alienate heteropatriarchy and liberal ideology. If the second apotheosis of liberalism encouraged the normalization of culture and agency as part of national liberation, we can cite women of color feminist reformulations of culture and agency as antagonisms to contemporary globalization. Along with the increase in technological innovations, the transfer of populations, and the global circulation of commodity forms, the diverse cultural, intellectual, and political formation known as women of color feminism was a feature of contemporary globalization. If contemporary globalization arose as a disruption to national authority, women of color feminism, as a formation that critiqued national authority, owes part of its genesis to that disruption. Put differently, if modern globalization challenges the claims of nationalist formations, positing national narratives as ideological and discursive,[16] then women of color feminism, in general, and black feminist formations, in particular, were part of analyses that posited culture and nation as constructed, imaginative, and heterogeneous, rather than as natural, objective, and homogeneous. Discussing the place of critical endeavors within the contemporary juncture, Arjun Appadurai argues,

> The image, the imagined, the imaginary—these are all terms which direct us to something critical and new in global cultural processes: the imagination as a social practice. No longer mere fantasy (opium for the masses whose real work is elsewhere), no longer simple escape (from a world defined principally by more concrete purposes and structures), no longer elite pastime (thus not relevant to the lives of ordinary people) and no longer mere contemplation (irrelevant for new forms of desire and subjectivity), the imagination has become an organized field of social practices, a form of work (both in the sense of labor and of culturally organized practice) and a form of negotiation between sites of agency ("individuals") and globally defined fields of possibility.[17]

As critical formations emerging out of the contradictions of liberation movements, U.S. women of color feminism helped to designate the imagination as a social practice under contemporary globalization. In a moment in which national liberation movements and Western nation-states disfranchised women of color and queer of color subjects, culture, for those groups, became the obvious scene of alternative agency. In the process, these subjects reformatted culture as a site of oppositional agency that eschewed nationalism, rather than facilitated it. Culture became the field from which to imaginatively work against the disfranchisements of nationalism and the debilities of global capital.

In the late 1970s and during the 1980s, black lesbians were most prominent in critiques of heterosexuality and patriarchy.[18] In their work as activists, cultural workers, critics, and theorists, black lesbian feminists tried to wrest culture from the normative confines of nationalism at the moment that the authority of nationalist culture was being challenged worldwide. In terms of black feminism, black lesbians went farthest in retheorizing culture so that it would reflect a gender and sexual disruption to heteropatriarchy and inspire practices and formulations that were alternative to nationalism. Rearticulating culture meant that the presumably "nonpolitical language"[19] of a cultural text like *Sula* provided black lesbian feminists with a model for alternative subjectivities. The imaginative terrain of culture became a politicized site for women of color feminists during a historic moment in which liberal nationalism, cultural nationalism, revolutionary nationalism, and hegemonic feminism usurped the meaning of the political to suppress racialized differences of gender and sexuality. Black lesbian feminists helped to render the imagination into a social practice that utilized cultural forms precisely because of the overlapping gender, sexual, class, and racial exclusions that constituted forms of nationalism.

Locating women of color feminism within the contradictions of contemporary globalization means that we must position its oppositional properties within *and* outside the global parameters of the second apotheosis and its normalization of gender and sexual regulations. We must understand that women of color feminism attempted to negate the normalization of heteropatriarchal culture and agency by an inchoate global economy. Indeed, black lesbian feminist articulations of difference, queer identity, and coalition bear traces of this negation. Theorizing negation in his preface to *Reason and Revolution*, Herbert Marcuse states,

> The negation which dialectic applies to [concepts imposed by common sense] is not only a critique of a conformist logic, which denies the reality of contradictions; it is also a critique of the given state of affairs on its own grounds—of the established system of life, which denies its own promises and potentialities.[20]

The second apotheosis of liberalism was an attempt to neutralize race, gender, and sexuality as overlapping differences that suggested rupture and critique. As forms of nationalism attempted to neutralize those differences through gender, sexual, and racial regulation, they were in fact acting according to the logic of globalization. As women of color and black lesbian feminists invested racialized gender and sexual differences with negative potentials, they were actually opposing the logic of globalization, naming it as a new ground of exploitation *and* emergence. The negative articulation of categories such as "lesbian," "coalition," and "difference" represented an attempt to cease appropriating culture to demonstrate the accoutrements of national identity—homogeneity, equivalence, normativity, and essence. These categories came about as a way to theorize capital and culture as racialized sites of gender and sexual heterogeneity. Put simply, women of color feminism, generally, and black lesbian feminism, particularly, attempted to place culture on a different path and establish avenues alternative to the ones paved by forms of nationalism.

The Moynihan Report and Black Nationalism

If the convergence of national liberation and liberal ideology marked the rise of contemporary globalization, we can actually see the intersections of black nationalism and liberal ideology through the discourse of black matriarchy, formalized in the Moynihan Report and propagated, in part, by black power spokespersons. The discourse of black matriarchy simultaneously enabled leftist and conservative formations within the United States. Leftist and conservative investments in black matriarchy served as the linchpin that sustained black nationalist formations and animated neoconservative ones.

The Negro Family: The Case for National Action was published in 1965, a year after the Civil Rights Act of 1964. The report was written by sociologist (and future U.S. senator) Daniel Patrick Moynihan for the U.S. Department of Labor's Office of Policy Planning and Research. The report attempted to place the African American family—particularly female-headed families—within national policy discourse. Popularly known as the Moynihan Report, it framed itself as a document interested in advancing the aims of civil rights. The report stated that the gains won by civil rights belied the fact that "the gap between the Negro and most other groups in American society [was] widening." "The fundamental problem," according to the Moynihan Report, "[was] that of family structure." As I argued in the preceding chapter, the contradictions of capital in the 1940s were displaced onto African American gender, sexual, and familial relations. Similarly, Moynihan displaced the contradictions that framed the civil rights era onto the African American family. For Moynihan, African American nonheteronormative relations were *the* impediment to such a transformation. The virus of racism had afflicted blacks such that they could not meet the competitive challenges of a liberal capitalist society. While racist prejudice might be irrational, there were objective differences that prevented black achievement. For the sociologist, African American familial arrangements and their nonheteronormative disfigurements spawned those differences.

The Moynihan Report attempted to address these material contradictions by questioning whether legal maneuvers could socialize African Americans for a competitive society. He began, "Liberty and Equality are the twin ideals of American democracy. But they are not the same thing. Nor, most importantly, are they equally attractive to all groups at any given time; nor yet are they always compatible, one with the other."[21] Indeed, for the Moynihan Report, the difference between equality and liberty is a racialized one, a difference that takes on particular meaning in the period of civil rights agitation. It states,

> The demand for Equality of Opportunity has been generally perceived
> by white Americans as a demand for liberty, a demand not to be excluded
> from the competitions of life—at the polling place, in the scholarship
> examinations, at the personnel office, on the housing market. Liberty does,
> of course, demand that every one be free to try his luck, or test his skill in
> such matters. But these opportunities do not necessarily produce equality:
> on the contrary, to the extent that winners imply losers, equality of oppor-
> tunity almost insures inequality of results. (3)

For the Moynihan Report, citizens instantiate the ideal of liberty by compet-
ing in the political, educational, and economic spheres. Liberty preserves
competition but does not imply equality of outcome. As such, a society could
be liberated and have inequalities that manifest as racial, gender, and class
hierarchies, but those inequalities would be the outcome of competition,
rather than power and domination. The differences that result from competition represent the objective outcomes of that competition. For this reason,
"equality of opportunity could insure inequality of results" without suggesting racist, classist, or patriarchal dynamics.

African Americans, according to the report, misunderstand liberty's
relationship to equality. Moynihan states, "The point of semantics is that
equality of opportunity now has a different meaning for Negroes than it has
for whites. It is not (or at least no longer) a demand for liberty alone, but
also for equality—in terms of group results" (3). For Moynihan, this misunderstanding has to do with the ambiguity that inheres within civil rights
laws, an ambiguity that violates the distinction between equality and liberty.
He writes, "Some aspects of the new laws do guarantee results, in the sense
that upon enactment and enforcement they bring about an objective that
is an end in itself, e.g., the public accommodations title of the Civil Rights
Act" (3). Provisions such as the ones dealing with voting, he goes on to
state, "will achieve an objective that is an end in itself . . . but the exercise
of those rights will no doubt lead to further enlargements of the freedom of
the Negro American" (3). The ability of the laws to guarantee some results,
however, should not suggest that this is their principal character: "[B]y and
large, the programs that have been enacted in the first phase of the Negro
Revolution—Manpower Retraining, the Job Corps, Community Action, et
al.—only make opportunities available. They cannot insure the outcome"
(3). Civil rights laws, while giving the impression that they can ensure equality
of outcome, can only grant equality of opportunity, according to the report.
In other words, the law can protect and guarantee the subject's right to com-

pete within the political, academic, and economic terrains of the American
nation-state, but the law does not ensure that the subject will attain the
rewards and privileges of those terrains. Therefore, African Americans are
mistaken inasmuch as they assume access without competition. The next
phase of the civil rights revolution, he wrote, would be to correct this assumption by making "certain that equality of results will now follow. If we
do not, there will be no social peace in the United States for generations"
(3). As he understood it, "The time, therefore, is at hand for an unflinching
look at the present potential of Negro Americans to move from where they
now are to where they want, and ought to be" (4).

Equality of outcome and indeed peace, the report suggested, depended
on the gender and sexual compliance of African American culture. Like *An
American Dilemma* before it, the Moynihan Report regarded the African
American family as that institution that suggests the African American's distance from the normative ideals of American citizenship:

> That being the case, it has to be said that there is a considerable body of
> evidence to support the conclusion that Negro social structure, in particu-
> lar the Negro family, battered and harassed by discrimination, injustice,
> and uprooting, is in the deepest trouble. While many young Negroes are
> moving ahead to unprecedented levels of achievement, many more are fall-
> ing further and further behind. (4)

It is important to note that Moynihan actually inherited his thesis about
the African American family from E. Franklin Frazier's writings on black
families and the problems of black matriarchies.[22] Basing the problems of
African American social structure on the troubles of the African American
family, the Moynihan Report renders African American intimate arrangements into the obstacle to equality of outcome. As the family was imagined
as that institution that prevented many African Americans from "moving
ahead," family became that institution that determined the direction of mobility, socializing its members to competitive ideals and practices and granting them equality of results only as the family yielded to heteropatriarchal
dictates.

According to the text, the history of racial exclusion stretching back
to slavery and reconstruction accounts for the so-called gender and sexual
devastations of African American families, devastations evinced by the
number of female-headed households, "outcomes that worked against the
emergence of a strong father figure."[23] The Moynihan Report draws on a
notion that masculinity is innate to men and biologically driven, declaring that "the very essence of man is to strut" (16). For Moynihan, this
masculinity is integral to American national character. Hence, the history

of racist violence has castrated African American men, preventing them from realizing a masculinity that is fundamental to all men. While Park's "Temperament, Tradition, and Nationality" may have articulated liberalism through sentimental notions of the "Negro as the lady among the races," the Moynihan Report enunciated liberal ideology through an identification with and conception of the African American male as castrated and therefore bereft of heteropatriarchal entitlements.

For the text, this gender and sexual devastation did not simply remove the male from the head of the household. To compound the matter, it replaced the male patriarch with a female head, retarding "the progress of the group as a whole and [imposing] a crushing burden on the Negro male and, in consequence, on a great many Negro women as well" (29). As a familial formation that "retards progress" because of its nonheteronormative conformity, the female-headed household impedes the march of civil rights. The designation of the female-headed household as an impediment typifies the normative underpinnings of civil rights. While imagining the female-headed household as the antithesis of civil rights, the document argues that it is the matrix of urban and social ills, producing a "tangle of pathology" (29).

Masculinization, hence, had to come from outside African American culture. The report designated the armed forces as an institution that could masculinize black men, placing black men in an idealized context in which "'Negro' and 'white' do not exist" (42). The Moynihan Report cast racial exclusion as fundamentally feminizing. If exclusion is the trace of feminization, then equality can only be won by recovering the heteropatriarchal loss suffered under racism. Set in the moment of imperialist wars within Asia, this argument was a way of arguing that black men could resolve their alleged gender insufficiency by participating in those wars. Since the U.S. government was drafting young African American men for the war, the Vietnam War was a contentious issue that placed African Americans at the heart. The government's drafting of African American men was a bitter source of protest for the BPP especially.[24] Instead of black men being used for the aims of U.S. imperialism, the BPP countered that black people, especially black men, should commit themselves to the revolutionary struggle of the National Liberation Front in Vietnam. As Eldridge Cleaver stated, "The black man's interest lies in seeing a free and independent Vietnam, a strong Vietnam which is not the puppet of international white supremacy. If the nations of Asia, Latin America, and Africa are strong and free, the black man in America will be safe and secure and free to live in dignity and self-respect."[25]

The Moynihan Report attempted to transform a presumably "pathological" culture into one that was suitable for gender and sexual conformity and compliant with heteropatriarchal regulation. As evidenced by the text's argument about the military, the state would take the place of the absent patriarch in the African American family and would regulate African American familial practices.[26] Only a "national effort . . . directed towards the question of family structure could resolve the problems that inhibited African American progress."[27] United States policies would have to be designed to "strengthen the Negro family so as to enable it to raise and support its members" as other families supported their members (47–48).

U.S. policies and practices that targeted African American families were both distorting and invasive. Confronting the ways the discourse of black matriarchy disfigured black women, Johnnie Tilmon, chairwoman of the National Welfare Rights Organization, stated, "There are a lot of other lies that male society tells about welfare mothers; that AFDC (Aid to Families with Dependent Children) mothers are immoral, that AFDC mothers are lazy, misuse their welfare checks, spend it all on booze and are stupid and incompetent."[28] As the discourse of black matriarchy presented black mothers as unscrupulous and "incompetent," it also justified practices of surveillance in which "welfare detectives" would apparently wake up black women and their children to look through dirty clothes hampers and refrigerators in search of black men.[29]

The Moynihan Report actually is an important genealogical node in successive and hegemonic discourses about minority communities within the United States. These discourses, George Lipsitz argues, emerged after the passage of the 1964 and 1965 Civil Rights Acts. Such discourses suggested that "the problems facing communities of color no longer stem primarily from discrimination but from the characteristics of these communities themselves, from unrestrained sexual behavior and childbirths out of wedlock, crime, welfare dependency, and a perverse sense of group identity and group entitlement."[30] These discourses owe their origin and coherence to the Moynihan Report.

The discourse of black matriarchy was founded on assumptions that presumed heteropatriarchal culture as the appropriate and regulatory norm. As such, the discourse provided sanctuary for liberal, leftist, and soon-to-be conservative formations. For instance, black nationalist groups, while they contested Moynihan's argument about the state being the appropriate catalyst to masculine agency, agreed with Moynihan's thesis about the emasculating effects of black women and the need for black men to resume their role as patriarchs. To Moynihan's list of pathologies caused by black matriarchy, black nationalists like Eldridge Cleaver would add homosexuality. According to Cleaver, the antagonisms of class society and "a dying culture and civilization" had produced homosexuality, and the black revolution could achieve heteropatriarchal status by ending class antagonisms and subsequently homosexuality.[31] In supporting heteropatriarchal regulation, black nationalists like Cleaver and Nathan Hare facilitated the triumph of liberalism. The ideological affiliations between black nationalists and Moynihan were actually part of a global phenomenon in which national liberation was establishing fellowship with the normative claims of liberal ideology. Cheryl Clarke sheds light on this fellowship in her remarks about the homophobic alliances between the Family Protection Act, a bill proposed to the U.S. Congress in 1981, and the First National Plenary Conference on Self-Determination in December of that same year. Clarke draws our attention to the ways in which the bill and the conference flyer respectively denounce homosexual organizations as unworthy of federal funding from the U.S. nation-state and refute homosexuality as "a threat to our survival as a [black] people and as a nation."[32] Clarke's illustration is much more than an isolated incidence. It is, in fact, typical of the alliances between national liberation and modern state-formation during the second apotheosis.

The discourse of black matriarchy bears the trace of a hegemonic formation, one in which sociological discourse, black nationalist movements, civil rights, and neoconservative alliances are entangled. In addition to seducing black nationalists, that discourse facilitated a conservative blockade of social welfare policy in the United States, a blockade that began in the late 1970s.[33] Displacing the contradictions of capital onto African American female-headed households established the moral grammar and the political practices of the very neoconservative formations that would roll back the gains of civil rights in the 1980s and 1990s and undermine the well-being of black poor and working-class families. Hence, the Moynihan Report and the pathologizing of black mothers as nonheteronormative provided the discursive origins for the dismantling of welfare as part of the fulfillment of global capital by the millennium's end.

With the advent of a world recession resulting from the oil crisis in the 1970s, the pressures of a global economy bore heavily on welfare states like the United States and Britain.[34] In a context in which the budgetary practices of welfare states were questioned, private enterprise increasingly understood welfare state institutions as fetters to capitalism. Moreover, private enterprise acted as the discursive incubator for neoconservative formations.[35] Neoconservative ideologies emerged within a context in which public spending that exceeded economic growth produced imbalances between revenues and expenditures. The weakening economic power of welfare states compromised the budgetary aims of those states and undermined a Keynesian logic that public spending would inspire economic growth.[36] Such disruptions to the power of welfare states and to prior economic logic produced an electoral situation that favored the rise of neoconservative administrations.[37]

The pathological image of nonheteronormative formations like the female-headed household played a key role in this conservative resurgence. Neoconservatives explicitly based their objections to public spending on the discourse of black matriarchy, arguing that black "welfare queens" were getting fat off liberal social policies and producing destructive urban environments in which young blacks had no regard for competition and honest work.[38] For neoconservatives, both the welfare state and African American communities were outcomes of a misunderstanding about the distinction between liberty and equality. Neoconservatives inherited this presumption about African Americans' perverse sense of entitlement, which abolished all competitive drive. Once imagined as buffers for the underdogs of global economic transformations, welfare states, according to neoconservatives, now abolished competition as a necessary factor in everyday life. For neoconservatives, the absence of a competitive ethos originated within an insufficiently regulatory and therefore nonheteronormative minority culture.

"Lesbian" as Negation of Identity Politics

The discourse of black matriarchy was part of the genealogy of black feminist formation, in general, and black lesbian feminist formation, in particular. Ostensibly a discourse about an aberrant heterosexuality, the discourse encouraged, as Cheryl Clarke suggests, the suppression of other nonheteronormative formations. In the context of the 1970s and 1980s, black lesbians pointed out the ways in which the discourse of black matriarchy regulated a range of racialized gender and sexual formations. We may look to their interaction with a cultural text like Toni Morrison's *Sula* as an indication of how black lesbian feminists engaged the gender and sexual heterogeneity of African American culture. We may then understand those engagements as ways of negating the commonsense understandings of that culture and of gesturing toward the potentialities that inhered in a global economy.

Sula begins with the Peace family, represented by Sula, her matriarchal grandmother Eva, and her mother Hanna. On the surface it would seem that the novel repeats the narrative contours of the black matriarchate discourse: Eva raises her children without her husband, who runs away early in the novel. Hannah raises Sula without a father. In the banal language of that discourse, it would appear that the Peace family exemplifies the vicious cycle of the female-headed household. But the novel suggests alternative readings of the Peace family, readings that black lesbians seized to construct a politics that was feminist, queer, antiracist, and coalitional. In a 1983 interview, Audre Lorde considered the main character's quest for agency within the confines of a social world that was thoroughly heteropatriarchal. She stated,

"*Sula* is a totally incredible book. It made me light up like a Christmas tree. I particularly identified with the book because of the female-outsider idea. That book is one long poem. Sula is the ultimate black female of our time, trapped in her power and her pain."[39] Black lesbian feminists' engagement with *Sula* represented a process of negation in which an apparently non-political literary text about two black women became a resource for epistemological and political practices that could express alternatives to existing social movements. Devising such practices meant resuscitating nonnormative difference as the horizon of epistemological critique, aesthetic innovation, and political practice.

The second apotheosis expanded liberal ideology and its normative investments, in part, through national identity. In such instances, citizenship was not the only nationalist articulation of identity. The category "woman" and its suppression of racial, class, and sexual heterogeneity represented such an articulation. "Colonized man" as the suppression of gender and sexual difference within relations of race expressed yet another articulation. We may also add that the category "worker," inasmuch as it obscured gender, racial, and sexual differences within capitalist relations of production, expressed yet another articulation of national identity. It is important to note that these nationalist articulations of identity were "important models of social and political unity necessary for coherent liberation struggles."[40] For our current historic moment, it is just as important to address the ways in which the women's, civil rights, black power, and labor movements neglected to conceptualize the multiple specificities and differences that constituted their various subjects. In doing so, they normalized the suppression of subaltern gender, racial, and sexual identities and revealed their investments in nationalism.

Rendered invisible by the political subjects of hegemonic feminism, minority nationalism, and marxism, women of color feminists attempted to articulate identity formations that would work to negate the nationalist presumptions and protocols of identity. As Gladys M. Jiménez-Munoz observes, women of color feminism intervened into the question of identity by refusing to posit identity as a goal, "a site empty of social contradictions, or unhelpful constructions. Rather, it is the space where these other social contradictions can be addressed and worked through, insofar as it is the space where these contradictions become visible."[41] Jiménez-Munoz remarks further that "[i]t is this place of departure, of creating and reinventing spaces, that is crucial because as lesbians of color oftentimes this meant being located in positions in which one could not take for granted the social solidarity characteristic of racially oppressed/cultural-national families and communities in Europe and North America."[42] In other words, lesbian of color feminism contributed to the theorization of identity by arguing that if identity is posed, it must be constantly contravened to address the variety of social contradictions that nationalism strives to conceal.

An example of this effort at negation can be found in Barbara Smith's classic essay, "Towards a Black Feminist Criticism." Much has been written about the presumed failures of the essay, that it reduces "Black feminist criticism . . . to an experiential relationship that exists between black women as critics and black women as writers who represent black women's reality."[43] Such critiques appropriately attend to the identity politics within the piece, but there is a politics of difference at work within Smith's essay as well, a politics that disrupts identity's presumptions of equivalence and verisimilitude. This politics expresses black lesbian feminist practices of negation. Indeed, we may locate Smith's essay within black lesbian feminist attempts to devise another politics, "one which engages with rather than suppresses heterogeneities of gender, class, sexuality, race, and nation, yet [one] which is also able to maintain and extend the forms of unity that make common struggle possible—a politics whose vision is not the origin but the destination."[44] To reiterate, these attempts to formulate a politics of difference took place within a moment in which a nascent global capital was working to disrupt the promises and the stability of national identity.

We can see the epistemological articulation of this disruption within Smith's use of the category "lesbian." She writes,

> Despite the apparent heterosexuality of the female characters, I discovered in re-reading *Sula* that it works as a lesbian novel not only because of the passionate friendship between Sula and Nel, but because of Morrison's consistently critical stance toward the heterosexual institutions of male/female relationships, marriage and the family. Consciously or not, Morrison's work poses both lesbian and feminist questions about black women's autonomy and their impact upon each other's lives.[45]

While Smith does not clarify what she means by "lesbian novel,"[46] what is striking is the way that Smith deploys "lesbian" outside the boundaries of identity. She defines "lesbian" not in terms of identity, but in terms of a set of critiques of heterosexuality and patriarchy. Rather than naming an identity, "lesbian" actually identifies a set of social relations that point to the instability of heteropatriarchy and to a possible critical emergence within that instability. Another way of stating this would be to say that Smith's use of "lesbian" designates the ways in which heteropatriarchal relations are rife with unrest and contradiction and that these disruptions rebuke heteropatriarchal ideals and claims. As Smith's use of the category "lesbian" explains social relations rather than identity, it disrupts the heterosexual/homosexual dyad. Interpreting *Sula* as an allegory of such a disruption, Smith writes, "Sula's presence in her community functions much like the presence of lesbians everywhere to expose the contradictions of supposedly normal life."[47] In the historic moment of the novel's production and circulation, "normal life" was the hegemonic articulation of nationalist discourses. Situating *Sula* in the wake of Addison Gayle's cultural nationalist anthology, *The Black Aesthetic,* Madhu Dubey argues, "Nel and Sula's union constitutes the novel's strongest challenge to Black Aesthetic discourse. As we have already seen, one of the functions of black women writers, as prescribed by the Black Aesthetic, was to depict black male-female relationships as necessary, complementary unions."[48] As the material presence of black lesbians exposed the contradictions of "normativity," between the presumed universal nature of normativity and the actual discrepant fact of nonnormativity, black lesbian existence became a practice of negation.

Inasmuch as black lesbian difference functioned as a force of negation that illuminated the very heterogeneous formations that nationalist ideologies worked to conceal, this difference negated identitarian presumptions about authorial intention, presumptions that constructed an equivalence between the author and the cultural form. We can see this negation at work in Smith's comments about Morrison and *Sula*. Smith states,

> If one sees Sula's inexplicable "evil" and nonconformity as the evil of not being male-identified, many elements in the novel become clear. The work might be clearer still if Morrison had approached her subject with the consciousness that a lesbian relationship was at least a possibility for her characters. Obviously Morrison did not intend the reader to perceive Sula and Nel's relationship as inherently lesbian. However, this lack of intention only shows the way in which heterosexist assumptions can veil what may logically be expected to occur in a work.[49]

As Mikhail Bakhtin argues, "Language is not a neutral medium that passes freely and easily into the private property of the speaker's intentions; it is populated—overpopulated—with the intentions of others."[50] Smith suggests that black lesbian feminist critique negates the presumption that *Sula* is the private property of Morrison's intentions. Instead she suggests that the text is populated with interests that Morrison could not imagine. Indeed, the socially heteroglot world that locates Sula as a cultural form, a world characterized by gender and sexual heterogeneity, frustrates authorial intention. An essentialist notion of identity would have compelled Smith to assume that Morrison as a black woman had a lesbian identification. Indeed, Smith seems to be more concerned with the ways in which Morrison's text spirals away from Morrison's intentions, and in that spiraling connects to black female subjects that Morrison did not imagine.

Indeed, the essay arose from and produced heterogeneous circumstances that made it difficult for the category "black woman" to speak a logic of equivalence. Black lesbian feminist organizations and activists came from a diverse range of social movements—the women's, the antiwar, the civil rights, the black power movements, and so forth. The black lesbian feminist group the Combahee River Collective illustrates the heterogeneous composition of black lesbian feminism. Founded in Boston in 1974, the Combahee River Collective formed after the first eastern regional meeting of the National Black Feminist Organization (NBFO), in part as an alternative to the "bourgeois feminist stance of the NBFO and their lack of a clear political focus."[51] Conceived out of the intersections of civil rights, black power, and socialist feminism, the Combahee River Collective attempted to construct a notion of black woman that was simultaneously queer, antiracist, feminist, and socialist. Salsa Soul Sisters Third World Womyn Inc. was organized in 1974 as a third-world lesbian organization including African American, African, and Caribbean women, as well as Asian American woman and Latinas. In the 1980s, Sapphire Sapphos emerged as a black lesbian organization with a heterogeneous class composition made up of women in and around Washington D.C.[52] The class, national, ethnic, political, sexual, and racial diversity that made up black lesbian feminist organizations compelled articulations of black feminism and black womanhood that allowed for such multiplicity.

The heterogeneous composition of black lesbian feminism inspired a politics of difference that could critique the nationalist underpinnings of identity and challenge the racial regulation and gender and sexual normativity that composed the second apotheosis. In this way, women of color feminist negations were very different from the politics of negation that national liberation proffered. National liberation negated Western national identity by substituting subaltern identities. This negation was one in which identity was retained as both the vehicle for and the destination of national emancipation. Contrary to national liberation's preservation of national identity, women of color feminism negated both Western nationalism and national liberation by working to theorize the limits of subaltern identity. They did so within a moment in which ethnic and feminist movements' deployment of identity proved their complicity with the normative claims of liberal ideology. Commenting on lesbian of color attempts to theorize those limits, Jiménez-Munoz states, "[There] are difficult matters that lesbian writers of color have assumed and that further problematize the issue of identity from the perspective of women of color: this is the question of how an oppressed subject can also, simultaneously, be an oppressing subject."[53] This theorization of identity as both enabling and fraught was theorized into the practices of black lesbian feminist organizations. Those organizations engaged those questions particularly within the often difficult context of coalitional work, as it necessitated engaging racial and national differences many times governed by divisive discourses of race. Women of color feminism had to express a politics of negation and difference in which identity was a point of departure since the gendered and sexual regulations of national liberation proved that women of color, in general, and lesbians of color, in particular, could not take comfort in the presumed accommodations of nationalism.

Sula and the Upward and Downward Expansion of Minority Social Structure

Sula was published within the period that occasioned the upward and downward expansion of black social structures. The economic changes of the 1970s launched some African Americans into middle-class lifestyles and locked others into poverty.[54] The polarization of social structures was not specific to the United States. Indeed, it was part of a general global trend reached as the economies of highly industrialized countries shifted toward service. As sociologist Saskia Sassen notes, the shift to a service economy, coupled with the "redeployment of manufacturing and office jobs to less developed areas," has "directly and indirectly . . . created a significant increase in the supply of low-wage jobs, particularly female-typed jobs, in highly developed countries."[55] As sociologist Rose Brewer has argued, for African American women, the shift toward a service economy within the United States has helped to segregate black women in service and clerical jobs, working in hospitals, nursing homes, fast food outlets, and cafeterias.[56] As the polarization of African American social structure became a context for normalization, it helped constitute the normative character of the second apotheosis.

We must address this polarization of social structure not simply as an economic phenomenon, but as a social phenomenon with normative implications as well. The discourse of black matriarchy may have preceded the polarization that characterized the beginnings of contemporary globalization, but in the context of the United States it helped to constitute the ideological and discursive climate for the shift toward postindustrialization. We can think of Moynihan's argument that civil rights legislation was helping to advance some blacks and not others as a way of foreshadowing the normative polarization of African American social structure. We may say that African American social structure in the polarizing moments of the 1970s inherited the normative ideologies of civil rights, canonical sociology, and national liberation. As the discourse of black matriarchy justified reinvestments in heteropatriarchal discourse—reinvestments that occasioned the regulation of black single mothers and black lesbians alike—that discourse helped to constitute the upward and downward expansion of African American social structure as the polarization of heteronormative and nonheteronormative African American social formations. This polarization of African American social structure encompassed a period that simultaneously produced the single black mother and the black lesbian as the female-outsider in contradistinction to the normative black middle-class subject who could claim legitimacy within African American communities.

We may read the following scene as an allegory of the polarizations that were beginning to take place within African American communities, divisions over heteronormative belonging and nonheteronormative exclusion. Sula—after returning to the Bottom, the black section of the town called Medallion—has just placed her grandmother Eva in a nursing home, slept with Jude, her best friend Nel's husband, and has built a reputation as sexually and culturally transgressive. The narrator states,

> When the word got out about Eva being put in Sunnydale, the people in the Bottom shook their heads and said Sula was a roach. Later, when they saw how she took Jude, then ditched him for others, and heard how he bought a bus ticket to Detroit (where he bought but never mailed birthday cards to his sons), they forgot all about Hannah's easy ways (or their own) and said she was a bitch. . . .
>
> But it was the men who gave her the final label, who fingerprinted her for all time. They were the ones who said she was guilty of the unforgivable thing—the thing for which there was no understanding, no excuse, no compassion. The route from which there was no way back, the dirt that could not ever be washed away. They said that Sula slept with white men. It may not have been true, but it certainly could have been. She was obviously capable of it. . . .
>
> So they laid broomsticks across their doors at night and sprinkled salt on porch steps. But aside from one or two unsuccessful efforts to collect the dust from her footsteps, they did nothing to harm her. As always the black people looked at evil stony-eyed and let it run.[57]

By constructing Sula as other, her accusers can claim normativity for themselves. Moreover, Morrison establishes Sula's construction as other within the imperatives of heteropatriarchal privilege. It is the men who "fingerprint" her, marking her according to patriarchal law. This scene allegorizes the regulation of nonheteronormative difference as Sula is disciplined for inappropriate object choices—white men. Fingerprinting her is also meta-phoric for the ways in which national liberation regulated other nonhetero-normative formations. Moreover, it evokes the ways in which black nation-alists often assumed control over black women's bodies. As Sula was called "bitch," black lesbians and black single mothers were addressed at various times as "little men," "bulldaggers," and "matriarchs." In sum, the afore-mentioned scene points to multiple practices of fingerprinting and thereby gestures toward nonheteronormative strata within African American culture.

In addition to interpreting the scene through the history of national lib-eration, we may also read the passage as metaphorical for an emergent class formation among African Americans, a class formation that was equally as regulatory. Morrison points to the regulatory ethos of the period of national liberation in the chapter entitled "1965":

> Everything had changed. Even the whores were better then: tough, fat,
> laughing women with burns on their cheeks and wit married to their mean-
> ness: or widows couched in small houses in the woods with eight children
> to feed and no man. These modern-day whores were pale and dull before
> those women. These little clothes-crazy things were *always embarrassed.*
> *Nasty but shamed.* They didn't know what shameless was. They should
> have known those silvery widows in the woods who would get up from the
> dinner table and walk into the trees with a customer with as much embar-
> rassment as a calving mare.[58]

The aforementioned scene is striking inasmuch as 1965 has brought with it not only a new class formation, "young ones [who talk] about community, but [leave] the hills to the poor, the old, the stubborn—and the rich white folks," but a new sensibility, one organized around shame and embarrass-ment for nonheteronormative subjects. This shame, this embarrassment, we may read as the evidence of disciplinary techniques that were simultane-ous with a new class emergence among the people in the Bottom. We may go even further to say that the scene is metaphorical for a then advancing middle-class formation that negotiated the upward and downward expan-sion of African American social structure by regulating and differentiating persons that remained in the Bottom.

Something Else to Be: Coalition as a "Globally Defined Field of Possibility"

Sula allegorized not only the conditions of black women's gender and sexu-al regulation, but also a desire to formulate identities and social practices that could withstand and provide alternatives to those limitations. Morrison writes,

> Because each had discovered years before that they were neither white nor male, and that all freedom and triumph was forbidden to them, they had set about creating something else to be.[59]

Being "something else" was not a task restricted to the realm of personal identity but extended to social practice as well. We may see this extension in women of color and black lesbian feminist theorizations of coalition. Indeed, Smith attested that coalition building among women of color and third-world feminists was the "single most enlivening and hopeful development in the 1980s."[60] As with Smith's illumination of the heterogeneity that characterizes black women's experiences in her reading of *Sula,* black lesbian feminists desired and produced a political and theoretical engagement—at times tension-filled[61]—that acknowledged the heteroglot nature of women's identities and experiences and in doing so, disrupted essentialist articulations of blackness and womanhood. Those engagements indexed women of color and black lesbian feminist desires for modes of agency that departed from nationalist articulations of coalition. In addition, such interventions attested to the material and discursive conditions of an emergent and heterogeneous labor force. If negation, as Marcuse argues, partly refers to the forces that compel destruction, then we may say that black lesbian feminist writing and organizing pointed to capital's global phase as particularly exploitative for U.S. and third-world women of color. In the context of the rapid commodification of U.S. women of color and third-world female labor, the discourse of black matriarchy provided much of the normative syntax by which to regulate global capital's emergent labor force. Black lesbian and women of color feminist interpretations of coalition gestured toward regulatory modes that claimed the lives not only of black women, but of Asian, Asian American, Latina, and Caribbean women as well. In doing so, such theorizations of coalition traced the properties of capital's new phase and sought to address that mode as one that could produce unprecedented possibilities.

To understand how women of color feminists innovated understandings of coalition, we must contextualize those innovations within revolutionary nationalist articulations of coalition. For the Black Panther Party, as for many national liberation struggles, coalitions were based on nationalist alliances against imperialist domination. Nationalist theorizations of coalition thus became a way of extending the heteropatriarchal logic of national liberation. In doing so, coalitions based on anti-imperialist nationalism actually propagated the normative components of liberal ideology.

Women of color and black lesbian feminists took up the issue of coalition not to extend revolutionary nationalist theorizations, but to radically revise them. For instance, in the introduction to *Home Girls: A Black Feminist Anthology,* the first black lesbian feminist collection of writings, Smith draws a connection between the analysis of intersections and coalitional work. She argues, "Approaching politics with a comprehension of the simultaneity of oppressions has helped to create a political atmosphere particularly conducive to coalition building."[62] Indeed, the simultaneity of oppressions allowed passage away from national liberation and into a completely different understanding of alliances across difference. The Combahee River Collective statement offers a glimpse of this understanding:

> We realize that the liberation of all oppressed peoples necessitates the destruction of the political-economic systems of capitalism and imperialism as well as patriarchy. . . . We are not convinced, however, that a socialist revolution that is not also a feminist and anti-racist revolution will guarantee our liberation. We have arrived at the necessity for developing an understanding of class position of Black women who are generally marginal in the labor force, while at this particular time some of us are temporarily viewed as doubly desirable tokens at white-collar and professional levels. We need to articulate the real class situation of persons who are not merely raceless, sexless workers, but for whom racial and sexual oppression are significant determinants in their working/economic lives. Although we are in essential agreement with Marx's theory as it applied to the very specific economic relationships he analyzed, we know that his analysis must be extended further in order for us to understand our specific economic situation as Black women.[63]

Articulating class formations as significant in terms of racial and sexual oppression meant that the collective had to address capitalism and imperialism as processes that were formed according to those differences. In doing so, the collective refuted the disciplinary maneuvers of several critical formations. Unlike revolutionary nationalism, the collective did not privilege race and nation to the exclusion of gender or sexuality. Unlike traditional marxism, the group did not evoke class to occlude the significance of all other differences. And contrary to socialist feminism, it did not posit gender and class to deny race and sexuality. The Combahee River Collective and other black lesbian feminists were actually rearticulating coalition to address gender, racial, and sexual dominance as part of capitalist expansion globally. Rather than naming a process that crushes difference and particularity, globalization described the formation of economic modes from which critical differences burgeon and normativity incubates.

As black lesbian feminist theorizations of coalition implied, global capital was erecting regimes of normativity that would discipline a largely female labor force. To reiterate, the shift toward a service economy within the United States rendered the changes to African American social structures into one symptom of capital's new phase. Indeed, the expansion of service industries within this new phase entailed an increase in both low-wage and high-income jobs, making the polarization of social structures less of a U.S. phenomenon and more of a global one.[64] With the growth of service economies, more women were proletarianized. From 1970 to 1980, the number of women who worked in low-wage service jobs increased from 42 to 52 percent.[65] Connecting the feminization of labor under globalization to African American women's specific labor predicament, Brewer states, "[U]neven economic growth and internationalization have involved Black women in the complex circuitry of labor exchange of women nationally and globally."[66] Contradictorily, while many black women were concentrated in low-wage service jobs, still others in the 1970s and 1980s were pushed out of the job market altogether, as capital sought even cheaper third-world female labor outside the United States and within.[67] The devaluation of African American labor is thus directly tied to the proletarianization of third-world labor. U.S. capital could cease to rely on African American labor, generally, and black women's labor, specifically, as foreign investment from firms within highly industrialized countries developed export manufacturing in less economically advanced regions. In countries whose economies depended on export manufacturing, countries in Asia and the Caribbean for instance,[68] women often constituted the labor in manufacturing jobs.[69] As anthropologist Aihwa Ong notes, "In the 1960s developing countries greatly improved conditions for a new round of investments by foreign capital."[70] With tax-free privileges for foreign capital, goods manufactured in free-trade zones could be exported abroad (63). In these settings, third-world countries could bid for modern nation status by supplying workers for multinational capital. Ong summarizes the phenomenon:

> By the 1970s, a network of industrial zones scattered throughout Southeast Asia opened up the region to industrial investments by Japanese transnational companies, to be quickly followed by Western corporations. At about the same time, the implementation of the Maquiladora (assembly plant) program along the U.S.–Mexican border opened up Mexico to North American firms. (63)

As laborers entered commodity exchange, they would be thrust into a simultaneously racialized, gendered, and eroticized arena of normative regulation. An expanding service economy subjected many Chinese, Malaysian, Thai, Filipino, and Sri Lankan women to layoffs and low wages, pushing many into sex work (64). In the 1970s, U.S. firms pressed female employees in Malaysia and other parts of Southeast Asia to submit to gender normativity by dating, buying makeup from company stores, and participating in beauty pageants. As Ong states, "Such emphasis on Western images of sex appeal engendered a desire for goods that working women could satisfy only by increasing their commitment to wage work" (74). The reproduction of racialized gender and sexual regulation would thus facilitate the production of global capital.

In the context of the United States, sociological discourse provided the lexicon for the gendered and eroticized components of racial regulation for nonwhite surplus populations. In the 1980s and 1990s, specifically, the discourse of black matriarchy provided the language for regulating immigrant racial formations. From 1980 to 1995, roughly fifteen million Asians and Latinos immigrated to the United States.[71] During this period as well, neoconservative alliances assaulted public spending for racialized nonwhite immigrants. As ethnic studies scholar Lisa Cacho notes, "In 1996, a democratic president and a republican Congress passed the Illegal Immigration Reform and Immigrant Responsibility Act and the Personal Responsibility and Work Opportunity Act" (389). In the tradition of retrenchment practices, these bills "effectively eliminated public assistance to undocumented immigrants, severely cut and restricted aid to legal immigrants, imposed harsher penalties for illegal immigration (including immigrants seeking asylum), and relaxed deportation procedures" (389). These anti-immigrant measures were the outcome and cause of a discourse of white injury that was most powerfully exhibited in the 1994 passage of California's Proposition 187, which denied public expenditures (medical care, education, and so forth) to undocumented immigrants and their children (389). The discourse of white injury legalized through Proposition 187 and the congressional acts constructed nonwhite immigrants, particularly Latin immigrants, as financial and social burdens to white taxpayers. Like the discourse of black matriarchy, the discourse of white injury displaced the contradictions of capital onto the immigrant home. Writing about the construction of immigrant women of color under this discursive environment, Cacho argues, "The racialized female is . . . demonized along the lines of reproduction; mothers are cast as the harbingers and reproducers of social ills and pathology—providing children with empty folded tortillas that lead to lifetimes of crime" (400). Pathologizing women of color immigrants as wild reproducers, women who spawn communities with no regard for the distinctions between liberty and equality, became a way of justifying cuts to public spending and obscuring the ways in which the United States needed immigrant labor. The theory of black matriarchy, in other words, helped to generate discourses about other nonheteronormative racial formations, legitimating the exploitation of nonwhite labor and devastating the lives of poor and working-class communities of color.

But negation not only refers to the conditions of exploitation. It denotes the circumstances for critique and alternatives as well. More specifically, the commodification of female labor under globalization produced coalitions as a site of antiracist, feminist, and queer critique. In the context of capital's new economic phase, which depended on racialized gender and sexual discourses to manage an emergent female labor force, coalitions could only challenge these modes of regulation by making gendered, eroticized, and racialized exploitation the basis of political and intellectual intervention. In this context, coalition was based on women of color's subjection to simultaneous oppressions, oppressions constituted through normative undercurrents, modes of exploitation that would characterize globalization in the late twentieth century.

African American culture, as this book has attempted to illustrate, functions as one location that negates and critiques the normative itineraries of capitalist modes of production. The alternatives that African American culture offers owe their significance to the gender and sexual diversity that characterize that culture. This text has also attempted to address African American cultural forms as registers of that heterogeneity. In effect, such interpretations have departed from traditional (i.e., canonical) analyses of African American literature. In relation to those analyses, I have tried not to approach sociology as the discrete history of an academic discipline. Instead, we may read sociology as a discursive and ideological formation that has worked to establish the normative character of U.S. national culture, and has helped narrate and regulate nonheteronormative racial formations. The U.S. nation-state's claims to universality were indeed formed through a racialized normativity that belied the state's regulation of racialized nonnormative gender and sexual formations. With regard to African Americans, sociology has helped to produce the gendered and sexualized components of African American racial difference. The sociological production of racial knowledge about African Americans has thus intersected with capital's own production of and constitution through differences of race, gender, sexuality, and class. Because of their own normative underpinnings, oppositional forces like the black power movement fell prey to capital's new global mode as it sought to regulate a burgeoning labor pool through appeals to normativity. Within contemporary globalization, liberal ideology fed on national liberation movements, using their investments in normativity as a source of capital's nourishment. In this historic moment, probably more than any other, oppositional coalitions have to be grounded in nonnormative racial difference. We must look to the differentiated histories of women of color and queer of color critical formations to aid us in this enterprise.

Conclusion

Toward the End of Normativity

It has been more than thirty years since women of color feminists worked to articulate the complexities of nationalism. Other intellectual formations have since engaged those complexities as well. Through "postnationalist" projects, American studies has made nationalism an explicit object of the discipline. Examining nationalism has promoted critical efforts aimed at shattering narratives of discreteness that remove the United States from the history of Western imperialism. These efforts also involve lifting American studies out of a parochialism rooted in canonical understandings of literature and history. Critically engaging canonical formations corresponds to the type of queer of color engagement that I have attempted throughout this book. As queer of color analysis interrogates the normative and nonnormative articulations of social formations (political, economic, epistemological, and cultural), it has a direct interest in engaging American studies and its postnationalist articulations. As postnationalist projects assume new modes of interpreting this disciplinary formation, which has historically been both consistent with and divergent from forms of U.S. nationalism, postnationalist enterprises intersect directly with queer of color interests in the genealogy of social formations. American studies' contradictory relationship to nationalism begs us to constantly repose the question "What are the subjects of American studies?" We must ask this question not only of more canonical versions of American studies, but of its postnationalist versions as well. Queer of color analysis serves in this instance as a guide that can thus inspire caution and deliberation, especially about the ways in which postnationalist American studies may be outside the normative protocols of nationalism and within them. Another way of stating this would be to say that queer of color analysis confronts American studies by asking whether or not the subjects of American studies can address the complexity of relations taking place within our historic moment.

The interest of American studies and queer of color critique in the subject of history intersects with one of the main theoretical directives of historical materialism: to formulate the subject of history to express the complex engagements of society. Despite the ways in which categories such as "abstract

138

labor" and "the proletariat" have obscured intersecting relations of gender, sexuality, class, and race, historical materialism has traditionally demanded that the subjects of history be articulated in such a way that they illuminate the heterogeneous elements of social relations. Throughout this book, I have tried to show how this demand for historicity engages an analysis of the intersections of class, gender, sexuality, and race. Moreover, I have endeavored to show that the racialized regulations of gender and sexuality constitute political, economic, cultural, and epistemological formations. Contemporary social formations continue to be constituted through these regulations. These intersecting oppressions unfortunately cannot be addressed in the present iteration of postnationalist American studies. In its current form, postnationalist American studies obscures the ways in which state and capital have achieved and continue to achieve racial dominance through discourses of gender and sexual normativity. In doing so, it blinds itself to contemporary global social formations.

In the introduction to the anthology *Post-Nationalist American Studies,* the authors argue that "postnationalist" names the desire to contribute to a vision of American studies that is "less insular and parochial, and more internationalist and comparative." They write,

> Within the United States, moreover, it is important to distinguish between nationalisms which are aligned with the nation-state and those which challenge "official" nationalism. As George Lipsitz reminded us when he joined our seminar one week, despite their limitations, black and Chicano nationalisms, for instance, are not identical with or reducible to U.S. nationalism. In other words, we need to critique the limits and exclusions of nationalism without forgetting the differences between nationalisms or throwing all nationalisms into the trash of history.[1]

In its current iteration, postnationalist American studies attempts to conserve the revolutionary and cultural nationalist subjects of history. These subjects uphold history as the intertwining of racial, national, and class differences. As it arises out of cultural and revolutionary nationalisms, this version of history suppresses knowledge of the gender and sexual heterogeneity that composes social formations. Addressing this heterogeneity is especially crucial in this historic juncture. As contemporary globalization is in part the outcome of a convergence between national liberation movements and the normative components of liberal ideology, we must reconsider the appropriateness of basing postnationalist American studies on the subjects of those movements. Indeed, our current moment requires an analysis of social formations that can illuminate how the intersections of gender, class, and sexuality variegate racial and national formations within the current phase of capital.

Postnationalist American Studies and the Idealization of Cultural and Revolutionary Nationalisms

The preservation of cultural and revolutionary subjects through American studies warrants a consideration of the ideological premises of such a maneuver. In a chapter from *For Marx* entitled "Marxism and Humanism," Althusser takes up the ideological underpinnings of humanist theories of history and politics. He begins by positing two concepts—the idealism of the essence and the empiricism of the subject. Althusser states that the idealism of the essence posits "that there is a universal essence of man." Relatedly, this idealism suggests an empiricism—"that this essence is the attribute of 'each single individual' who is its real subject. Stating the relation between the two, Althusser writes, "an empiricism of the subject always corresponds to an idealism of the essence (or an empiricism of the essence to an idealism of the subject)."[2] Revolutionary nationalism and cultural nationalism have historically relied on and produced an idealism of the essence and an empiricism of the subject. With few exceptions, they have idealized heteropatriarchy as the essence of social relations and have presumed that heterosexual subjects and relations exist as absolute givens. Idealizing heteropatriarchy as the rational organization of society also meant defining antiracist agency through the recuperation of phallocentric loss. Again, women of color feminist formations emerged as an alternative to nationalist ideals and what they implied about social formations and agency. Like their African American counterparts, Chicana feminists, particularly Chicana lesbian feminists, challenged the idealization of heteropatriarchy within the Chicano movement, an idealism of heteropatriarchy and empiricism of heterosexual subjects that led Chicano nationalists to discipline Chicana feminists because of their gender and sexual estrangement from nationalist ideals.[3] In general, revolutionary and cultural nationalisms waxed empiricist as they measured the authenticity of subjects of color and defined the reality of minority cultures in terms of heteropatriarchy. This idealism and empiricism account for revolutionary and cultural nationalism's occlusion and suppression of gender, sexual, and political formations that contradicted the ideals of heteropatriarchy and shattered the image of minority cultures and communities that nationalist formations had constructed. Rescuing black and Chicano nationalisms implies certain ideals that embody black and Chicano nationalism. The preservation and cultivation of black and Chicano nationalism within American studies extends black and Chicano nationalism's idealism and empiricism. As cultural and revolutionary nationalist formations suppress the critical gender and sexual heterogeneity of minority communities, cultural and revolutionary nationalist formations conceal the very practices that constitute social formations. As postnationalist American studies works to preserve the revolutionary and cultural nationalist subjects, it promotes this idealism/ empiricism and authorizes their exclusions and regulations.

It is important to remember that the suppression of gender and sexual heterogeneity is part of historical materialism's legacy. As postnationalist American studies idealizes the revolutionary and cultural nationalist subjects, it accrues that legacy. We must also remember another aspect of historical materialism—its mission to explicate the complexity of social formations. To do so it demands that we rebel against its own normative legacy. The relations presumed by women of color feminism and queer of color critique provide the impetus for such a rebellion. Women of color feminists and queer of color critics historically have demanded that the social be reconceived in terms of the complex intersections of race, gender, sexuality, and class.

As they provide a critique of the idealism of the essence and the empiricism of the heteronormative subject, we may say that women of color feminism and queer of color critique provide the impetus for moving beyond the postulates of nationalist formations. A truly postnationalist American studies would be more appropriately based in these critical formations than in revolutionary and cultural nationalist ones. To do so, we must replace black and Chicano nationalism as the location of postnationalist American studies with new concepts. This move corresponds to what Althusser argues was Marx's replacement of bourgeois ideologies of man with concepts such as "forces of production" and "relations of production"—concepts that address the different levels of practice. For a newly invented postnationalist American studies, these concepts are ones that can address the intersections of race, gender, and sexuality as discursive and social formations within a given mode of production. As Marx broke with theories of history and politics based on the essence of man, we must break with theories of history and politics based on gender and sexual normativity. If we are to understand the normative and nonnormative formations that constitute our contemporary global moment, we must indeed discard the myth of nationalism's coherence and viability for understanding agency, culture, and subjectivity. As the character Woodridge in chapter 2 made clear in his critique of the college, everything depends on our knowledge of nationalist formations as ideologies and discourses premised on regulation and discipline. Ours is a moment in which the negation of normativity and nationalism is the condition for critical knowledge, and theorizations of postnationalist American studies must begin here.

Replacing humanism with new concepts, according to Althusser, was

Marx's attempt to designate society as the subject of history. For postnationalist American studies the subject of history must be society as well, but not "society" emptied of the racialized and classed particularities of gender and sexuality, but framed in terms of them. It must presume society as the culmination of the intersections of gender, sexuality, race, and class as its subject. This notion of society must also presume the production and disruption of normativity. These are the subjects suggested through women of color and queer of color analyses. These subjects present history as the intersections of race, nation, class, *and* gender and sexuality.

Black queer male formations during the 1980s and 1990s implied such an understanding of history and society, one that upheld the intersections of race, gender, sexuality, and class as an extension of the epistemic maneuvers of black feminist formations. In doing so, black queer men aligned themselves with the critical practices of women of color feminism and positioned themselves against the normative itineraries of cultural and revolutionary nationalisms. As Essex Hemphill writes,

> Perhaps the second Renaissance in African American literature occurred when black women claimed their own voices from the post-sixties, male-dominated realm of the "black experience," a realm that at times resembled a boxing ring restricting black women to the roles of mere spectators. What black women, especially out black lesbians, bravely did was break the silence surrounding their experiences. No longer would black men, the sole interpreters of race and culture, presume to speak for (or ignore) women's experiences. Black women opened up new dialogues and explored uncharted territories surrounding race, sexuality, gender relations, family, history, and eroticism. In the process, they angered some black male writers who felt they were being culturally castrated and usurped, but out of necessity, black women realized they would have to speak for themselves—and do so honestly. As a result of their courage, black women also inspired many of the black gay men writing today to seek our own voices so we can tell our truths. Thus, we are at the beginning of completing a total picture of the African American experience.[4]

Hemphill addresses the ways in which the category the "black experience" testified to an idealism and empiricism of an essence that disciplined black women and black queer men. In general, black queer male critical formations in the 1990s represented an attempt to outline the complexities of social practice within African American communities, doing so against cultural and revolutionary nationalist attempts at concealment. As Hemphill implies, heteropatriarchal interpellation of black nationalist formations prevented them from theorizing the diversity of interactions that composed black cultures. As a result, the gender and sexual regulations that descended on women and queers of color compelled critical interventions that would illuminate a more "total picture." This attempt to illustrate the heterogeneous elements of African American culture coheres directly with the aim of historical materialism. As liberal ideological formations compelled historical materialism to theorize the materiality of labor relations, the normative regulations of revolutionary and cultural nationalisms compelled queer of color critics to investigate the gendered and sexual specificity of racial formations.

A postnationalist American studies informed by women of color and queer of color social formations does not at all mean the idealization of the woman of color and queer of color subject. According to Althusser, bourgeois humanism begins with abstract man and therefore postulates humanist concepts such as freedom, dignity, rights—all the while obscuring the material conditions that contradict those postulates. Althusser argues that as Marx turned to "real man," Marx turned to society. The category "real man" then became the impetus for historical materialism's investigation of social formations. Althusser goes on to argue that substituting abstract man with real man results in the eventual dismissal of the category "man" entirely. He writes,

> [O]nce the scientific analysis of this real object has been undertaken, we discover that a knowledge of concrete (real) men, that is, a knowledge of the ensemble of the social relations is only possible on condition that we do completely without the theoretical services of the concept of man (in the sense in which it existed in its theoretical claims even before the displacement).[5]

This is in many ways analogous to the theoretical maneuvers of a postnationalist American studies reformulated according to the adjoining insights of women of color feminism and queer of color critique. As postnationalist American studies designates women of color and queers of color as the subjects of critique, it turns toward the intersections of gender, sexuality, race, and labor as the components of social relations. To designate them as the subjects of knowledge is also to dismiss the theoretical services of identity politics. Instead of identity driving critical interventions, the heterogeneous formations that make up the social drive critical interventions. Making the queer of color and the woman of color subjects the basis of critical inquiry means that we must imbue them with gestural rather than emulative functions. As subjects of knowledge, they point away from themselves and to the racialized, gendered, classed, and eroticized heterogeneity of the social, summoning critical practices appropriate for that heterogeneity.

Racialized Normative and Nonnormative Formations: New Subjects for Postnationalist American Studies

Marx's move toward "society" and away from "man" expresses another theoretical imperative of historical materialism: Our theoretical knowledge should be appropriate for the historic juncture that we engage. In this sense, we need to rejuvenate our understanding of intersectional analysis to address a moment in which capital must negotiate with differences of race and class as well as gender and sexuality to achieve itself. This is not a moment that can be understood through critiques that excise gender and sexuality from their theoretical armature. Ignoring differences of gender and sexuality prevents us from seeing how they are constitutive of normative processes that themselves are constitutive of contemporary globalization. More specifically, we need an analysis that can chart how the normative compromises of national liberation helped produce the normative itineraries of advanced capitalist and postcolonial sites.

To begin with, the failures of national liberation mark advanced capitalist and postcolonial formations. To restate the preceding chapter's argument, this failure has everything to do with how national liberation invested in heteropatriarchal ideals. These investments have produced present-day conditions in which advanced capitalist and postcolonial formations intersect through heteronormative regulation—that is, through the creation of a sometimes indigenous, sometimes diasporic, but usually regulatory middle class. In Trinidad, Tobago, and the Bahamas, anticolonial movements gave birth to postcolonial regimes in the Caribbean. These were state regimes managed by a middle class made up of former anticolonial elites. Those elites administered the transition from primarily agrarian economies to ones based on the growth of a service sector that relegates poor and working-class people to jobs as "housekeepers, cooks, maids, cleaners, and laundresses."[6] As M. Jacqui Alexander notes, postcolonial middle classes in these countries have based their managerial legitimacy on their ability to deliver indigenous economies and labor over to the needs of multinational corporations. That legitimacy cannot be separated from the needs of elites to construct themselves as ideally heterosexual and patriarchal, and therefore fit for governance. Constructing themselves as such has led to the criminalization of lesbians, prostitutes, and any others who deviate from heteropatriarchal ideals.[7] Indeed, we may think of managerial classes as the recipients of the normative genealogies of the liberal and revolutionary nationalist formations discussed in the introduction.

In the United States the transition from an industrial economy to a postindustrial economy has become the contemporary terrain on which struggles over race, sexuality, gender, and nationality are waged. Deindustrialization and postindustrialization in the United States, for instance, have led to a decline in manufacturing jobs and an increase in low-skilled positions in the service sector, processes that have spurred the proletarianization of African American labor. That decline and growth is also part of an increase in private sector and government jobs, which, conversely, promoted the development of elite formations among African Americans. As Cathy Cohen notes, "[W]hile significant numbers of African Americans found the economic restructuring of the 1970s devastating to themselves and their neighborhoods, the expansion of skilled employment allowed for the evolution of what has been called the 'new Black middle class.'"[8] As Cohen goes on to state, the new black middle class based its legitimacy on its ideological and often administrative role as the overseer of queer, poor, HIV-positive, and drug-addicted persons in black communities, becoming the normative antithesis to deviant African American subjects. The creation of the public sector within the Reagan administration situated the black middle class as the regulator of African American nonheteronormativity. By 1970, government employed 57 percent of college-educated black males and 76 percent of college-educated black females. The expansion of elite service jobs produced class privilege as the determinant of African American gender and sexual normativity.

The emergence of postindustrialization within the United States also shaped the needs of immigration policy and provided yet another context for struggles over queerness, race, and normativity. Post-1965 immigration legislation sought immigrant labor whose skills were often developed under postcolonial regimes.[9] In the context of South Asia, for instance, these policies helped to create a South Asian diaspora differentiated in terms of gender, ethnicity, religion, and national origin, as well as sexuality. The global migration of South Asians has made diaspora one location in which race, queerness, and national belonging are struggled over. Indeed, sexuality within this South Asian diaspora has become a site for contesting national belonging and diasporic identity. In her article, "Nostalgia, Desire, and Diaspora," Gayatri Gopinath discusses the confrontation between queer Indians and Indian nationalists over participation in the India Day Parade. That confrontation was waged between the Federation of Indian Assocations (FIA) (a group made up of Indian businessmen), the South Asian Lesbian and Gay Association (SALGA), and SAKHI for South Asian women (an anti–domestic violence women's group). In 1995, the FIA denied SALGA and SAKHI the right to march on the grounds that the groups were "antinational" and contradicted the idea that India is "Hindu, patriarchal, middle-class, and free of homosexuals."[10]

The contemporary moment is one in which the regulation and transgression of gender and sexuality are the twin expressions of racial formation.

Understanding investments in gender and sexual regulation to be the linch-pin between state, cultural, and revolutionary nationalisms means that we must simultaneously critique state formation and minority nationalism. State nationalism relegates particularities of race, gender, class, and sexuality to the private sphere and through this relegation is able to constitute itself as the terrain of universality. While cultural and revolutionary nationalisms have historically critiqued the state's relegation of race to the terrain of the private, calling attention to the state's illusory universality by exposing its surrepti-tious reliance upon racial difference, cultural and revolutionary nationalisms have colluded with the state by investing in gender and sexual normativity.

As canonical sociology helped to narrate migration and the expansion of commerce in earlier parts of the twentieth century, canonical sociology re-mains significant in this phase of globalization. For instance, we may locate William Julius Wilson's landmark 1987 text *The Truly Disadvantaged: The Inner City, the Underclass, and Public Policy* within the discursive and ideo-logical maneuvers of this historic juncture.[11] *The Truly Disadvantaged* chal-lenged a conservative thesis most powerfully posited by Charles Murray in *Losing Ground: American Social Policy, 1950–1980*. Arising out of the rac-ist discourse of the welfare queen, *Losing Ground* argues that Aid to Fami-lies with Dependent Children (AFDC) benefits appealed financially to poor and working-class women, encouraging them to forgo marriage and head households themselves instead of relying on men. *The Truly Disadvantaged* offered a critique of this argument, debunking the presumption that welfare benefits promote female-headed households. Its challenge to a conservative discourse notwithstanding, *The Truly Disadvantaged* actually abetted that discourse by presenting heteropatriarchy as the remedy to poverty. The text did so through its argument about the role of joblessness and female-headed households. According to Wilson, available evidence "suggests that the in-creasing rate of joblessness among black men merits serious consideration as a major underlying factor in the rise of black single mothers and female-headed households" (83). He continues,

> [W]e argue that both the delay in marriage and the lower rate of remar-riage, each of which is associated with high percentages of out-of-wedlock births and female-headed households, can be directly tied to the labor-market status of black males. As we have documented, black women, especially young black women, are facing a shrinking pool of "marriage-able" (i.e., economically stable) men. (91)

In making the problem the joblessness of black men and therefore their ineligibility for marriage, any recommendation for correcting joblessness au-tomatically becomes an attempt to recuperate heteropatriarchy and implic-itly demands the gendered and sexual regulation of the nonheteronormative racial difference of African American lower-class women. For instance, the text argues, "[T]he problem of joblessness should be a top-priority item in any public policy discussion focusing on enhancing the status of families" (105). Despite the text's caveats about the need to create opportunities for both sexes, reading joblessness as a sign of black men's deficiency as hetero-normative agents means that providing jobs works toward the ultimate aim of reconstituting the universality of heteropatriarchy.

Far from being a conservative response, the thesis of Wilson's text, as it universalizes heteropatriarchy, arises out of and continues the normative genealogy of leftist critique. Moreover, in a historic moment in which mi-nority middle classes ascend to power through appeals to normativity and thus become the regulators of working-class racial, gender, and sexual dif-ferences, Wilson's argument actually is the ideological and discursive patron of contemporary globalization. For instance, Wilson is careful to establish that female-headed households are only a sign of dependence in the case of African Americans. As Wilson states,

> Although marital dissolution means a substantial loss of income, and sometimes severe economic hardship—median income of white female-headed families in 1979 was $11,452, compared to $21,824 for white married-couple families—most white women can maintain their families above poverty with a combination of earnings and income from other sources such as alimony, child support, public-income transfers, personal wealth, and assistance from families. In 1982, 70 percent of white female-headed families were living above the poverty line. In addition, many white single mothers remarry. (77)

For Wilson, white female-headed households signify agency, as those families are the outcome of "economic independence" rather than "dependence." White women's class privilege normalizes them as single mothers, while the class difference of black inner-city single mothers denormalizes their gender and sexual particularity. As the text implies, white women's detachment from a male head does not disrupt or compromise their status as liberal subjects but confirms it. Put simply, white women can inhabit the position of the liberal subject because of their economic independence. As the state universalizes the marriage form, *The Truly Disadvantaged* upholds that form by granting white women a privilege previously associated with men, the privileged to be unattached. On the other hand, the text denies black women this privilege and any proximity to the liberal subject. As the text is ironi-cally focused on black male joblessness in an investigation of black women's poverty, it is ultimately concerned with constituting black men as appropri-ate liberal subjects, portraying no such concern for black women. In fact, the text implies that black women function to consummate black men as liberal subjects, arguing for the universalization of black men through access to black women's bodies. Given a historical context in which middle classes are positioned as the regulators of the intertwining gender, sexual, and racial differences of lower classes, Wilson's argument implies not only a difference between black lower-class women and white middle-class women, but suggests an equivalence between white and black middle-class subjects. It is important to recognize that this equivalence is brokered against the nonheteronormative difference of African American working-class subjects, particularly women. An equivalence between white and black middle classes implies that both can claim, to varying degrees, normative privilege against the denigrated status of black poor women, in particular.

In a context such as this, middle-class status fortifies normative privilege for African Americans who can claim it, ostensibly purifying racial difference of its nonheteronormative hues, casting nonnormative racial difference as a gendered and eroticized phenomenon specific to black poor and working classes. As I argued in chapter 4, national liberation's bid for normativity coupled with the upward and downward expansion of social structures has produced crossracial alliances over middle-class access to normative privileges. As contemporary globalization polarized minority communities economically, it produced the social conditions whereby class differences could help establish the normative status of racial subjects.

Within this historic moment characterized by the normalization of racialized class formations, we need modes of analysis that can address normativity as an object of inquiry and critique. Cultural and revolutionary nationalism are fundamentally incapable of posing such an inquiry as they arise out of a genealogy of normativity. Cultural and revolutionary nationalisms have no mind for gender and sexual normativity. But if it is to study society in its fullest complexity, postnationalist American studies must mind this very phenomenon. We need a postnationalist American studies that can address the complex formations obtained in this moment of globalization, formations whose racial, gender, sexual, and class differences obtain their distinctions through engagements with normativity. In the preface of this book I asked where the familiar faces of black queer subjects were in the picture of my hometown. It is worth asking where the faces of queer of color subjects are within postnationalist American studies. Where, for instance, is the transgendered man who wore Levi's held up by suspenders, or the sissy who played for us on Sunday mornings? It is not enough to merely recognize their existence. In this moment of transgressions and regulations, we must approach these subjects as sites of knowledge.

Notes

Preface

1. The web address for the site is http://lcweb2.loc.gov/ammem/aaohtml/exhibit/ aointro.html.

Introduction

1. Queer of color analysis, as I define it in this text, interrogates social formations as the intersections of race, gender, sexuality, and class, with particular interest in how those formations correspond with and diverge from nationalist ideals and practices. Queer of color analysis is a heterogeneous enterprise made up of women of color feminism, materialist analysis, poststructuralist theory, and queer critique.

2. Chandan Reddy, "Home, Houses, Nonidentity: 'Paris Is Burning,'" in *Burning Down the House: Recycling Domesticity,* ed. Rosemary Marangoly George (Boulder: Westview Press, 1997), 356–57.

3. Ibid., 357.

4. José Esteban Muñoz, *Disidentifications: Queers of Color and the Performance of Politics* (Minneapolis: University of Minnesota Press, 1999), 25.

5. Louis Althusser argues, "Historical materialism is the science of social formations." See *For Marx,* trans. Ben Brewster (London and New York: Verso, 1993), 251.

6. Muñoz, *Disidentifications,* 5.

7. Louis Althusser and Étienne Balibar, *Reading Capital,* trans. Ben Brewster (London: Verso, 1979), 88.

8. Raymond Williams, *Marxism and Literature* (Oxford: Oxford University Press, 1977), 18.

9. Karl Marx and Frederick Engels, *The German Ideology,* trans. Dirk J. Struik (New York: International Publishers, 1974), 43–44. Emphasis mine.

10. David Theo Goldberg. *Racist Culture: Philosophy and the Politics of Meaning* (London: Blackwell, 1993), 63.

11. Karl Marx, *Pre-Capitalist Economic Formations,* trans. Jack Cohen (New York: International Publishers, 1964).

12. Ibid., 49.

13. Karl Marx, *Economic and Philosophic Manuscripts of 1844,* ed. Dirk J. Struik, trans. Martin Milligan (New York: International Publishers, 1964), 134.

14. Ibid., 121.

15. The modern conception of subjectivity and agency (liberal and revolutionary) are thoroughly normalized. David Theo Goldberg, for example, makes the following

argument: "Moral notions tend to be basic to each sociodiscursive order, for they are key in defining the interactive ways social subjects see others and conceive (of) themselves. Social relations are constitutive of personal and social identity, and a central part of the order of such relations is the perceived need, the requirement for subjects to give an account of their actions. These acounts may assume the bare form of explanation, but they usually tend more imperatively to legitimate or to justify acts (to ourselves and others). Morality is the scene of this legitimation and justification" (*Racist Culture*, 14).

Indeed the modern conception of agency has historically and consequentially understood formations that fall out of the normative boundaries of morality as incapable of agency and therefore worthy of exclusion and regulation. One of the principal tasks of antiracist queer critique must be to account for those formations expelled from normative calculations of agency and subjectivity. Accounting for those formations means that we must ask what modes of engagement and awareness they enact, modes that normative conceptions of agency and subjectivity can never acknowledge or apprehend.

16. Marx, *Economic and Philosophic Manuscripts of 1844*, 133.

17. Ibid., 114.

18. Karl Marx, *Capital*, vol. 1, *A Critique of Political Economy*, trans. Ben Fowkes (London: Penguin Classics, 1990), 482.

19. Thomas Laquer, "Sexual Desire and the Market Economy during the Industrial Revolution," in *Discourses of Sexuality: From Aristotle to AIDS*, ed. Donna Stanton (Ann Arbor: University of Michigan Press, 1992), 185–215.

20. Ibid., 208.

21. Ibid.

22. Ibid., 189, quoting Flora Tristan, *London Journal*, trans. Denis Palmer and Giselle Pincetl (1840; reprint, London: George Prior, 1980), 79.

23. Ibid., 208.

24. Ibid., 190, quoting Frederick Engels, *The Condition of the Working Class in England: Karl Marx and Frederick Engels on Britain* (Moscow: Foreign Languages Publishing House, 1962), 61.

25. Anne McClintock, "Screwing the System: Sexwork, Race, and the Law," *Boundary 2* 19, no. 2 (1992): 80–82.

26. Evelyn Brooks Hammonds, "Toward a Genealogy of Black Female Sexuality: The Problematic of Silence," in *Feminist Genealogies, Colonial Legacies, Democratic Futures*, ed. M. Jacqui Alexander and Chandra Talpade Mohanty (New York and London: Routledge, 1997), 172.

27. Laquer, "Sexual Desire and the Market Economy," 210–11.

28. Karl Marx, "On the Jewish Question," in *The Marx-Engels Reader*, ed. Robert C. Tucker (New York: W. W. Norton and Company, 1978), 33.

29. Lisa Lowe, *Immigrant Acts: On Asian American Cultural Politics* (Durham: Duke University Press, 1996), 25.

30. Michel Foucault, *The History of Sexuality*, vol. 1, *An Introduction*, trans. Robert Hurley (New York: Vintage Books, 1990), 37.

31. Marx, *Capital*, 763.

32. Marx, "On the Jewish Question," 34.

33. George Sanchez, "Go after the Women," in *Unequal Sisters: A Multicultural Reader in U.S. Women's History,* ed. Vicki L. Ruiz and Ellen Carol Du Bois (New York: Routledge, 1994), 285.

34. Ibid, 291–92. Gloria Anzaldúa writes that the borderland is the place for the "squint-eyed, the perverse, the queer, the troublesome, the mongrel, the mulatto, the half-breed, the half dead; in short, those who cross over, pass over, or go through the confines of the "normal" (*Borderlands: The New Mestiza-La Frontera* [San Francisco: Aunt Lute Books, 1999], 25).

35. See Nayan Shah, "Perversity, Contamination, and the Dangers of Queer Domesticity," in *Contagious Divides: Epidemics and Race in San Francisco's Chinatown* (Berkeley and Los Angeles: University of California Press, 2001).

36. Kevin Mumford, *Interzones: Black/White Sex Districts in Chicago and New York in the Early Twentieth Century* (New York: Columbia University Press, 1997), xviii.

37. Sanchez, "Go after the Women," 289.

38. Marx, *Capital,* 782.

39. Ibid., 784.

40. By arguing that capital produces gender and sexual heterogeneities as part of its racialized contradiction, I wish neither to privilege a discourse of repression, nor to assume a corollary formulation—that capital is the site of equivalences or uniformities. Indeed, this material and discursive production of surplus is the racialized production of nonheteronormative—and therefore racially differentiated and nonequivalent—sexualities.

41. Lowe, *Immigrant Acts,* 23.

42. Marx, *Capital,* 795–96.

43. Althusser defines contradiction as "the articulation of a practice . . . into the complex whole of the social formation" (*For Marx,* 250). Althusser goes on to state that the accumulation of contradictions may produce the "weakest link" in a system: "If this contradiction is to become 'active' in the strongest sense, to become a ruptural principle, there must be an accumulation of 'circumstances' and 'currents' so that whatever their origin and sense . . . they 'fuse into a ruptural unity'" (*For Marx,* 99).

44. For the theory of overdetermination, see ibid.

45. I thank Grace Hong for making this implication clear to me. Robert Park cites Marx as the theorist who inspired an engagement with social transformation. As Park states in "Race Ideologies," "What students of society and politics know about ideologies and about revolutions seems to have its source, for the most part, in the literature inspired by Karl Marx and by the writers who inherited the Marxian tradition." Robert Ezra Park, *Race and Culture: Essays in the Sociology of Contemporary Man* (New York: Free Press, 1950), 303.

46. Anthony Giddens, *Modernity and Self-Identity: Self and Society in the Late Modern Age* (Stanford: Stanford University Press, 1991), 2.

47. Craig Calhoun, *Critical Social Theory: Culture, History, and the Challenge of Difference* (Oxford: Blackwell, 1995), 43.

48. Goldberg, *Racist Culture,* 150.

49. Giddens, *Modernity and Self-Identity*, 14.

50. Thomas Pettigrew, *The Sociology of Race Relations: Reflection and Reform* (New York: The Free Press, 1980), xxi.

51. James McKee, *Sociology and the Race Problem: The Failure of a Perspective* (Urbana and Chicago: University of Illinois Press, 1993), 128.

52. Kobena Mercer, *Welcome to the Jungle: New Positions in Black Cultural Studies* (New York: Routledge, 1994), 150–51.

53. As Rose M. Brewer argues in "Black Women in Poverty: Some Comments on Female-Headed Families," "Most analyses of the underlying causes have been filled with normative assumptions about what is proper and improper familial behavior, and, consequently, social scientists often have labeled the family formation practices of the black population 'inappropriate'" (*Signs: Journal of Women in Culture and Society* 13 [1988]: 331). See also Angela Davis and Fania Davis, "The Black Family and the Crisis of Capitalism," *Black Scholar* 17, no. 5 (September/October 1986): 33–40. The work of black queer intellectuals extends this discussion to show how the labeling of black familial forms as inappropriate denies families formed out of same-sex unions any positive regard, labeling them "immoral" and "threatening." See especially Cheryl Clarke's "The Failure to Transform: Homophobia in the Black Community," in *Home Girls: A Black Feminist Anthology*, ed. Barbara Smith (New York: Kitchen Table-Women of Color Press, 1983). See also Isaac Julian and Kobena Mercer's "True Confessions: A Discourse on Images of Black Male Sexuality," in *Brother to Brother: New Writings by Black Gay Men*, ed. Essex Hemphill (Boston: Alyson Publications, 1991).

54. For a discussion of the family's place within liberal ideology, see Wendy Brown, "Liberalism's Family Values," in *States of Injury: Power and Freedom in Late Modernity* (Princeton: Princeton University Press, 1995), 135–65.

55. As Sheila Rowbotham noted, "The family under capitalism carries an intolerable weight: all the rags and bones and bits of old iron the capitalist commodity system can't use. Within the family women are carrying the preposterous contradiction of love in a loveless world. They are providing capitalism with the human relations it cannot maintain" (*Woman's Consciousness, Man's World* [Harmondsworth, Middlesex: Penguin, 1973], 77), quoted in Brown, "Liberalism's Family Values," 151.

56. David L Eng and Alice Y. Hom, eds., *Q & A: Queer in Asian America* (Philadelphia: Temple University Press, 1998), 5.

57. I thank Judith Halberstam for helping me arrive at this argument.

58. Foucault, *The History of Sexuality*, 5.

59. Steinberg, *Turning Back*, 26–29.

60. Lisa Lowe and David Lloyd, eds., *The Politics of Culture in the Shadow of Capital* (Durham: Duke University Press, 1997), 1.

61. Henry Louis Gates, Jr., *Figures in Black: Words, Signs, and the "Racial" Self* (Oxford: Oxford University Press, 1987), xxiv.

62. Morroe Berger, ed. and trans., *Madame De Staël: On Politics, Literature, and National Character* (Garden City, N.Y.: Doubleday and Company, Inc., 1964), 142–45.

63. Goldberg, *Racist Culture*, 30.

64. Alexis de Tocqueville, *Democracy in America*, trans. George Lawrence (Garden City, N.Y.: Doubleday, 1966), 11.

65. My distinction between the "rational citizen" and the "irrational other" is analogous to Immanuel Wallerstein's use of the "citizen" and the "barbarian" in "The Insurmountable Contradictions of Liberalism: Human Rights and the Rights of Peoples in the Geocultures of the Modern World-System" (*The South Atlantic Quarterly* 94, no. 4 [fall 1995]: 1161–78).

66. Gates, *Figures in Black*, 8.

67. My use of "ambivalence" is borrowed from Zygmunt Bauman, who in his chapter "Philosophy and Sociology" argues that establishing discursive authority means making the boundary of the "organic structure" sharp and clearly marked, which means "excluding the middle," suppressing or exterminating everything ambiguous, everything that sits astride the barricade and thus compromises the vital distinction between *inside* and *outside*. Building and keeping order means making friends and fighting enemies. First and foremost, however, it means purging ambivalence (Bauman, *Intimations of Postmodernity* [London: Routledge, 1992], 120).

68. See Avery Gordon, *Ghostly Matters: Haunting and the Sociological Imagination* (Minneapolis: University of Minnesota Press, 1997), and Pettigrew, *The Sociology of Race Relations*.

69. See "Angela Davis: Reflections on Race, Class, and Gender in the U.S.A.," in Lowe and Lloyd, *The Politics of Culture*.

1. The Knee-pants of Servility

1. Robert E. Park, *Race and Culture: Essays in the Sociology of Contemporary Man* (London: The Free Press of Glencoe, 1950), 138–51.

2. Ibid., 36–51.

3. Stow Persons, *Ethnic Studies at Chicago: 1905–1945* (Urbana and Chicago: University of Illinois Press, 1987), 68.

4. Ibid., 63.

5. Ibid.

6. Robert E. Park, "Human Migration and the Marginal Man," in *Race and Culture*, 354.

7. James Barrett and David Roediger, "Inbetween Peoples: Race, Nationality, and the 'New Immigrant' Working Class," in *Journal of American Ethnic History* (spring 1997): 11.

8. Ibid., 8.

9. Ibid., 12.

10. Ibid., 14.

11. Ibid.

12. Lowe, *Immigrant Acts*, 13–14.

13. During the eras of Prohibition and vice reform, prostitution and alcohol consumption were thought to be in tandem with each other. The association was made, in large part, because the saloon was the location for the purchase of both alcohol

and sex. After Prohibition, the saloon was supplanted by the modern speakeasy and black and tan, both of which offered sexual release for their patrons. As Kevin Mumford argues, "[P]rohibitionism . . . stemmed from deeper anxieties toward the changing gender norms of sexual propriety and gender comportment" (*Interzones*, 158–59). As Antonio Gramsci observes, there is also a symbolic instrumental relation between alcoholism and sexuality: "The sexual question is again connected with that of alcohol. Abuse and irregularity of sexual functions is, after alcoholism, the most dangerous enemy of nervous energies, and it is commonly observed that 'obsessional' work provokes alcoholic and sexual deprivation" (*Selections from the Prison Notebooks* [New York International Publishers, 1971], 304).

14. Robert Park, Ernest W. Burgess, and Roderick D. McKenzie, *The City* (Chicago and London: University of Chicago Press, 1925), 106–7.

15. Ibid.

16. Ibid., 109.

17. William I. Thomas and Florian Znaniecki, *The Polish Peasant in Europe and America* (Urbana and Chicago: University of Illinois, 1984), 280.

18. Park, Burgess, and McKenzie, *The City*, 44.

19. Gwendolyn Mink, *The Wages of Motherhood: Inequality in the Welfare State, 1917–1942* (Ithaca and London: Cornell Univesity Press, 1995), 123–50.

20. Ibid.

21. Ibid., 140.

22. Ibid., 146.

23. Karl Marx, *Economic and Philosophic Manuscripts of 1844*, 125.

24. Mink, *The Wages of Motherhood*, 143.

25. Mumford, *Interzones*, 11.

26. Ibid, 17.

27. My use of "polymorphous perversions" diverges from Foucault inasmuch as I am interested in how the perverse is a racialized and gendered category that emerges out of economic change.

28. See Mumford, *Interzones*, 38–40.

29. Conrad Bentzen, "Notes on the Homosexual in Chicago," 14 March 1938. Ernest Burgess Collection, box 145, folder 10.

30. Ironically enough, in Park's mind, the mulatto was the "marginal man," the personality who epitomized the cultural hybridity engendered by migration as well as the regulatory ideals of heteronormativity. Existing between two cultures and objectively observing them both, the marginal man was the "citizen of the world," the "city man," and the "cosmopolite." In Park's words they were "the cultural advanced guard and the leaders of the Negro people" (381). Sociologists like Park believed that the supposed racial and cultural superiority of the mulatto was maintained through "social and sexual selection" (385). Indeed, to the extent that sociologists argued that the mulatto vanguard depended on the "addition of the best blood," they conceived of the mulatto as an idealization of heterosexual and patriarchal norms within an industrializing United States. In a moment in which industrialization was precipitating an upheaval in racially defined sexual mores, the mulatto aristocracy was defined as

upholders of the regulatory regimes of the heteropatriarchal household. As such, the mulatto was proximate to the racialized heteronormativity of whiteness and distant from the nonheteronormative presumptions about African American sexuality.

31. Park, Burgess, and McKenzie, *The City,* 43.

32. Allan H. Spear, *Black Chicago: The Making of a Negro Ghetto, 1890–1920* (Chicago and London: University of Chicago Press, 1967), 24–25.

33. Bentzen, "Notes on the Homosexual in Chicago."

34. Ibid., italics mine.

35. Park, Burgess, and McKenzie, *The City,* 32.

36. Mumford, *Interzones,* 112.

37. Cedric Robinson, *Black Marxism: The Making of the Black Radical Tradition* (Chapel Hill and London: University of North Carolina, 1983), 289.

38. Richard Wright, "I Tried to Be a Communist," in *The God That Failed,* ed. Richard Crossman (New York, 1949), 116, quoted in Russell C. Brignano, *Richard Wright: An Introduction to the Man and His Works* (Pittsburgh: University of Pittsburgh, 1970), 52.

39. Michel Fabre, *The Unfinished Quest of Richard Wright,* trans. Isabel Barzun (Urbana and Chicago: University of Illinois, 1993), 13–14.

40. Abdul JanMohamed, "Sexuality on/of the Racial Border: Foucault, Wright, and the Articulation of 'Racialized Sexuality,'" in *Discourses of Sexuality: From Aristotle to AIDS,* ed. Donna Stanton (Ann Arbor: University of Michigan Press, 1992), 107.

41. Richard Wright, introduction to St. Clair Drake and Horace Cayton, *Black Metropolis: A Study of Negro Life in a Northern City* (New York: Harcourt, Brace, and World, 1945), xviii.

42. Bernard Bell, *The Afro-American Novel and Its Tradition* (Amherst: University of Massachusetts Press, 1987), 151.

43. Fabre, *The Unfinished Quest of Richard Wright,* 142.

44. Richard Wright, "Blueprint for Negro Writing," in *Within the Circle: An Anthology of African-American Literary Criticism from the Harlem Renaissance to the Present,* ed. Angelyn Mitchell (Durham and London: Duke University Press, 1994), 97; italics mine.

45. Paula Rabinowitz, "Margaret Bourke-White's Red Coat; or, Slumming in the Thirties," in *Radical Revisions: Rereading 1930s Culture,* ed. Bill Mullen and Sherry Linkon (Urbana and Chicago: University of Illinois Press, 1996), 196.

46. Wright, "Blueprint for Negro Writing," 102.

47. Ibid., 100.

48. Richard Wright, *Black Boy: A Record of Childhood and Youth* (New York and London: Harper and Brothers, 1945), 14.

49. Richard Wright, *Native Son* (New York: Perennial Classics, 1991), 437.

50. JanMohamed, "Sexuality on/of the Racial Border," 108.

51. Drake and Cayton, *Black Metropolis,* 589.

52. Saunders Redding argues that Wright's characters are taught the meaning of the better life "from the movies, the picture magazines, and the screaming headlines in the daily press." See "The Alien Land of Richard Wright," in *Soon One Morning:*

New Writing by American Negroes, 1940–1962, ed. Herbert Hill (New York: Alfred A. Knopf, 1969), 54.

53. See Lizabeth Cohen's *Making a New Deal: Industrial Workers in Chicago, 1919–1935* (Cambridge: Cambridge University Press, 1990).

54. Park, McKenzie, and Burgess, *The City,* 108.

55. Kenneth Kinnamon, "How *Native Son* Was Born," in *Richard Wright, Critical Perspectives Past and Present,* eds. K. Anthony Appiah and Henry Louis Gates (New York: Amistad, 1993), 119. See also Wright, *Native Son,* 30.

56. I thank Richard Morrison for pointing this out to me. Wright, *Native Son,* 30.

57. Walter Reckless, *Vice in Chicago* (Montclair: Patterson Smith, 1969), 222.

58. Park, McKenzie, and Burgess, *The City,* 108.

59. Ibid., 107–8.

60. By "friend," Mary means communist or the "friend of the Negro." Wright, *Native Son,* 64.

61. Kinnamon, "How *Native Son* Was Born," 120.

62. Wright, *Native Son,* 11–12; italics mine.

63. JanMohamed, "Sexuality on/of the Racial Border," 107.

64. Wright, *Native Son,* 8.

65. Ibid., 105–7.

66. JanMohamed, "Sexuality on/of the Racial Border," 108. For a discussion of Bessie's place and the construction of black women in the novel, see Barbara E. Johnson, "The Re(a)d and the Black," in *Reading Black, Reading Feminist: A Critical Anthology,* ed. Henry Louis Gates Jr. (New York: Meridian Press, 1990), 145–54.

67. Wright, *Native Son,* xxiv.

68. Wright, *Blueprint for Negro Writing,* 101.

69. Ibid., 100.

70. In this regard, I agree with Sherley Anne Williams. She writes, "With the publication of *Native Son* in 1940, Richard Wright turned the impulse to protest in another direction. Rather than showing whites and Blacks what could happen with the help of a strong Black leader, he begins the trend in Black literature whose chief characteristic is its fierce indictment of American society because of the society's brutalizing effect on Black people. Wright and his followers and imitators 'protested,' as did many other Black writers, against a coercive and racist environment. . . . It may seem surprising that Bigger Thomas is not included in the list of rebel heroes, for (Edward) Margolies credits Bigger with being a 'metaphysical revolutionary,' (Eldridge) Cleaver calls him 'a Black rebel of the ghetto' and his creator speaks often of Bigger's 'revolt.' Bigger is an aborted hustler, a boy too out of touch with himself to understand the yearnings of his own heart, too alienated from his people and their past to find a way of bridging the gap between the rural, religion-haunted South of his family and the seemingly traditionless North" (*Give Birth to Brightness: A Thematic Study in Black Literature* [New York: The Dial Press, 1972], 74–75).

71. I do not evoke the word "read" in the generic sense of "get the meaning of," but in the vernacular sense evoked by black drag culture. The late black drag queen Dorian Corey defines this sense of read as "Reading is the real art form of insult. . . .

You get in a smart crack and everyone laughs because you found a flaw, then you've got a good read going" (Jennie Livingston, *Paris Is Burning* [New York: Fox Lorber Home Video, 1992]). In this sense, nonheteronormative subjects read normative formations to expose their flaws and to illustrate the absurdities that normative ideals mistake as truth and profundity.

2. The Specter of Woodridge

1. Farah Jasmine Griffin, *Who Set You Flowin: The African American Migration Narrative* (New York: Oxford University Press, 1995), 3–4.

2. See Ellison's "Strange Words for a Startling Occasion," in *Shadow and Act* (New York: Vintage, 1964).

3. Ellison, *Shadow and Act,* xx.

4. For more on Ellison's relationship to sociology, see his review of Myrdal's *An American Dilemma,* entitled *"An American Dilemma:* A Review," in *Shadow and Act.*

5. Persons, *Ethnic Studies at Chicago,* 60.

6. Stanford Lyman, *Militarism, Imperialism, and Racial Accommodation: An Analysis and Interpretation of the Early Writings of Robert E. Park* (Fayetteville: University of Arkansas, 1992), 290–305.

7. Ibid., 291.

8. Ibid., 110.

9. Robert Park and Ernest W. Burgess, introduction to *The Science of Sociology* (Chicago: University of Chicago Press, 1921), 139.

10. Ibid.

11. Ibid.

12. Park, "Education in its Relation to the Conflict and Fusion of Cultures," in *Race and Culture,* 283.

13. See Lisa Lowe, "Canon, Institutionalization, Identity: Asian American Studies," in *Immigrant Acts.*

14. Ralph Ellison, *Invisible Man* (New York: Modern Library, 1952), 89–93.

15. Ibid., 27.

16. Ibid.

17. Foucault, *The History of Sexuality,* 28.

18. Kenrick Ian Grandison, "Negotiated Space: The Black College Campus as a Cultural Record of Postbellum America," *American Quarterly* 51 (1999): 251–62.

19. Ralph Ellison, unpublished chapter from earlier version of *Invisible Man,* Ralph Ellison Papers, container 50, box "Woodridge," Library of Congress, Washington, D.C., 163.

20. John M. Reilly, "The Testament of Ralph Ellison," in *Speaking for You: The Vision of Ralph Ellison,* ed. Kimberly Benston (Washington, D.C.: Howard University Press, 1987), 54.

21. Ellison, unpublished chapter, 171.

22. Ellison, *Invisible Man,* 72.

23. Ibid.

24. Foucault, *The History of Sexuality,* 73.

25. Ellison, *Shadow and Act,* 43–44

26. Ralph Ellison, *Going to the Territory* (New York: Random House, 1986), 317–18; italics mine.

27. Ellison, *Shadow and Act,* 182.

28. David Lloyd, "Genet's Genealogies: European Minorities and the Ends of Canon," *Telos: A Quarterly Journal of Critical Thought* 70 (winter 1986–87): 161–85.

29. Ibid., 171–72.

30. Ibid.

31. Ellison, *Invisible Man,* 11.

32. Ibid., 433–34.

33. Ibid., 435–36.

34. See Sucheng Chan, *Asian Americans: An Interpretive History* (Boston: Twayne Press, 1991).

35. See Victor Viesca, "Straight Out the Barrio: Ozomatli and the Importance of Place in the Formation of Chicano/a Popular Culture in Los Angeles," *Cultural Values* 4, no. 4 (October 2000), 450.

36. Ibid., 451.

37. Lowe, *Immigrant Acts,* 42.

38. Foucault, *The History of Sexuality,* 59–64.

39. Ellison, *Invisible Man,* 36.

40. Ibid., 41.

41. Foucault, *The History of Sexuality,* 59.

42. Ibid., 63.

43. Ibid., 110.

44. One might argue that the main character is referring to the hegemony of exteriority in defining African American culture and identity when he states, "When they approach me they see only my surroundings, themselves, or figments of their imagination—indeed, everything and anything except for me" (Ellison, *Invisible Man,* 3).

45. James B. McKee, *Sociology and the Race Problem: The Failure of a Perspective* (Urbana and Chicago: University of Illinois Press, 1993), 148.

46. John Dollard, *Caste and Class in a Southern Town* (Garden City, N.Y.: Doubleday, 1937), 275.

47. Griffin, *Who Set You Flowin,* 104.

48. See Hammonds, "Toward a Genealogy of Black Female Sexuality." See also Hazel Carby, *Reconstructing Womanhood: The Emergence of the Afro-American Woman Novelist* (New York: Oxford University Press).

49. Ellison, *Invisible Man,* 3.

50. Ellison, "That Same Pain, That Same Pleasure: An Interview," in *Shadow and Act,* 16–17.

51. Foucault, *The History of Sexuality,* 25.

52. Ibid.

53. Ibid, 25–26.

54. Ibid 5–6.

55. Ellison, *Invisible Man*, 37.

56. Ibid.

3. Nightmares of the Heteronormative

1. Herbert Marcuse, "Industrialization and Capitalism," in *Max Weber and Sociology*, ed. Otto Stammer (New York: Harper Torchbooks, 1971), 135.

2. H. H. Gerth and C. Wright Mills, *From Max Weber: Essays in Sociology* (New York: Oxford University Press, 1958), 343.

3. Ibid., 344.

4. Ibid., 347.

5. Ibid., 349.

6. Max Weber, *The Protestant Ethic and the Spirit of Capitalism* (New York: Scribner's, 1958), 158.

7. Ibid.

8. Reddy, "Home, Houses, Nonidentity," 357.

9. Weber, *The Protestant Ethic*, 26.

10. Charles I. Nero, "Toward a Black Gay Aesthetic: Signifying in Contemporary Black Literature," in *Brother to Brother: New Writings by Black Gay Men*, ed. Essex Hemphill (Boston: Alyson Publications, 1991), 233–34.

11. Ibid., 233.

12. Ibid., 234.

13. Katherine Franke, "Becoming a Citizen: Post-Bellum Regulation of African American Marriage," *Yale Journal of Law and the Humanities* 11 (1999): 251.

14. Ibid.

15. Maxine Baca Zinn, "Feminist Rethinking from Racial-Ethnic Families," in *Women of Color in U.S. Society*, ed. Maxine Baca Zinn and Bonnie Thornton Dill (Philadelphia: Temple University Press, 1994), 303–14.

16. Ibid.

17. Lawrence Glickman, "Inventing the 'American Standard of Living': Gender, Race, and Working-Class Identity, 1880–1925," in *Labor History* 34, nos. 2–3 (spring/summer): 221–35.

18. Angela Davis, *Blues Legacies and Black Feminism: Gertrude "Ma" Rainey, Bessie Smith, and Billie Holiday* (New York: Vintage Books, 1998), 9.

19. See Steven Steinberg, *Turning Back: The Retreat from Racial Justice in American Thought and Policy* (Boston: Beacon Press, 1995); and Serge Guilbaut, *How New York Stole the Idea of Modern Art: Abstract Expressionism, Freedom, Cold War*, trans. Arthur Goldhammer (Chicago: University of Chicago Press, 1983).

20. Peggy Pascoe, "Miscegenation Law, Court Cases, and Ideologies of 'Race' in Twentieth Century America," *The Journal of American History* (June 1996): 44–69.

21. Steinberg, *Turning Back*, 25.

22. Gunnar Myrdal, *An American Dilemma: The Negro Problem and Modern Democracy* (New York and London: Harper and Brothers Publishers, 1944), 928–29.

23. Steinberg, *Turning Back,* 23–24.

24. Cheryl Sanders, *Saints in Exile: The Holiness-Pentecostal Experience in African American Religion and Culture* (New York: Oxford University Press, 1996), 4.

25. Theophus Smith, *Conjuring Culture: Biblical Formations of Black America* (Oxford: Oxford University Press, 1994), 3.

26. Myrdal, *An American Dilemma,* 937.

27. Ibid., 934.

28. Kimberlé Crenshaw, "Race, Reform, and Retrenchment: Transformation and Legitimation in Antidiscrimination Law," in *Critical Race Theory: The Key Writings That Formed the Movement,* ed. Kimberlé Crenshaw, Neil Gotanda, Gary Peller, and Kendall Thomas (New York: New Press, 1995), 112.

29. Eileen Boris, "'You Wouldn't Want One of 'Em Dancing with Your Wife': Racialized Bodies on the Job in World War II," *American Quarterly* 50 (1998): 81.

30. Ibid., 82–98.

31. Robin D. G. Kelley, *Race Rebels: Culture, Politics and the Black Working Class* (New York: The Free Press, 1994), 164.

32. Boris, "'You Wouldn't Want One of 'Em Dancing with Your Wife,'" 85.

33. Ibid., 93.

34. Myrdal, *An American Dilemma,* 519.

35. James B. McKee, *Sociology and the Race Problem: The Failure of a Perspective* (Urbana and Chicago: University of Illinois Press, 1993), 240.

36. Stanford Lyman, *Color, Culture, Civilization: Race and Minority Issues in American Society* (Urbana: University of Illinois Press, 1994), 47.

37. Robert Park, *Race and Culture,* 350.

38. Ibid., 351.

39. Ibid., 353.

40. James Baldwin, "An Interview with James Baldwin," interview by Studs Terkel, 1961, in *Conversations with James Baldwin,* ed. Fred L. Standley and Louis H. Pratt (Jackson and London: University Press of Mississippi, 1989), 5.

41. C. L. R. James, "Abyssinia and the Imperialists," in *The C. L. R. James Reader,* ed. Anna Grimshaw (Oxford: Blackwell Publishers, 1993), 63; italics mine.

42. Ibid.

43. Paul Gilroy, *The Black Atlantic: Modernity and Double Consciousness* (Cambridge: Harvard University Press, 1993), 29.

44. Malcolm Preston, "The Image: Three Views—Ben Sahn, Darius Milhaud, and James Baldwin Debate the Real Meaning of a Fashionable Term," 1962, in Standley and Pratt, *Conversations with James Baldwin,* 26.

45. Ibid., 26.

46. James Baldwin, "Everybody's Protest Novel," in *Notes of a Native Son* (Boston: Beacon Press, 1955), 19.

47. James Baldwin, "Many Thousands Gone," in *Notes of a Native Son,* 24–25.

48. Baldwin, *Notes of a Native Son,* 17.

49. Myrdal, *An American Dilemma,* 929.

50. James Baldwin, "Preservation of Innocence," *Zero* 1 (summer 1949): 22.

51. Weber, *The Protestant Ethic,* 69.

52. Bernard Bell, *The Afro-American Novel,* 189.

53. Griffin, *Who Set You Flowin,* 3.

54. Kevin Mumford, "Homosex Changes: Race, Cultural Geography, and the Emergence of the Gay," *American Quarterly* 48 (1996): 395–414.

55. Ibid., 402.

56. Nathan I. Huggins, *Harlem Renaissance* (London: Oxford University Press, 1973), 89.

57. Ibid.

58. James Baldwin, *Go Tell It on the Mountain* (New York: Dell Press, 1981), 18–19.

59. Sanders, *Saints in Exile,* 5.

60. Bell, *The Afro-American Novel,* 225.

61. Baldwin, *Go Tell It on the Mountain,* 21–22.

62. Phyllis Palmer, *Domesticity and Dirt: Housewives and Domestic Servants in the United States* (Philadelphia: Temple University Press, 1998), 138.

63. Reddy, "Home, Houses, Nonidentity," 356–57.

64. Ibid.

65. Ibid.

66. Mink, *The Wages of Motherhood,* 46.

67. See George Lipsitz, *The Possessive Investment in Whiteness: How White People Profit from Identity Politics* (Philadelphia: Temple University Press, 1998).

68. Wasserman tests were used to detect syphilis. See Boris, "'You Wouldn't Want One of 'Em Dancing with Your Wife,'" 94.

69. Baldwin, *Go Tell It on the Mountain,* 72.

70. Davis, *Blues Legacies and Black Feminism,* 10.

71. Baldwin, *Go Tell It on the Mountain,* 215.

72. Smith, *Conjuring Culture,* 4.

73. Ibid., 124–25.

74. Baldwin, *Go Tell It on the Mountain,* 83.

4. Something Else to Be

1. Audre Lorde, *Sister Outsider: Essays and Speeches* (Trumansburg, N.Y.: Crossing Press, 1984), 115.

2. Chela Sandoval, *Methodology of the Oppressed* (Minneapolis: University of Minnesota Press, 2000), 42.

3. Wallerstein, "The Insurmountable Contradictions of Liberalism," 1173.

4. Ula Taylor, "The Historical Evolution of Black Feminist Theory and Praxis," *Journal of Black Studies* 29, no. 2 (November 1998): 242.

5. Wallerstein, "The Insurmountable Contradictions of Liberalism," 1173.

6. Huey Newton, "Huey Newton Talks to the Movement about the Black Panther Party, Cultural Nationalism, SNCC, Liberals, and White Revolutionaries," in *The Black Panthers Speak,* ed. Philip S. Foner (New York: Da Capo Press, 1995), 50.

7. Amilcar Cabral, "National Liberation and Culture," in *Colonial Discourse*

and Postcolonial Theory: A Reader, ed. Patrick Williams and Laura Chrisman (New York: Columbia University Press, 1994), 55.

8. Ibid., 59.

9. Frantz Fanon, *The Wretched of the Earth* (New York: Grove Weidenfeld, 1963), 245–46.

10. See Goldberg, *Racist Culture.*

11. Newton, "Huey Newton Talks to the Movement," 58–59.

12. Fanon, *The Wretched of the Earth,* 247–48.

13. Frances Beale, "Double Jeopardy: To Be Black and Female," in *The Black Woman: An Anthology,* ed. Toni Cade Bambara (New York: Signet, 1970), 90–91.

14. See Taylor, "The Historical Evolution of Black Feminist Theory and Praxis."

15. Michael Hardt and Antonio Negri, *Empire* (Cambridge: Harvard University Press, 2000), 132–34.

16. See David Held and Anthony McGrew, "The Great Globalization Debate: An Introduction," in *The Global Transformations Reader,* ed. David Held and Anthony McGrew (Malden, Mass.: Blackwell), 1–45.

17. Arjun Appadurai, "Disjuncture and Difference in the Global Cultural Economy," in Williams and Chrisman, *Colonial Discourse and Postcolonial Theory,* 327.

18. Taylor, "The Historical Evolution of Black Feminist Theory and Praxis," 249.

19. Herbert Marcuse in "A Note on Dialectic" argues, "The negation is determinate if it refers the established state of affairs to the basic factors and forces which make for its destructiveness, as well as for the possible alternatives beyond the status quo. In the human reality, they are historical factors and forces, and the determinate negation is ultimately a political negation. As such, it may well find authentic expression in nonpolitical language, and the more so as the entire dimension of politics becomes an integral part of the status quo." *The Essential Frankfurt School Reader,* ed. Andrew Arrato and Eike Gebhardt (New York: Continuum, 2000), 449.

20. Marcuse, "A Note on Dialectic," 445.

21. Daniel P. Moynihan, "The Negro Family: The Case for National Action" (Washington, D.C.: Office of Policy Planning and Research, United States Department of Labor, 1965), 2.

22. See E. Franklin Frazier's *The Negro Family in the United States* (Chicago and London: The University of Chicago Press, 1966). See also Patricia Bell Scott's "Debunking Sapphire: Toward a Non-Racist and Non-Sexist Social Science," in *All the Women Are White, All the Blacks Are Men, But Some of Us Are Brave,* ed. Gloria T. Hull, Patricia Bell Scott, and Barbara Smith (New York: The Feminist Press, 1982), 85–92.

23. Moynihan, "The Negro Family," 16.

24. See Foner, introduction to *The Black Panthers Speak.*

25. Eldridge Cleaver, "The Black Man's Stake in Vietnam," in *The Black Panthers Speak,* 102.

26. As Kay Lindsey argued, "An inordinately high proportion of Black women become welfare mothers, usually without a husband, in the household at least, and

while the white agency outwardly deplores the absence in the household of a father figure, it does not take long to realize that the state has created an artificial family, in which it, via the welfare check, takes the place of the husband and can thus manipulate the 'family' more directly" ("The Black Woman as a Woman," in Bambara, *The Black Woman*, 88).

27. Moynihan, "The Negro Family," 47.

28. Taylor, "The Historical Evolution of Black Feminist Theory and Praxis," 247.

29. Ibid., 246.

30. George Lipsitz, *The Possessive Investment in Whiteness*, 24.

31. Eldridge Cleaver, *Soul on Ice* (New York: McGraw-Hill, 1968), 176–90.

32. Cheryl Clarke, "The Failure to Transform: Homophobia in the Black Community," in Smith, *Home Girls*, 198.

33. For an analysis of this blockade as part of the responses to capital's new global phase, see Paul Pierson, *Dismantling the Welfare State? Reagan, Thatcher, and the Politics of Retrenchment* (Cambridge: Cambridge University Press, 1994), 1–9.

34. See Pierson, *Dismantling the Welfare State?* and Elmar Rieger and Stephen Leibfried's "Welfare State Limits to Globalization," in Held and McGrew, *The Global Transformations Reader*, 332–37.

35. Ibid.

36. See Pierson, *Dismantling the Welfare State?*

37. Ibid.

38. See Dorothy Robert's *Killing the Black Body: Race, Reproduction, and the Meaning of Liberty* (New York: Vintage Books, 1997).

39. Audre Lorde, interview by Claudia Tate, in Tate, *Black Women Writers at Work* (New York: Continuum, 1983), 113.

40. Lowe, *Immigrant Acts*, 152.

41. Gladys M. Jiménez-Munoz in *Moving beyond Boundaries*, ed. Carol Boyce Davies and Molara Ogundipe-Leslie (New York: New York University Press, 1994–1995), 120.

42. Ibid.

43. Hazel Carby, *Reconstructing Womanhood: The Emergence of the Afro-American Woman Novelist* (New York: Oxford University Press, 1987), 16.

44. Lowe, *Immigrant Acts*, 153.

45. Barbara Smith, "Toward a Black Feminist Criticism," in *Within the Circle: An Anthology of African American Literary Criticism from the Harlen Renaissance to the Present*, ed. Angelyn Mitchell (Durham, N.C.: Duke University Press, 1994), 417–18.

46. See, for instance, Madhu Dubey, "'No Bottom and No Top': Oppositions in *Sula*," in *Black Women Novelists and the Nationalist Aesthetic* (Bloomington and Indianapolis: Indiana University Press, 1994).

47. Smith, "Toward a Black Feminist Criticism," 420.

48. Dubey, "'No Bottom and No Top': Oppositions in *Sula*," 55.

49. Smith, "Toward a Black Feminist Criticism," 423.

50. Mikhail Bakhtin, *The Dialogic Imagination: Four Essays,* ed. Michael Holquist and trans. Caryl Emerson and Michael Holquist (Austin: University of Texas Press, 1981), 294.

51. "The Combahee River Collective Statement," in Smith, *Home Girls,* 279.

52. Tania Abdoulahad, Gwendolyn Rogers, Barbara Smith, and Jameelah Waheed, "Black Lesbian/Feminist Organizing: A Conversation," in Smith, *Home Girls,* 293.

53. Jiménez-Munoz, *Moving beyond Boundaries,* 117.

54. Jacqueline Jones, *Labor of Love, Labor of Sorrow: Black Women, Work, and the Family from Slavery to the Present* (New York: Vintage Books, 1995), 301.

55. Saskia Sassen, *Globalization and Its Discontents: Essays on the New Mobility of People and Money* (New York: The New Press, 1998), 120.

56. Rose Brewer, "Theorizing Race, Class, and Gender: The New Scholarship of Black Feminist Intellectuals and Black Women's Labor," in *Theorizing Black Feminisms: The Visionary Pragmatism of Black Women,* ed. Stanlie M. James and Abena P. A. Busia (New York: Routledge), 19–21.

57. Toni Morrison, *Sula* (New York: Plume, 1973), 112–13.

58. Ibid., 164.

59. Ibid., 52.

60. Smith, introduction to *Home Girls,* xix–lvi.

61. Coalition was never regarded as a process free from tension and conflict. Salsa Soul Sisters, for instance, held outreach programs for women of color in Asian and Latino communities, all the while acknowledging the difficulty of such efforts at coalition and indeed making them the subject of public discourse. See Tania Abdulahad, Gwendolyn Rogers, Barbara Smith, and Jameelah Wahled, "Black Lesbian Feminist Organizing: A Conversation," in Smith, *Home Girls.*

62. Smith, *Home Girls,* xxxiii.

63. The Combahee River Collective, "The Combahee River Collective Statement," 277.

64. Sassen, *Globalization and Its Discontents,* 121.

65. Ibid., 121–22.

66. Brewer, "Theorizing Race, Class, and Gender," 19.

67. Ibid., 21.

68. As Sassen notes, Mexico and Colombia have also experienced such trends. See *Globalization and Its Discontents,* 118.

69. Ibid., 113.

70. Aihwa Ong, "The Gender and Labor Politics of Postmodernity," in Lowe and Lloyd, *The Politics of Culture in the Shadow of Capital,* 62.

71. Lisa Cacho, "'The People of California are Suffering': The Ideology of White Injury in Discourses of Immigration," *Cultural Values* 4, no. 4 (October 2000): 390.

Conclusion

1. Barbara Brinson Coriel et al., introduction to *Post-Nationalist American Studies,* ed. John Carlos Rowe (Berkeley and Los Angeles: University of California Press, 2000), 2.

2. Louis Althusser, *For Marx* (London: Verso, 1993), 228.

3. See Aida Hurtado, "'Sitios y Lenguas': Chicanas Theorize Feminisms," *Hypatia* 13, no. 2 (spring 1998): 134.

4. Essex Hemphill, introduction to *Brother to Brother*, ed. Essex Hemphill (Boston: Alyson Publications, 1991), xxvii.

5. Althusser, *For Marx*, 243.

6. M. Jacqui Alexander, "Not Just Any Body Can Be a Citizen," *Feminist Review* 48 (fall 1994): 5–23.

7. Ibid.

8. Cathy Cohen, *The Boundaries of Blackness: AIDS and the Breakdown of Black Politics* (Chicago: University of Chicago Press, 1999), 88.

9. Kulvinder Arora, "Mapping Religion, Culture, and Education in the Production of South Asian Immigrant Space in the United States," *Hitting Critical Mass: A Journal of Asian American Cultural Criticism* 5, no. 2 (fall 1998): 1–11.

10. Gayatri Gopinath, "Nostalgia, Desire, Diaspora: South Asian Sexualities in Motion," *Positions* 5, no. 2 (1997): 459.

11. William J. Wilson, *The Truly Disadvantaged: The Inner City, the Underclass, and Public Policy* (Chicago and London: The University of Chicago Press, 1987). That Wilson's *The Truly Disadvantaged* has become a part of canonical sociology in no way implies that the discipline has overhauled canonical boundaries. Indeed, it would seem that canonical sociology positions this work in such a way as to confirm those boundaries. While *The Truly Disadvantaged* enjoys a certain renown within sociology, that renown does not necessitate an excavation of the types of critiques that black sociological formations would bring to bear on the restrictions and normative presumptions of canonical sociology.

Index

Roderick A. Ferguson is assistant professor of American studies at the University of Minnesota.